Minority Access to Federal Grants-in-Aid

John Hope, II

The Praeger Special Studies program—utilizing the most modern and efficient book production techniques and a selective worldwide distribution network—makes available to the academic, government, and business communities significant, timely research in U.S. and international economic, social, and political development.

Minority Access to Federal Grants-in-Aid

The Gap between Policy and Performance

Praeger Publishers New York Washington London

PRAEGER SPECIAL STUDIES IN U.S. ECONOMIC, SOCIAL, AND POLITICAL ISSUES

Library of Congress Cataloging in Publication Data

Hope, John, 1909-
    Minority access to Federal grants-in-aid.

    (Praeger special studies in U.S. economic, social, and
political issues)
    Bibliography: p.
    Includes index.
    1. Grants-in-aid—United States.   2. Minorities in the
civil service—United States.   I. Title.
HJ275.H66   336.1'85   75-19794
ISBN 0-275-55920-3

PRAEGER PUBLISHERS
111 Fourth Avenue, New York, N.Y. 10003, U.S.A.

Published in the United States of America in 1976
by Praeger Publishers, Inc.

Printed in the United States of America

To the John Hope clan, a determined and resourceful family who for at least three generations to my certain knowledge has abhorred injustice and unwarranted domination of one group by another, has striven for a rational approach to eliminating these twin inequities, has stubbornly rejected arrogance and demogoguery as solutions, has tried to counteract them both in their subtle private and blatantly public forms, and has clung to the seemingly faded concept that "man is his brother's keeper" despite the growing evidence that this may no longer be true.

To my parents, John Hope and Lugenia Burns Hope, a winning team in the cause of education, community organization, and social, political, and economic growth aimed at full racial parity; loving and supportive parents who worked unceasingly to improve the harsh moral environment in which they had to live and make their mark.

To my beloved wife, Elise Oliver Hope, who has been a full partner in all that I have tried to do for some four decades.

To our three children, John, Richard, and Linda and their spouses, who carry on the struggle perhaps in different arenas and sometimes with different tools but for the same broad ends.

In the United States where the population is not homogeneous, differences in race, color, and national origin often cause minority group members to get smaller rewards for their contributions to the productive process and less benefit from federally funded programs than otherwise comparable majority group members. On the basis of background characteristics of potential beneficiaries, decisions are made by officials in federal, state, and local governments which result in minority group members' receiving less than their fair share of the services and programs supported by federal grants-in-aid. Although discrimination in grants-in-aid benefits on the grounds of race, color, and national origin was made unlawful by Title VI of the Civil Rights Act of 1964, there has been a significant and continuing gap between the policy of nondiscrimination avowed by the law and its application.

The research for this book explored in some detail the actions and inactions of decision-making managers of grant programs at all levels of the federal governmental hierarchy from the Executive Office of the President down to the line management unit making the day-to-day operating decisions. It was found that the amount of services reaching members of minority groups falls short of the promise of equal access and nondiscriminatory treatment. Basically this happens because of the forces set in motion when one or more groups in a society are considered subordinate and another group dominant. Knowingly and unknowingly decisions are made favoring the dominant group over the subordinate groups. The findings point very strongly to the necessity for federal granting agencies, agencies receiving funds, and other elements of the service-delivery system to recognize the fact that their managers often make decisions on the basis of legally irrelevant traits of their clients and beneficiaries. The top executives in the service-delivery system need to develop managerial strategies for changing the present ways of operating their programs so that all eligible beneficiaries enter and participate in a manner approaching that which would exist were the population homogeneous.

The more actions relating to the allocation of assistance among various groups are based on decisions that reflect a perception of difference in these groups by officials, the greater the gap between policy and performance is likely to be. The converse is also true. In this sense the role of management in the implementation of civil rights policies has been critical in the failure to carry out the laws passed more than a decade ago.

An explanation is in order for use of data on blacks in the study to the exclusion of other racial and ethnic minorities, women, and the physically and mentally handicapped. The principal reason is that the government has collected data on blacks for a longer period of time than for the other racial and ethnic minorities included in the federal civil rights and equal opportunity laws and regulations. Women and the handicapped have been too recently included in amendments to the civil rights law to provide an adequate body of data for the period covered by the research. Since I sought to observe the relationship between policy and practice over time and to appraise the size and significance of the deviation from policy, I avoided unnecessary complications by confining the subject matter to non-blacks and blacks, for whom data have been available for the longest time and are in a form providing maximum comparability in time, place, and among the various federal departments and agencies.

I began the research when I was on leave from the Office for Civil Rights of the Department of Health, Education, and Welfare in 1971-72 and have continued through 1975. I am indebted to the Brookings Institution, and particularly to Fordyce Luikart, Alice M. Rivlin, and Kermit Gordon, for awarding me one of the approximately ten federal fellowships given to senior federal civil servants annually to use as they see fit. I am also indebted to the Office for Civil Rights, and particularly to J. Stanley Pottinger, then its director, for granting me the leave of absence to take advantage of this opportunity. The Office for Civil Rights has contributed further to this project in a variety of ways, both voluntary and inadvertent.

I would like to express special appreciation to the some forty heads of federal civil rights units and agencies who submitted to in-depth interviews on their perceptions of their roles and functions as civil rights executives. I am also grateful to other government agency people who gave generously of their time in discussing various aspects of my research: Andrew F. Brimmer, Jean Fairfax, Eli Ginsberg, Dale Heistand, Harold Howe, William Taylor, and Charles V. Willie.

My background of work experience in government and private agencies concerned with equal opportunity and civil rights was an aid to making observations and judgments. I have worked in four federal agencies, in three of them in executive capacities, in an effort to apply the civil rights policies of the federal government. During World War II I was a fair employment practices examiner for the President's Committee on Fair Employment Practices. During the Kennedy-Johnson years I was director of the federal employment program of the President's Committee on Equal Employment

Opportunity until its demise. In both of these agencies I was concerned with reducing discrimination against employees or applicants for employment in the federal bureaucracy. In order to get a first-hand view of the way the principle of equality of opportunity worked in the service-delivery area I moved from the President's Committee to the Department of Health, Education, and Welfare, the largest source of grants-in-aid benefits in the federal government. This has given me an opportunity to observe the granting process as a regional office executive and as a headquarters executive and as a liaison officer without enforcement responsibilities.

I am indebted to the United States Commission on Civil Rights for assembling and publishing the types of accurately detailed information about government civil rights/ethnic origin (CR/EO) policies and practices from which students of minority-majority problems can continuously draw. I used its published reports extensively and gleaned much from the expertise of the staff. Particularly helpful from the commission staff were John A. Buggs, Jeffrey M. Miller, Cynthia N. Graae, and John Hope III.

I am grateful for general indispensable help ranging from the nurturing of the idea to the development of concepts given freely by Kenneth B. Clark, Hylan Lewis, Richard O. Hope, Mercer Cook, and Lester C. Thurow. Others who read and commented helpfully on the manuscript or otherwise contributed to the overall project were Harold C. Fleming, Linda Hope Lee, Ray Marshall, Amelia Perazich, J. Saunders Redding, Morton S. Sklar, and Ivan E. Taylor. Mary Symons Strong persisted in helping me formulate my ideas more clearly and took responsibility for guiding the manuscript from its original form through to publication. I am deeply grateful for her optimism and expertise. My assistant, Barbara Williams, and my secretary, Marie Lockard, cheerfully, faithfully, and unstintingly gave of their talents in innumerable ways from the beginning of my research efforts to the very end.

While many have been helpful to me in this undertaking, the views expressed are my own and I take full responsibility for them.

CONTENTS

LIST OF TABLES

THE GAP IN THE DELIVERY OF FEDERALLY-FUNDED SERVICES
TO MINORITIES

Although the Civil Rights Act of 1964 has been in operation for more than a decade, minority group participation in the benefits of the vast federal grants-in-aid programs has fallen far short of the objectives and guarantees of equal treatment provided by Title VI of the act. This gap, if not chasm, between statutory commitment and actual performance has been the outcome of managerial decisions and action at all levels of the administration of federal financial assistance programs. Despite the explicit and unambiguous requirements of Title VI, the executive branch of the federal government from top to bottom has failed to provide equal access to the benefits of such federally-financed programs to people of all racial and ethnic minority backgrounds. Both lack of leadership and ineffective management in carrying out the safeguards against discrimination have characterized the performance of the White House, the rest of top federal management, and the departments and agencies directly responsible for Title VI programs.

Among the various provisions for ending discrimination contained in the Civil Rights Act of 1964, Title VI was one of the most important because it placed a broad ban on racial and ethnic discrimination in any program or activity receiving financial assistance from the federal government. Title VI stated:

> No person in the United States shall, on the ground of race, color, or national origin, be excluded from participation in, be denied the benefits of, or be subjected to discrimination under any program or activity receiving Federal financial assistance. [Civil Rights Act of 1964, section 601]

In its coverage Title VI was limited to programs and activities which obtained federal assistance "by way of grant, loan, or contract of insurance or guarantee" (Civil Rights Act of 1964, section 602).

While these programs and activities covered by Title VI differed widely in their purposes and functions, they had one important element in common: they operated through loans and grants made to intermediaries who were called "recipients" rather than directly to the people who were supposed to benefit from the federal financial assistance. These so-called recipients might be either public or private organizations, but most frequently they were state and local governments that received grants and loans from the federal government to help finance statewide and local programs of many different sorts. These were the familiar programs into which federal funds were channeled through federal departments and agencies to governments and private organizations throughout the fifty states. The grants and loans were used for the support of educational, health, welfare, and many other sorts of social and economic programs.

Of the more than $25 billion of such federal grants-in-aid payments made in 1968, the bulk of the money, $18 billion, went to state and local governments. Such assistance to state and local governments probably exceeded $30 billion in 1970 and, with the emphasis on decentralization under the Nixon and Ford administrations, was easily in the neighborhood of $50 billion by 1975.

Upon receiving these huge amounts of financial assistance from Washington, state and local governments and other public and private organizations had a great deal of discretion in making decisions about how their programs were to operate and how the benefits were to be distributed. Although detailed guidelines for preventing discrimination in providing services and other benefits were typically written into the legislation and administrative regulations governing the operations of the programs, the local governments in the various states which received the money frequently ignored the antidiscrimination rules and were permitted to do so by the federal agencies granting the funds. The result has been that, contrary to the statutory requirements of Title VI, executive orders of the presidents, and other regulations, the intended beneficiaries of the programs have been discriminated against and denied services and money on account of their race, color, and national origin.

The discrimination in these programs has been widespread and has continued for years. Blatant discrimination against minorities has occurred time and time again in all kinds of programs funded by federal money. Some of the discriminatory practices have been reported in the press, but many have never been exposed. Their occurrence was so common that they were not newsworthy. They took place in programs supported by all the federal departments and agencies with Title VI responsibilities. In the Cooperative Extension Service which was jointly funded by federal, state, and county agencies, for example, the assistance given white farmers has been greater than that given black farmers who were qualified for an equal amount of aid. In public housing programs, local housing authorities receiving federal financial assistance have chosen sites for public housing projects that promoted segregation and employed tenant assignment policies that denied minority families an equal chance to rent apartments in the projects. In public welfare programs for which state and local governments have received substantial federal assistance, there are many cases in which officials of state and local welfare agencies have imposed higher eligibility requirements on black and other minority families than on whites. All of these discriminatory practices were clearly in violation of the law.

Funds for grants-in-aid and loan programs were voted and appropriated by Congress, and their administration was the task of the executive branch. The responsibility for this improper use of federal monies rested ultimately with the chief executive and his staff. The president is supposed to fulfill this statutory obligation by establishing full surveillance of the operations of all departments and agencies with major civil rights duties. By necessity presidents have made use of their powers to delegate the responsibility for supervising the execution of programs to particular members of their White House staffs. When efforts lag in carrying out programs, White House staffers are known to put pressure on operating agencies to mend their ways. When presidents have wanted something done by the bureaucracy, their staffs have never been hesitant about relaying their message. Departmental executives at various levels have either received or been aware of telephone calls from the White House, sometimes made more or less anonymously but other times not, venturing suggestions or demanding action. These calls come from the White House staff informally or from the Bureau of the Budget or its successor, the Office of Management and Budget, as a part of their formal oversight and monitoring functions.

Unfortunately supervision and prodding by the White House and the Bureau of the Budget (BOB) and Office of Management and Budget (OMB) staffs have been sorely lacking in the case of Title VI. In fact, the reverse signals have often been given. There were a number of management units below the White House itself which could have made the grant-awarding units in the departments accountable for their Title VI responsibilities. At the top of this hierarchy and most powerful were the BOB and more recently the OMB which was created by executive order of President Richard M. Nixon in 1970. They were established to oversee and monitor the executive management of the federal bureaucracy and to act on the president's behalf to see that the departments and agencies carried out presidential policies and priorities. This made them the keystone to the implementation of civil rights laws. In both BOB and OMB most control over the executive branch was lodged in their major role in the budget-making process. The BOB could have made a significant positive impact on the government's civil rights effort. It could have accomplished a great deal through its power to review and approve all legislative proposals and agency proposals for the collection of data for the purpose of monitoring and evaluating the results of programs. But it did not.

In 1970 the Office of Management and Budget received an even stronger mandate with greater powers than those given the BOB to determine how policies should be carried out and to monitor how well they were being administered. With its pivotal supervisory and executive roles, the OMB could have influenced the staffing, structure, and policy development of departments and agencies with Title VI programs in such a way that they would have kept the recipients of the funds in compliance with equal opportunity requirements. But the OMB has not done so.

The intermediate management unit below the OMB which was given specific responsibility for Title VI enforcement was the Department of Justice (DOJ). Seven months after the passage of the Civil Rights Act of 1964, the Justice Department was assigned the job of coordinating all Title VI activities of the departments and agencies with grants-in-aid programs. In this position, the DOJ's potential impact on the implementation of Title VI by federal grant managers was enormous. The attorney general and his department's interpretation of the role of coordinator turned out to be critical in a negative sense, because they chose to define their powers as mainly advisory rather than supervisory.

Beneath the White House, the OMB, and the Department of Justice, the levels of management with Title VI responsibilities were the heads of the federal departments and agencies which made the grants and the civil rights specialists in these departments and agencies. Their particular involvement varied from zero all the way to full time. The policies and decisions of the departmental secretaries impinged heavily on their division and agency heads who were the line executives in charge of the financial assistance programs. Supervision by the secretaries of the departments was often not continuously given, inconsistent in content, or unevenly executed, but these top administrators created the climate of work for line officials making the daily decisions about who was to get funded and who was not and whether or not the recipients were required to use the money equitably.

Many members of a racially and ethnically mixed society think and act in terms of "we" versus "they" or "those people;" majority versus minority, black versus white, and so forth. Such patterns of thought and behavior frequently influence the decisions and actions of government officials, whether consciously or not. In their most aggressive and virulent forms, they are expressed in racist and chauvinist behavior. Whatever the causes for their existence, they often lead to irrational, biased, and short-sighted decisions which reflect institutional and personal prejudices. The extent to which the host of decision makers, whether in the White House or in the smallest operating unit in the bureaucracy, have such attitudes and act upon them influences the country's civil rights and equal opportunity policies and practices. Although laws and regulations do not have the ability to change attitudes, at least not immediately, they can outlaw the expression of them in the official acts of government officials. The practice of discrimination in the administration of federal financial assistance was made illegal by the Civil Rights Act.

In the long run, the perfect application of an equal opportunity policy by government officials would result in the delivery of services to Americans of different racial and ethnic backgrounds as if there were no differences based on minority status impinging on making equitable market decisions. The decision makers would assume that there are no differences among eligible beneficiaries or participants based on racial or ethnic characteristics. These differences would be ruled out as elements taken into consideration when the benefits of grants-in-aid are distributed. In fact, the machinery set up to implement the equal opportunity and civil rights laws requires that people involved in activities covered by the laws act this way in areas where discrimination is proscribed.

Public policy outlawing discriminatory behavior in certain areas was adopted several decades before the civil rights acts of the 1960s. Antidiscrimination measures in federal public employment were initiated as early as World War II, and more recently the ban on discrimination in employment was extended to private employers having government contracts. The Civil Rights Acts enlarged the definition of equal opportunity. Among other things, they made discrimination illegal in all the programs and activities receiving financial assistance from the federal treasury.

Passing the civil rights laws, however, did not bring about a new pervasive pattern of equity and fair play. It is safe to say that federal agency executives vary in the assumptions they employ in making decisions about the distribution of government services to minorities. How are decisions made to deliver services to members of groups who are identical in eligibility, qualifications, and other pertinent economic characteristics? Decisions about the distribution of the services of a program may be based on one of the following assumptions:

First, that beneficiaries similar in all other aspects except their racial or ethnic characteristics will be differentiated in the delivery of this assistance in such a way that some groups will receive a proportionately larger amount of assistance than others, that is, consciously discriminatory distribution of assistance.

Second, that assistance will be distributed with complete disregard for the racial and ethnic differences between the present beneficiaries, that is, a complete absence of conscious differentiation between economically homogeneous units. Under this assumption, the manager will give no consideration to the results of past discrimination against racial and ethnic groups.

Third, that beneficiaries not only are not differentiated by racial and ethnic group in the present, but that temporary compensation is provided for past discrimination in order to assure that after a period of correction, the condition described in the second assumption will prevail in the long run.

Given the necessary data for analysis one could develop a coefficient of differentiation (or conversely a coefficient of integration or homogeneity) as an indicator to measure the degree of deviation from complete compliance with the equal opportunity policy of the government. The variations in decision-making would cover the span ranging from complete differentiation between groups on the basis of racial and ethnic characteristics to the complete absence of such differentiation with all of the gradations in between.

In addition to those judgmental factors influencing the decisions of managers which might arise from personal prejudices or systematic, institutional discrimination and racism, the decisions of a manager might be affected pro or con by the objective data available for his use in making his decisions. Two alternative assumptions might be made by a manager regarding the presence of racial/ethnic differentiation among the beneficiaries of grants made in his agency. First, he might assume the absence of such differentiation and conclude that there is no need for the collection of racial/ethnic data about who is getting the benefits of his program. Second, he might assume the presence of such differentiation and recognize the importance of collecting information in order to describe the size and character of the discrimination being practiced. It is not uncommon for managers of federal, state, and local offices, agencies, and other units to assume uncritically the absence of discrimination within their jurisdictions either because of a lack of information or the desire to deny the presence of discrimination and thus avoid efforts to solve the problem.

There is no general federal policy requiring the executive departments and agencies involved in the enforcement of equal opportunity policy to collect data classified by racial/ethnic groups to whom grant funds and other services have been distributed. This is true despite the fact that discrimination based on irrelevant characteristics such as race, color, national origin, and sex is rampant, and that Title VI requires the elimination of this artificial barrier to equal treatment. The Office of Management and Budget has actively resisted the adoption of this tool of management even though it is the titular authority on the effectiveness of management in the executive branch. The OMB has the power to make such a requirement government-wide and uniform and to judge performance based on objective data.

The result of this negative policy is to encourage the management units (who need to know whether government services distributed by them are allocated without arbitrary differentiation according to the racial/ethnic group) not to gather and use such information for making decisions about the management of the Title VI compliance status of their programs. For those agency executives who might recognize the need for such data as a tool for Title VI grants-in-aid management and try to collect it without the backing of OMB, the lack of a general federal policy accentuates the obstacles to such collection systems and limits the area of its use and acceptance as a tool of management. Some departments have such a policy in some form but most of them do not.

Title VI requires that no person "shall, on the ground of race, color, or national origin, be excluded from participation in, be denied the benefits of, or be subjected to discrimination under any program or activity receiving Federal financial assistance." Though well-meaning people may recoil from the idea that applicants and users of government services and "free goods" be identified as white, black, people of Spanish origin, Mexican-American, and so forth, it simply is the only way to monitor the administration of programs supported by federal money, whether they be schools, universities, hospitals, parks, extension services, vocational rehabilitation centers for the disabled, or other. The collection of racial and ethnic data is the only objective means of knowing whether such public and private institutions are complying with equal opportunity laws and whether the gap between minority and majority access to the benefits of federally financed services is being narrowed. The true extent of the gap cannot even be known without the data. The official who gives out services may not realize how much his unconscious biases and old habits of work and the folkways of his immediate community affect the decisions he makes for his clients. When a record is kept on a racial and ethnic basis, however, there is no ignoring the facts. No product manager in private enterprise would allow an employee to convince him on the basis of intuition that all was well when complaints were pouring in about unsatisfactory service. By the same token, action to remedy unfair service to the citizen of minority background can be taken only on the basis of the actual distribution record identifying the individual who is eligible for benefits by racial and ethnic group.

It is often the case that management systems of public institutions tend to ignore or underestimate the cost of discrimination, inequity, and prejudice to the government itself as well as the cost to minorities directly affected by differential access to government benefits. One important way to assure that management is both efficient and just is to have qualified representatives from the various racial and ethnic groups participate in the decision-making process. They should hold positions in the middle and upper range of the federal, state, and local administrations so that they can take part in preparing the data required for making decisions, in evaluating them, in making the actual decisions, and in directing implementation of decisions.

Management at all levels faces a basic operational problem in implementing the equal opportunity policy of the country. If the gap between avowal and performance is to be narrowed, managers at all levels have to get into the habit of making all decisions on the assumption that there are various subgroups, each one of which should be kept in mind in making all decisions, not simply in making decisions directly and distinguishably affecting particular minorities as a group. The results in terms of fairness and effectiveness depend on the decisions made, the action taken, and the policies applied on the basis of these decisions. Such questions as the following are important for management to raise and answer:

First, are the goals and objectives which affect and protect minorities within the management unit (both as employers, employees, and clients) clearly formulated and conveyed to all levels of management for application within their respective spheres and levels of management?

Second, are the managers required to develop and apply specific means for accomplishing these goals, and, failing this, must they give clear and explicit reasons why they have not achieved such objectives? When evaluated do the systems work? Have random sampling or other systems of collecting information been used? Is there periodic monitoring of the actions of operational managers to determine whether they are reaching the objectives set by higher level management in a timely manner, and, if not, are these operational managers required to give reasons for the failure so that this particular management unit will reach its goal in the future? Do operational managers negotiate changes in goal based on existing circumstances and the feasibility of attaining the goal?

Third, are operating managers required to recommend alternatives for consideration by higher level policy-making management in those situations where it is not felt that the goals and objectives imposed by this higher level are appropriate or attainable?

This book attempts to examine the philosophies and practices of the various managerial levels of the federal executive in their administration of the federal grants-in-aid programs which have Title VI bans on discrimination in the delivery of services. In Part I,

Management of Grants to Minorities, attention is given to the wide gap between the mandate of the executive branch to prevent discrimination in programs assisted by federal funds and the actual performance of these responsibilities at each level of the administrative structure. Chapter 1 discusses the pivotal leadership and executive roles of the president and the Office of Management and Budget and its predecessor, the Bureau of the Budget, in setting the direction of civil rights and equal opportunity policies, particularly Title VI, and monitoring their execution. Chapter 2 analyzes the powers and responsibilities of the Department of Justice in its role of coordinator of the Title VI programs of departments with authority to make grants-in-aid to state and local governments and private organizations and with responsibility for insuring compliance with Title VI. Chapter 3 describes the organizational structures and mechanisms employed by the departments and agencies of the federal executive branch for enforcing Title VI and highlights their accomplishments and failures. Chapter 4 outlines and analyzes the compliance techniques and complaint procedures established for securing compliance with Title VI by recipient agencies, pointing out the flaws in their conception of enforcement and their failure to make systematic attempts to require timely compliance by the funded bodies.

In Part II, Administration of Civil Rights/Equal Opportunity Policies in Grant Programs, Chapter 5 investigates the organizational status, staffing, and management practices of the civil rights units within departments and agencies which make grants-in-aid to recipient state and local agencies. Chapter 6 provides a profile of the civil rights/equal opportunity manager who has overall departmental or agency responsibility and nominal authority in Title VI compliance efforts.

Part III, Minority Managers in the Federal Bureaucracy, gives a detailed statistical picture of the employment of blacks at the white collar level of the federal civil service. Particular attention is given to the presence of blacks in the upper managerial and professional categories. This is stressed because of the importance of minority participation in decision making in the upper echelons of management. Chapter 7 takes up the subject of the underemployment of blacks in the higher categories of federal employment at the headquarters offices in Washington, while Chapter 8 describes how many blacks hold decision-making and managerial positions in the various regional offices of the bureaucracy. The gap between the avowed policy of equal employment opportunity in federal jobs and the actual numbers holding such jobs is shown by comparing the penetration rates of blacks with their white counterparts in government employment and with the total number of blacks in the population.

Part IV, Management Tools for Title VI Enforcement, is about the use of racial and ethnic data as management tools for enforcing compliance with Title VI. Chapter 9 discusses the systems of collection of racial and ethnic data and the experience of some departments and agencies in gathering racial and ethnic data. Chapter 10 presents the limited attempts of departments and agencies to use racial and ethnic data for monitoring and compelling compliance with Title VI in federally assisted programs. The closing chapter gives an overview and evaluation of a decade of experience in the administration of the civil rights aspects of programs of federal financial assistance. The chasm between policy and performance, still so wide, threatens to become even wider as a result of the trend toward local control and decentralization of the supervision of federal monies in the revenue sharing programs.

MANAGEMENT OF GRANTS TO MINORITIES

As head of the executive branch of the government, the president has the ultimate responsibility for implementing the civil rights and equal opportunity laws. As early as World War II, presidents issued executive orders and created special advisory bodies to help them develop civil rights policies and programs and to maintain control over operating departments and agencies with civil rights responsibilities. By and large, these new instrumentalities created by various presidents were of limited value and frequently were short lived. In the 1960s, President John F. Kennedy resorted to the advice of his Sub-Cabinet Group on Civil Rights. President Lyndon B. Johnson set up a President's Council on Equal Opportunity shortly after the passage of the Civil Rights Act of 1964, but civil rights coordination was actually handled on an ad hoc basis during the last three years of the Johnson administration.

Like his immediate predecessors, President Richard M. Nixon initially relied on members of his immediate White House staff for advice on civil rights issues, but when the Office of the President was reorganized in 1970 civil rights matters were included in the new executive structure, which created the Domestic Council and the Office of Management and Budget (OMB). The mandate of the OMB included a stronger emphasis on management functions than its predecessor, the Bureau of the Budget (BOB), had been given. However, the differences in the powers and responsibilities of the BOB failed to explain its very limited role in assuring or, at least, encouraging the execution of civil rights statutes by federal departments and agencies. BOB had been granted broad jurisdiction in overseeing executive management that made it one of the most powerful agencies in the federal bureaucracy. It was given the central role in the budget submission process. It also had authority to review and approve all legislative proposals and the plans for data collection by departments and agencies. Yet it neglected to use these tools to insure the enforcement of civil rights laws. It neglected to include civil rights concerns systematically in budget reviews; it did not recommend the collection of data to determine how effectively civil rights programs were working. In reviewing legislation which had important civil rights components, such as proposed housing and education statutes, it rarely inquired into the civil rights aspects of such proposed legislation.

In contrast with this very restricted conception of its role in civil rights matters on the part of BOB, the first director of the Office of Management and Budget, Dr. George P. Shultz, declared his intention "to build into OMB's institutional process an ongoing concern with civil rights so that this concern becomes a part and parcel of the regular activity of the agency."[1] In the same office memorandum of March 25, 1971, Shultz wrote:

> Last October, I stressed the importance of identifying civil rights issues in the budget process and evaluating agency performance in this critical area. In order to insure that this initial step is followed up throughout the year, a number of additional actions are needed. Otherwise, there is considerable danger that the civil rights thrust will recede under the press of other considerations.
>
> Rather than attempt to establish a single civil rights unit, it is much more desirable to insure that all OMB examiners and Management staff are conscious of their civil rights responsibilities in the course of their regular assignments. On the other hand, a central point for the review of the OMB effort to insure that the appropriate actions are being taken is essential. Mark Alger, Chief of the General Government Programs Division, will monitor the overall program outlined below and report to me on the progress of this effort.

In this manner, Shultz rejected the dichotomy between responsibilities for a program on the one hand and responsibilities for civil rights as a separate and special concern on the other. At the same time, he set definite monitoring responsibilities and made specific and coordinated civil rights assignments for "all major functional areas within OMB."

Shultz followed up and reinforced this statement of his position some seven months later in his memorandum of October 19, 1971, to the OMB staff:

> Ultimately, though, it is the job and responsibility of
> each representative of the Office of Management and
> Budget to insure that the full attention of agency man-
> agement is being devoted to this important area of con-
> cern and that this concern extends equally to all
> minorities.

Clearly delineating the civil rights responsibilities of the management
and budgeting staff and of the departments and agencies, he went on to
state that:

> Office staff should familiarize themselves with the
> civil rights considerations outlined in the attachment.
> Within the Executive branch, the administration of
> civil rights responsibilities is essentially reserved
> to the departments and agencies. Oversight and co-
> ordination of these activities rests with the Office of
> Management and Budget and the Civil Rights Com-
> mittee of the Domestic Council. [2]

Finally, Shultz gave guidance to OMB staff as to how they could
effectively carry out this mandate through their reviews and evaluations of agency and department civil rights performance. He
attached a detailed list of civil rights considerations to which he
directed specific attention, with the reminder that this responsibility
be met in conjunction with the other assignments which they were
carrying out.

On the basis of the explicit statements of philosophy and operational policy made by the first director of OMB, some changes for the
better in the implementation of the civil rights aspects of government
programs seemed to be in the offing. Indeed, OMB did make some
progress in its effort to institutionalize its civil rights program. It
attempted to focus the attention of its professional staff more sharply
on civil rights through semiannual memoranda. The regular Spring
Reviews and Fall Director's Previews treating civil rights issues,
the Special Analyses of Federal Civil Rights Activities and the Civil
Rights Seminars conducted for the staff presumably contributed to
broadening and deepening the staff's awareness of civil rights issues.

On the other hand, it was evident that OMB's failure to integrate
the normal consideration of the civil rights aspects of specific programs by budget examiners and management reviewers with the usual
program elements of their reviews forestalled effective evaluation of
civil rights activities within the structure of program and budget
monitoring.

Moreover, the agency did not develop what its bulletin called "adequate mechanisms" for making its staff "accountable for carrying out, or even identifying, the civil rights aspects of their assignments." As a result, the manner and extent to which civil rights requirements were exacted or ignored by the OMB examining staff were functions of the level of interest, training, and attitude of the particular OMB representative involved.

Instead, a pathetically understaffed Civil Rights Unit was created to do the job within OMB. Its staff consisted of only two professional members who were employed at civil service grade levels General Schedule (GS) 13 through 15, which reflected their lack of status in relationship to other members of the OMB. The Unit itself was placed at the division level, which removed it from direct contact with top policy makers. In fact, it reported to the chief and deputy of the General Government Programs Division, both of whom were mainly engaged in duties outside the civil rights area. As a consequence, those most heavily involved in the practical aspects of civil rights in OMB were virtually cut off from civil rights policy making in the agency.

Such a small staff in the Civil Rights Unit meant that its members were spread thin over many tasks and grossly overworked. In addition to their main duties connected with budget examinations of particular civil rights agencies and technical advice to various management divisions, they served as staff to the Civil Rights Committee of the Domestic Council, participated in the work of the Equal Opportunities Coordinating Council, and engaged in miscellaneous other ad hoc tasks. These various activities, however important each one might have been, detracted from the sharpness of focus, intensity of guidance, and technical assistance that the budget examiner and management people needed if OMB was to create an effective civil rights, equal opportunity arm.

Assuming that the integrated-program-for-civil-rights approach was accepted as OMB's philosophy in this area, its successful application would require a civil rights unit trained to give technical assistance, and with adequate resources and authority to direct all of OMB's enforcement and evaluation responsibilities. But OMB failed to create such a unit, even though its role in oversight and evaluation of federal programs through its fiscal, legislative, and statistical controls gave it a unique ability to influence the execution of the federal civil rights laws and policies. The civil rights staff's apparent lack of line authority to take action also raised serious questions about OMB's intent to use its influence in determining the policy developments and staffing of federal agencies to enable civil rights laws to be enforced. It was questionable whether there was any intention to achieve de facto inclusion of civil rights responsibilities as part of their assignments by all examiners and management staff, not to mention the positive discharge of these obligations.

The limitations in implementing the announced policies of OMB and the civil rights laws made poor performance inevitable. The executive they were to report to was never clearly identified. The processes for making policy decisions and for taking action on civil rights matters were not spelled out. In addition, there was a virtual absence of civil rights directives governing the conduct of budget examiners and management specialists. The prevailing atmosphere of permissiveness in implementing the civil rights requirements imposed by law on both OMB and the agencies they supervised contributed to the poor performance.

While the stated OMB philosophy dictated that budget examiners and management personnel should appraise the civil rights aspects of each program to which they were assigned, there was little evidence that they were qualified to make such appraisals. Nor were the training opportunities for such personnel adequate to insure that they had or could acquire the needed competency within a reasonable length of time. Civil rights training was optional and offered in only limited amounts. Training was less extensive in the management divisions than in the examination divisions, although many management staff activities were weakened by insufficient background in civil rights. Moreover, the Bureau of the Budget had passed on such a low "state of the civil rights art" to its successor that there was little likelihood for improvement as long as it depended on the limited expertise in civil rights of members of the tenured senior and executive staff, who would be at their posts for many years before retirement.

A change seemed to be signaled when, in 1973, the responsibility for monitoring and coordinating the civil rights activities of OMB was assigned to the deputy director. This appeared to be a recognition of the importance of the backing of top policy makers in civil rights matters. However, the wide range of his other duties seriously limited his ability to guide the civil rights aspects of the program. Nor has it been evident that he officially delegated this function to other executives with the expertise, status, and tenure necessary for effective and sustaining leadership.

Following Shultz' ringing affirmation of civil rights enforcement at the highest level of administration, the management arm of the president failed to produce the promised results. In the following section there is a review of the small and hesitant beginnings made by OMB to implement its civil rights and equal opportunity obligations. The federal budget process, the director's previews and reviews of civil rights, special analyses of federal civil rights activities, Circular A-11, performance management systems, legislative reviews, and the coordination of federally assisted programs are discussed in some detail to show the more specific mechanisms employed or neglected by OMB in their oversight and control of executive management by the bureaucracy in the civil rights area, particularly in Title VI responsibilities.

THE FEDERAL BUDGET PROCESS

For the White House agency whose major function was to determine how federal expenditures were actually made and how they could best be made, the examination of the budgets of federal departments and agencies was its central task. Such examinations were mandatory for all government agencies, but, until recently, budget examination of the civil rights elements of an agency's program were either excluded or left to the discretion of a particular budget examiner.

In order to understand civil rights policies and their proper application, it is important to have some understanding of the federal budget process in broad outline. Budgeting per se is a continuous process which all major government agencies pursue in some phase or other throughout the year, whether by executive preparation and submission, legislative authorization and appropriation, execution, or audit. The fundamental nature of budgeting in the executive branch is that there is a two-way flow of decisions up from the departments and agencies and then back down from the OMB and the president.

The first phase of the federal budget process, that of executive preparation and submission, is of critical importance in civil rights matters because it is at this juncture that actions taken and not taken affect the nature and size of every departmental budget and, therefore, have a profound effect on the civil rights and equal opportunity budget of every department. Because OMB is the representative of the president in all budget negotiations with the federal departments and agencies, it makes or breaks effective action in civil rights matters in departments and agencies throughout the entire federal establishment. The policy intentions and directions of the incumbent president are give concrete expressions in what comes out of this phase of the budget process. [3]

What happens to federal monies spent for grants-in-aid has been set on its initial path during the budget-making process. Civil rights implementation was not a line item in most agency budgets and, until the advent of OMB, the review of agency budgets placed little emphasis on assessing their civil rights performance. However, as a result of OMB directives and the activities of the Civil Rights Unit, increasing attention has been given to such issues in interviews between OMB examiners and federal agencies in budget submissions and in budget hearings.

However, only a small proportion of examiners have affirmatively pressed civil rights issues as a part of the examination of their assigned agencies, while a much larger group has continued to ignore or minimize civil rights matters. Generally speaking they have failed to report agency civil rights problems that were not settled at the program level and, as a result, top management of OMB has not been

effectively apprised of the extent to which discrimination prevailed in
government programs.

Such failures have been attributed to "pressures from other
priorities, lack of encouragement from supervisors, and incomplete
understanding of the particular civil rights enforcement problems facing
their agencies. The most serious problem, however, is the fact that
examiners still consider procedures for civil rights review ad hoc and
discretionary."[4]

To solve this procedural problem, the U.S. Commission on Civil
Rights recommended the following:

> To systematize these procedures, OMB should require, for
> the budget examination process, that each agency review its
> civil rights jurisdiction, giving close attention to the relation-
> ship between civil rights enforcement and its assistance pro-
> grams. Each agency should be required to set long-range
> goals for civil rights enforcement. Examiners should assess
> the adequacy of agency objectives and make certain that agen-
> cies have instituted effective mechanisms for accomplishing
> their goals. They should regularly review enforcement pro-
> grams to see if agencies are obtaining the desired results.[5]

Further evidence of OMB management's permissiveness in civil
rights aspects of their agency budget examination was its reluctance to
require examiners to furnish either their supervisors or the Civil
Rights Unit with an enumeration of the issues to be reviewed or a report on their progress in dealing with these issues. It was OMB's
position that such close supervision was not in line with its current
examination procedures and that it did not intend to formalize the process. As a consequence, OMB staff and other federal officials doubted
that OMB was committed to strengthening the federal civil rights enforcement effort in significant ways.

DIRECTOR'S PREVIEWS AND REVIEWS OF CIVIL RIGHTS

OMB top management initiated some techniques for increasing
the level of awareness and comprehension of civil rights issues among
its staff although this was not the main reason for these innovations.
In 1973 selected civil rights problems were reviewed in the Fall Director's Review and Spring Preview. Through this process critical
issues were treated in formal papers presented by staff members for
consideration by the senior members of the decision-making staff.
Insofar as the Spring Preview succeeded in bringing to the surface
crucial civil rights issues, it might foster the inclusion of such topics

by senior staff among the priority items to be included in the budget for the next fiscal year.

However, the Commission on Civil Rights has raised some question as to whether the director's reviews and previews have effectively focused on the civil rights problems that should be the direct responsibility of examiner and management staffs in their dealings with their client agencies. These director's reviews and previews have been long-standing tools of the budgeting process, antedating OMB. The purpose of such analyses has been to advise the president on policy issues arising in the budgeting and management operations of the executive branch.

Consequently, civil rights issues have appeared only as OMB policy-making management has recognized civil rights policies to be an integral part of overall program policy. This is a very recent phenomenon. It is questionable whether this evolution has gone far enough and whether the treatment accorded civil rights in these documents has been immediately applicable to the problems with which OMB budget examination and management analysis staffs were required to deal in their day-to-day association with federal departments and agencies. It has been suggested that the Civil Rights Unit be required to review the unresolved civil rights issues of specific agencies with the examiners in order to identify the most significant government-wide problems so that these problems could be brought to the attention of top OMB officials.

SPECIAL ANALYSIS OF FEDERAL
CIVIL RIGHTS ACTIVITIES

The Special Analysis of Federal Civil Rights Activities was a highly significant innovation of OMB which became a part of the 1973 budget and has presumably become a regular annual feature of the president's budget. It assembled data on federal expenditures for civil rights enforcement and federal assistance programs directed solely to minorities. As another illustration of OMB's laudable efforts to institutionalize the civil rights aspects of its operations, it was an added manifestation of the rather fundamental limitations of this effort to date. It was primarily an enumeration of federal outlays without a corresponding report on the results of these outlays, and with even less concern about the relationship between outlay and results. Time was the only measure of change used in the present and future estimates.

Evaluation of the issue of equity, so central to all considerations of civil rights and equal opportunity, was absent. Do these expenditures represent an equitable share for minorities as compared with the dominant group? This is the core of the civil rights issue, not merely the comparison of outlays for minorities from year to year, as important as this is for other purposes.

CIRCULAR A-11

Circular A-11 described the procedure by which agency budgets were to be prepared and submitted to OMB. In order to improve the quality of the civil rights data to be used for the preparation of the next Special Analysis of Federal Civil Rights Activity, Circular A-11 was revised to add a request that civil rights enforcement and minority assistance programs submit narrative, budgetary, and beneficiary data. But this request was so qualified as to purpose, timing, and area of permissiveness that it could not permanently lock into the agency budget either submission requirements or the racial and ethnic data necessary for objective determination of the allocation of program resources by racial and ethnic group of the beneficiaries.

In the first place, the submission of beneficiary data was optional, thus relieving the agency of the responsibility of beginning to collect it. Secondly, this was a special purpose, one-time request for use in the Special Analysis and since the submission date was made after the budgeting hearings, it could not be a factor in determining the federal budget, even for one year.

Thus in regard to civil rights the OMB has made significant gestures toward recognizing the need for requiring each agency to submit information on its civil rights budget for OMB examination and ultimate approval, only apparently to shrink from a bold application of its policy in the end. It has not asked for the effects of a program on beneficiaries who are minorities, or that a program be committed to making a maximum effort to reach minorities, or that plans be initiated to overcome failures to serve minority beneficiaries.

PERFORMANCE MANAGEMENT SYSTEM

At the hub of OMB's mechanisms for carrying out the mission assigned to it by the president, the Performance Management System (PMS) was organized as a way of evaluating programs in order to improve federal management processes. PMS was a system by which the widely known managerial technique called "management by objective" could be brought to bear on program administration from top to bottom of the government hierarchy. Potentially it was a means by which the effectiveness of federal management and even managers could be appraised and presumably measured objectively. Program

goals, timetables for executing them, and data collection systems could
be reviewed and revised by the OMB so that agencies' progress toward
meeting these goals could be measured.

Since OMB policy considered civil rights matters an integral part
of agency programs, and one of the major innovations of OMB required
by the president was to give emphasis to program evaluation, it was
reasonable to expect that the PMS would include evaluation not only of
agencies whose major activities were specialized civil rights and equal
opportunity programs, but also evaluation of the civil rights aspects of
general agency programs not addressed specifically or uniquely to minorities.

In the president's designation of the type of evaluation OMB
should make, there was a statement that should assess the extent to
which programs are actually achieving the intended results, and delivering the intended services to the intended recipients."[6] Furthermore, the OMB director in a memorandum to the OMB staff of March
25, 1971, directed that the PMS should be employed "to insure that
the achievement of civil rights goals is clearly and specifically included among the performance responsibilities of program managers."[7]

Despite support for the policy by management at this high level,
its development as a tool for evaluation was slow and very limited in
scope, and had virtually no impact on the promotion of equal opportunity
in grants-in-aid programs. Its application to civil rights programs was
almost non-existent. In fact, the prospects for its use were foreclosed
by the government's racial and ethnic data collection policy: OMB made
regulations for the collection of racial and ethnic data discretionary
rather than mandatory. This meant that PMS did not have a viable
nationwide basis for monitoring the delivery of services to minorities
by state and local governments and private groups receiving grants-
in-aid from the federal government. It precluded the prospect of
government-wide use of the technique for the purpose of evaluating the
civil rights aspects of these programs.

Under these conditions, only those agency programs whose sole
purpose was either assistance to minorities or enforcement of equal
opportunity laws and regulations were likely to collect racial and ethnic
data adequately. Those agencies that considered they were serving the
general public were less likely to be motivated to do so. Predictably,
then, PMS as a system has to date been applied to the Equal Employment Opportunity Commission (EEOC) and to the Office of Minority
Business Enterprise (OMBE) but not to equal opportunity programs of
the major grant-administering agencies such as the Departments of
Health, Education, and Welfare, Housing and Urban Development,
Labor, and Transportation.

In the specifically equal opportunity-oriented agencies, the possible managerial improvements from the PMS were increased efficiency, higher productivity, and effectiveness in rendering a particular

kind of service to a more or less homogeneous group of beneficiaries. But the more significant possible improvement in the major grant-administering departments would have been the more equitable allocation of total benefits among beneficiaries differing in racial and ethnic characteristics. The disinclination of OMB operational management to implement a sound civil rights policy in the latter group deprived the agency of a potent tool for achieving civil rights goals in all programs. Although OMB's principal responsibility was to evaluate the effectiveness of federal programs and to make an assessment of the extent to which they reached their intended beneficiaries, it did not institute a systematic evaluation of whether minorities have achieved equal access to the benefits of federal financial assistance.

LEGISLATIVE REVIEW

One of the functions of OMB as well as its predecessor was to assist the president "by clearing and coordinating departmental advice on proposed legislation and by making recommendations as to presidential action on legislative enactments."[8] This direction gave OMB a good chance to ensure that legislative programs of the respective departments were in tune with current civil rights edicts and with OMB civil rights policy. Circular A-19 stated the procedures for such clearance. In a transmitted memorandum attached to this Circular in July 1971, "provisions for reviewing civil rights implications of proposed legislation" were stated. It directed departments and agencies to find out whether legislative proposals would implement present civil rights laws, and whether these laws were "consistent with the Administration's civil rights policies and directives."

However, this memorandum had little influence on the legislative clearance process. OMB did not put pressure on agencies to comment on the probable impact of proposed statutes on minorities. OMB staff members have not been able to recall any examples in which civil rights considerations were included in the review of substantive legislation.

A year later, in July 1972, a revised Circular A-19 directed government departments and agencies to take into account certain specified civil rights laws when reviewing legislation, that is, Title VI of the Civil Rights Act of 1964, Titles VIII and IX of the Civil Rights Act of 1968, and Executive Orders 11246, 11478, and 11512. However, once again limitations on the nature and scope of the implementation of the operational directive demonstrated the nature of the gap between civil rights policy and practices.

COORDINATION OF FEDERALLY ASSISTED PROGRAMS

One of the new functions of OMB which was not a part of BOB's responsibilities was "to assist in developing efficient coordinating mechanisms to implement government activities and to expand inter-agency cooperation."[9] The coordination of federally assisted programs was a means of achieving decentralization of government activities and increased cooperation with state and local governments. Until now, however, the application of civil rights policy has been very limited and optional where applied. In March 1972 in a transmittal memorandum to Circular A-95, OMB directed that, in reviews of applications for federal assistance, the civil rights implications of such programs be considered. But these provisions were not mandatory requirements of the applicants, and Circular A-95 did not give specific standards for review of applications or make mandatory the treatment of civil rights considerations. The question as to whether the Organization and Management Systems Division intended to act positively and af-firmatively in civil rights matters was raised by the following situa-tion: the state, metropolitan, and regional clearing houses which were the planning agencies that circulated submitted applications were not required to submit them to civil rights organizations that would have a direct concern with the final disposition of applications. The Organ-ization and Management Systems Division which oversaw the evalua-tion, review, and coordination of federally assisted programs and projects is only now at the point of considering whether the uniform application form for all federal aid should require a statement by the applicant on the impact on minorities of the proposed program or project.

In examining the serious deviations of OMB's civil rights im-plementation from its avowed policy, one must not lose sight of OMB's rather remarkable beginnings in recognizing the civil rights aspects of its program over a wide range of issues. Dr. Shultz unquestionably left a sound policy legacy in his ground-breaking memoranda on the civil rights responsibilities of top management. But the record of OMB in this area discloses an inexcusable emphasis on discretionary action in areas where systematic development of mandatory approaches are needed and frequently are required by law. Limitation of resources is hardly a justification for this emphasis on discretionary action. A recognition of responsibility in the civil rights area and a systematic application of required enforcement procedures—even if they are on a limited demonstration basis—should be coupled with sampling tech-niques that would allow a gradual but systematic phasing-in of mandatory programs under the supervision of the powerful Office of Management and Budget.

NOTES

1. Center for National Policy Review, Establishing a Federal Racial/Ethnic Data System, Vol. II, Appendix B. A Report of the Inter-agency Racial Data Committee, Morton H. Sklar and Margaret A. Cotter, Co-Chairmen (Washington, D. C. : The Center for National Policy Review, School of Law, The Catholic University of America, 1972), p. 76. (See also Appendix A1.)

2. Ibid. , pp. 80-85. (See Appendix A2.)

3. See also Ott, David J. and Attiat F. Ott, Federal Budget Policy (Washington, D. C. : The Brookings Institution, 1969), pp. 22-42.

4. United States Commission on Civil Rights, The Federal Civil Rights Enforcement Effort—A Reassessment (Washington, D. C. : Government Printing Office, 1973), pp. 17-20.

5. Ibid. , p. 20.

6. United States Commission on Civil Rights, To Know or Not to Know: Collection and Use of Racial and Ethnic Data in Federal Assistance Programs (Washington, D. C. : Government Printing Office, 1973), pp. 66-67. See also, U. S. President, Public Papers of the Presidents of the United States (Washington, D. C. : Government Printing Office, 1971), Richard M. Nixon, 1970, pp. 257-63.

7. Ibid. , p. 73.

8. General Services Administration, U. S. Government Organ-ization Manual, 1971-72 (Washington, D. C. : Government Printing Office, 1971), p. 60.

9. Ibid.

2

As the government's chief law enforcement agency, the Department of Justice has played a central role in the federal civil rights effort, particularly in litigation. But it has also been assigned another kind of role in the civil rights area—that of providing for the "coordination by the Attorney General of enforcement of Title VI of the Civil Rights Act of 1964."* By Executive Order 11247 issued on September 24, 1965, President Lyndon B. Johnson transferred the responsibilities for coordination of the enforcement of Title VI from the President's Council on Equal Opportunity to the Department of Justice:

> The Attorney General shall assist Federal departments
> and agencies to coordinate their programs and activities
> and adopt consistent and uniform policies, practices,
> and procedures with respect to the enforcement of Title
> VI of the Civil Rights Act of 1964. He may promulgate
> such rules and regulations as he shall deem necessary
> to carry out his functions under this Order. [1]

---

*The Department of Justice is, in effect, the agency of last resort where noncompliance is found and sanctions either are unavailable to the federal agencies (as in the case with EEOC under Title VII of the Civil Rights Act of 1964) or the sanctions available (such as withholding of federal welfare payments from an entire state) are deemed less appropriate than the bringing of a lawsuit. Further, the Department of Justice passes on the legality of significant new civil rights policies proposed by all other federal departments and agencies.

Although the President's Council on Equal Opportunity had been given
the jurisdiction of a super agency covering the entire federal establishment in relation to their grants-in-aid programs and employment
practices (Civil Rights Acts of 1957 and 1964), during the council's
life of about seven months it exerted very limited influence over these
programs and actions, its work being confined very much to merely
assisting and coordinating.

THE COORDINATING FUNCTION:
INTERPRETATION AND IMPLEMENTATION

How the role of coordinator of Title VI was interpreted and acted
upon by the Department of Justice would be of critical importance for
minorities' access to federal grants-in-aid programs. In its position
as the last link in the chain of command above the line agencies, DOJ
was the management arm closest to the grant-administering agencies.
Title VI required that no person be denied the benefits of or be discriminated against in any program or activity receiving federal financial
assistance. How would the DOJ carry out its mandate to coordinate
Title VI enforcement activities?

Assignments involving coordinating responsibilities more or less
similar to DOJ's, but in very specific civil rights program areas, had
been given to other agencies at a lower level in the bureaucratic hierarchy. The Office of Federal Contract Compliance (OFCC), for example, had been designated under Executive Order 11246 as the coordinating agency for all equal employment opportunity activities of
government contractors and made a part of the Department of Labor.
The Civil Service Commission (CSC) under Executive Order 11478 of
1968 (which superseded Executive Order 11246) and the Equal Employment Opportunity Act of 1972 performed similar services in assuring
equal employment opportunity within the federal government. Under
Title VIII of the Civil Rights Act of 1968, the Department of Housing
and Urban Development (HUD) was given coordinating responsibilities
covering the fair housing activities of all federal agencies. In 1974
the Office for Civil Rights (OCR) became the government-wide coordinating agency for the enforcement of the bans on discrimination
against the physically and mentally handicapped.

The nature and scope of the function of coordination varied from
agency to agency, depending on the provisions of the particular executive order under which it operated, the social and political climate
prevailing at the time the order was issued, the nature and depth of
commitment to equal opportunity of the executive in charge, and other
considerations. The question was, what kinds of civil rights management decisions was the Department of Justice empowered by law

to make? By comparison with the coordinating functions assigned to
some of the other departments, the DOJ seemed to have been given
less authority. The Department of Labor and its Office of Federal
Contract Compliance, for example, seemed to have a stronger mandate
and more affirmative power for dealing with minority employment
policies and practices of private contractors doing federal work under
its executive order:

> The Secretary of Labor shall be responsible for the ad-
> ministration of Part II and III of this Order and shall adopt
> such rules and regulations and issue such orders as he deems
> necessary and appropriate to achieve the purposes thereof.[2]

Likewise, in the case of the Civil Service Commission, the strength
of managerial authority granted by law and regulations was much greater
than that given the DOJ. Moreover, the authority of CSC was increased
with the passage of the Equal Employment Opportunity Act of 1972 above
that provided in the executive order of 1969, which had provided that the
CSC "shall provide leadership and guidance to departments and agencies." The wording of the 1972 Act was more specific and demanding:
"The Civil Service Commission shall have authority to enforce the
provisions . . . through appropriate remedies, including reinstate-
ment or hiring of employees with or without back pay . . . and shall
issue such rules, regulations, orders and instructions as it deems
necessary and appropriate to carry out its responsibilities."[3]
The coordinating function in these civil rights programs between
1965 and 1972 had been moving from a non-management consultative
posture toward a management role of increasing specificity and vigor.
In contrast, the DOJ had clung tightly to a strict interpretation of the
scope of its authority. David Norman, assistant attorney general for
civil rights (Civil Rights Division), from 1971-73 defined the situation
this way:

> The executive order having placed the coordinating re-
> sponsibilities in the attorney general is otherwise very
> unspecific, and different people around government and
> outside the government construe coordinating respon-
> sibilities in different ways. We have operated for the
> most part from the beginning of the exercise of the
> authority under the executive order in a capacity of
> assisting other agencies with legal and technical prob-
> lems. . . . That has been the basic role of the DOJ
> with respect to Title VI. . . . The controversy has
> been about what is coordination, what should the DOJ
> be doing in its coordination. Critics say that we should
> take an aggressive, more or less stronger stand than

other agencies—tell them what they have to do and how
they have to shape up their civil rights Title VI programs.[4]

From the outset, the Justice Department saw its scope of
authority for coordinating the Title VI requirements in federal
financial assistance as a very limited one. This was apparent from
the way its civil rights work in this domain was structured and staffed.
Soon after Executive Order 11247 was activated, the former general
counsel of the President's Council on Equal Opportunity, David V.
Filvaroff, became special assistant to the attorney general for Title
VI at grade GS-17. A professional staff of two attorneys and one research assistant constituted the staff of the Office of the Special
Assistant. The special assistant reported directly to the attorney
general, but his office became a part of the Civil Rights Division for
administrative purposes.
    Conflict appeared from the beginning between the approach of
the special assistant to the attorney general for Title VI, who advocated
that the department adopt a broad view of its responsibilities, and officials of the Civil Rights Division of the Department of Justice, who
considered Title VI basically as a litigation tool. Even contact between
these two offices was not mandatory and regular, but was carried on
on an ad hoc basis.
    Filvaroff resigned in August 1966 and was not replaced, but his
functions were assumed on a part-time basis by the first assistant to
the assistant attorney general for the Civil Rights Division. Shortly
thereafter (December 1966) the position of special assistant to the
attorney general for Title VI was established at GS-16 level and the
Civil Rights Division's chief trial attorney was appointed. During his
four month tenure only one part-time attorney was added to the staff
of this office, and in April 1967, eight months after the first special
assistant resigned, another Department of Justice staff member,
David F. Rose, assumed the role of special assistant to the attorney
general. Upon assuming these duties Rose's grade was raised from
GS-15 to GS-17.
    During Rose's 2.5 years in this post the staff of his office in-
creased from two attorneys and one research assistant to eight attorneys and two research assistants, but the responsibilities of this
office were broadened and the emphasis on Title VI decreased during
his tenure. With this change the office became an integral part of the
Civil Rights Division, and unlike his predecessors Rose reported to
the assistant attorney general for civil rights rather than directly to
the attorney general. Moreover, Rose's office became the focal point
for all Department of Justice contact with other federal agencies on
civil rights matters, whether or not related to Title VI. It was given
the department's legislative drafting responsibilities and became

concerned with a good deal of litigation. Some of it dealt with Title VI matters, but most did not. In any case, the added functions more than consumed all the additional personnel resources added to this office.

Approximately three months later, in July 1969, the Title VI functions of the Justice Department were further downgraded and blurred in the process of another merger which eliminated any semblance of independence of the office or the existence of a special assistant to the attorney general. The Office of the Special Assistant for Title VI was merged with the internal Office of Planning and Coordination of the Justice Department by the assistant attorney general of the Civil Rights Division. In announcing this merger Rose stated that the new Office of Coordination and Federal Programs would be responsible for planning appeals and legislation, internal coordination, and the coordination of the civil rights programs of the federal agencies. But the staff time devoted to Title VI work did not increase, and the additional functions of the unit resulted in even less emphasis on Title VI matters.

Approximately two months later, in September 1969, the Title VI coordination functions of the Justice Department were pushed even farther down the list on the hierarchy of importance. The Civil Rights Division was reorganized, Rose was appointed chief of the Employment Litigation Section of the Civil Rights Division, and one of his staff members became director of the partly reorganized Title VI unit, now called the Office of Coordination and Special Appeals. The new director of this office, J. Harold Flannery, was not given the title of special assistant to the attorney general and, unlike his predecessor, did not report directly to the assistant attorney general, but rather to a senior deputy assistant attorney general. Only one full-time person was assigned to Title VI matters in this new office, which was composed of Flannery, his deputy, five staff attorneys, and one research assistant. Moreover, while both the director and his deputy had experience in the civil rights field, neither of these had any significant experience in dealing with Title VI matters.

Less than a year later, on July 1, 1970, the Coordination and Special Appeals Section was split into three parts upon the departure of its director and deputy director. A GS-15 attorney from the Civil Rights Division's Employment Section, Thomas Ewald, who had had no previous experience in dealing with Title VI matters, was made head of the Title VI unit. By this move the Title VI function was further downgraded; instead of being under the direction of a section chief it was made a small unit directed by a junior attorney who reported to one of the junior deputy assistant attorneys general.

Despite the obvious decline of Title VI matters in the hierarchy of management, Ewald and his office were given rather specific responsibilities and some resources for meeting them. The unit had a

staff of four full-time professionals working on Title VI coordination,
the development of the Title VI program, and litigation under Title VI.
The unit was also responsible for conducting the factual investigation
within the defendant agency and for coordinating the defendant officials
and the Department of Justice Civil Rights Division when federal officials were named defendants in suits alleging racial discrimination.
It continued to act as the division's liason with federal agencies in civil
rights matters, many of which did not involve Title VI.

Given the structure and staffing of the Justice Department's
Title VI coordinating machinery by 1970, one could not have expected
to find that the department had been meticulous and emphatic in carrying
out its coordination responsibilities. Furthermore, some of the apparent deficiencies of its coordination program may well have stemmed
from the extremely litigative bias of the agency, considering the fact
that virtually all of its staff were lawyers and legal assistants who
were frequently involved in protracted litigation and not in assisting
and coordinating the Title VI effort. The result was a failure to enforce the civil rights provisions in the granting of federal assistance,
since no one had taken the leadership necessary to end racial and
ethnic discrimination in the government's grants-in-aid programs.
At the end of 1971, the work to end discrimination, anticipated by the
executive order giving the job to the Justice Department, had been
both neglected and hobbled by lack of staff and by the large amount of
time devoted to litigation. The Civil Rights Commission analyzed the
causes of the abysmal performance of the Department of Justice in its
role of Title VI coordinator.

> The Title VI unit has never clearly identified Government
> enforcement goals and priorities; it has undertaken no pro-
> gram of systematic, indepth analysis of agency compliance
> potential; it has not routinely supported agency civil rights
> staffing requests before the Bureau of the Budget; it has
> not met regularly with agency personnel to discuss quarterly
> reports and to identify deficiencies in agency actions; it has
> not used all the means at its disposal to insure that agencies
> take strong and prompt administrative action where non-
> compliance is uncovered; and it has taken no steps to re-
> quire agencies to devote adequate manpower to the problems
> of the Spanish-speaking minority. Finally, instead of in-
> creasing manpower and expanding the effort to develop an
> effective uniform Government Title VI program, the Justice
> Department has cut back its Title VI staff, reduced the level
> of its Title VI office, and relegated it to the role of litigating
> Title VI suits and responding to agency requests for aid on
> an ad hoc basis. [5]

At the end of 1971, the major efforts of the Justice Department as coordinator of Title VI were the collection and analysis of Title VI quarterly reports, meetings with Title VI coordinators, the appointment of special interagency committees, assistance to agencies in the development of the system for establishing equal opportunity goals for each of their programs, ad hoc assistance to agencies in resolving particular problems, assistance in litigation, and the coordination of matters not related to Title VI.

The Title VI office continued a reporting system which had been established by the President's Council on Equal Opportunity, under which each agency with Title VI programs was required to submit quarterly reports, giving in detail the status of Title VI activities carried out by that agency. These reports were not in narrative form but consisted of a listing of data such as the number of assurances of compliance submitted by recipients, the number of complaints received and investigated, the number of complaint reviews undertaken, and the number and nature of actions taken on noncompliance situations. Unfortunately they had limited value because they provided only statistics and gave no explanation of the meaning of the statistics. Furthermore, they were not regularly reviewed by members of the Title VI office staff and they were rarely followed up.

ORGANIZATIONAL STRUCTURE AND STAFFING

During David Norman's tenure as assistant attorney general for civil rights of the Civil Rights Division of the Justice Department he increased the size of the Title VI staff and raised its status in the department. In 1971 the Title VI operation was raised from office status to the section level, giving it peer status with other civil rights and equal opportunity programs such as those in public accommodations, employment, voting, crime, housing, and education. Norman virtually doubled the Title VI staff: 21 positions (13 attorneys, three research analysts, and five clerical personnel) were authorized for 1973, a GS-16 section chief was made head of the program, and $296,000 was appropriated for running the section.

An innovation in the organization of the legal staff of Title VI was made. Lawyers, formerly sent to agencies on the basis of availability at the time of a request for assistance, were now assigned to a particular agency or group, so that their expertise would be cumulative and the rapport with the agency personnel with whom they worked on a regular basis would be reflected in more positive results. Attorneys from the Civil Rights Division had major involvement in Title VI matters with the Department of Agriculture, the Economic Development Agency in the Department of Commerce, the Department of

Health, Education, and Welfare, the Department of Housing and Urban Development, the Law Enforcement Assistance Administration of the Department of Justice, the Department of Labor, and the Department of Transportation. They had minor assignments with the American Revolution Bicentennial Commission, the Appalachian Regional Commission, ACTION, the Equal Employment Opportunity Commission, the Department of Defense, the Veterans Administration, the Department of Treasury's Office of Federal Revenue Sharing, and some of the federal financial regulatory agencies such as the Federal Home Loan Bank Board, the Federal Deposit Insurance Corporation, the Federal Research Board, and the Comptroller of the Currency.

These changes in structure, staffing, and organization of the Civil Rights Division seemed to signal a significant effort to reverse some of the negative movement in status and resources that had commenced before 1966, but they did not result in any more pressure on fund-granting agencies to end racial and ethnic discrimination. David Norman was asked in an interview whether his Title VI program had a monitoring role and answered:

> We do have a monitoring role though it is unstructured.
> There was a time when we required agencies to file
> reports with us periodically on what they were doing.
> That didn't do it and it seemed to me that this was not
> highly productive. It just added another nuisance to the
> agency that was trying to do some work. It compounded
> paper work. But we do monitoring on an informal basis
> by our people going to the appropriate people in an agency
> and sitting down and going over carefully what it is that
> they are doing and hopefully making constructive sugges-
> tions. [6]

This approach may have met the needs of agencies that were willing to try to meet their Title VI responsibilities and those that were aware of a need for assistance, but it made no contribution to bringing the willfully recalcitrant and the unaware agencies into compliance.

Norman was asked what the coordinating agency would do in a situation in which it had exhausted all of its efforts at technical assistance, guidance and advisory services, and no progress toward compliance was achieved. Would he consider the responsibilities of his agency completed? His reply was significant:

> No. I think that it would be an unlikely case if nothing
> improved, especially with time. There is never any
> point in time when you can say the matter is hopeless
> and there will never be any improvement. What we do
> is look back in on them in six months or later to see

what they are doing. If they need more suggestions,
they will get them. [7]

In this passive consultative role, the Title VI section appeared
to feel no responsibility for assuring prompt and full compliance on
the part of the agencies it advised. Moreover, not all agencies with
major Title VI responsibilities were required to ask DOJ for assistance
if they did not want to improve the quality and effectiveness of their
compliance effort or if they were so insensitive to the civil rights
obligations as to be unaware of the need for the assistance of DOJ's
Civil Rights Division.

COORDINATING ACTIVITIES:
SCOPE AND LIMITATIONS

The major Title VI coordinative activities of DOJ in 1972 were
summarized in the Civil Rights Division's annual report as follows:[8]
the increased staff used "substantial time" to provide services to
compliance programs of seven agencies with large Title VI responsibilities. The purpose of these services, according to the report, was
to help the agencies develop "more uniform and effective evaluation
procedures. " The staff also coordinated the adoption of uniform amendments to the Title VI regulations by 21 government agencies, and helped
others in their adoption of initial Title VI regulations. They also gave
advice on several proposed regulations and guidelines about matters
closely related to Title VI which were issued by various agencies for
their own use, and responded to requests from other agencies for
legal opinions on various subjects "including specific issues raised
in private litigation. " Finally, the division gave high priority to litigation against recipients of federal financial assistance charged with
discrimination, and as a result filed two cases against State Extension
Services "alleging denial of equal services to minority persons. "[9]
Indicative of the leisurely pace at which some of the DOJ Title
VI programs developed was its involvement in obtaining uniform Title
VI amendments to the original Title VI regulations. An interagency
task force concluded in July 1967 that such amendments were needed,
yet more than five years later these changes through amendment had
not been made. The amendments proposed by 20 federal agencies
were finally published in the Federal Register of December 9, 1971,
as a proposed rule-making procedure. After receiving comments
and criticisms the division recommended that 11 of the 20 agencies
make additional changes in the proposed amendments. By August
28, 1972, seven of the 11 agencies had changed the amendments and
sent them to the DOJ to be submitted to the president. [10]

The Title VI staff of DOJ also assisted several departments
and agencies in developing plans for improving their collection and
use of racial and ethnic data. After consulting with DOA personnel
on the applicability of the standards established by a court decision
against the Alabama Cooperative Extension Service to other state
extension services, Title VI staff helped DOA prepare affirmative
action requirements, which were submitted to all state extension
services in February 1972.

The Title VI staff also surveyed several agencies, prepared
analyses of the implementation patterns and practices of some, and
developed several plans for Title VI application. However, the Title
VI unit was unduly secretive about what it found in its surveys. Whatever information it uncovered about the funding practices of the agencies
as they related to compliance with Title VI, it did not release to other
agencies, particularly the Commission on Civil Rights. Instead of
shielding such agencies, the DOJ Title VI staff should have been doing
all it could to secure compliance with Title VI. It was highly questionable whether withholding information about the performance of these
agencies more than seven years after the responsibilities for Title
VI implementation were imposed on them would help secure compliance
by them. Although the Department of Justice reported that "the Title
VI Section had prepared analyses of Title VI implementation on the
part of certain federal agencies and had drafted several plans for
implementing Title VI, " neither the analyses nor the plans were made
available. DOJ maintained that "these documents were intended for use
by the Civil Rights Division or the agencies in question . . . [and]
release of copies would not be consistent with our function. "* Consequently, although the department had formulated specific plans to
assist agencies, the scope and quality of these plans were not made

---

*Attachment to letter from David L. Norman, Assistant Attorney
General, Civil Rights Division, Department of Justice, to Rev.
Theodore M. Hesburg, Chairman, U. S. Commission on Civil Rights,
September 15, 1972, at 4:00 p. m. "The department's refusal to make
such reports available severely limits the ability of the Commission
staff to evaluate the Title VI Section. Furthermore, such a position
is inconsistent with the Commission's legislative mandate, which
directs federal agencies to 'cooperate fully with the Commission to
the end that it may effectively carry out its functions and duties. '
According to DOJ officials, these surveys are only draft documents and
not official departmental positions. Even if they were final reports,
however, attempts by anyone other than the agency surveyed to secure
copies would be resisted on grounds that an attorney-client relation-

public* until 1975, when DOJ reversed its policy of secrecy and made available the requested documents describing the contents of agency reviews it had conducted. 11

Department of Justice officials still contended that their authority under Title VI was not broad enough to require other agencies to impose administrative or judicial sanctions. † Executive Order 11247 has been consistently interpreted by the department as giving it advisory powers only. Direction of agency activities by DOJ was viewed by DOJ as usurpation of agency powers. Although the Civil Rights Commission recommended that the executive order be amended to authorize the attorney general to direct agencies to take specific compliance and enforcement action, the recommendation was not acted upon. ††

The department's legal jurisdiction as the coordinating agency for the programs giving financial grants was defined again by a new executive order (11764) issued by President Nixon in early 1974, one which superseded the original enabling order. It gave the department broad authority to oversee the Title VI activities of all government agencies, authority that went beyond the old role of assisting. However, by mid 1975 the attorney general had not exerted firm managerial and directional authority over the some 25 federal agencies that collectively control the vast amount of federal monies in the grants-in-aid programs. Moreover, Assistant Attorney General for Civil Rights, J. Stanley Pottinger, who succeeded David Norman, faced direct challenges to his authority in 1975 by the Department of Agriculture and the Office for Civil Rights of HEW (of which he was director prior

---

ship exists, and that disclosure would have a chilling effect on the relationship between the department's Title VI personnel and the agencies. "

*The Commission on Civil Rights also requested DOJ to provide copies of any legal opinions concerning Title VI matters written after October 1971. The DOJ replied that the attorney general had not issued any such opinions, but that the department had responded to agency requests for its views concerning Title VI. The department declined to provide copies of these views, claiming that doing so would be inconsistent with its functions, but reversed its policy in 1975.

†On June 1, 1972, for example, letter from K. William O'Connor, Deputy Assistant Attorney General, Civil Rights Division, Department of Justice, to Harold C. Fleming, Leadership Conference on Civil Rights: " . . . we have not interpreted our coordinating function to authorize direction of the actions of the other federal agencies. "

††"The Department is considering whether the Title VI Section can be more effective with broader authority, as this Commission has urged. "12

to going to the Justice Department). In neither of these cases has
DOJ taken jurisdiction, as the Office of Federal Contract Compliance
did in a similar situation, nor at this writing has the department taken
any formal action. It is difficult to understand why it has not done so.
Is the Department of Justice a prisoner of its occupational preoccupa-
tion with the litigative as opposed to the firm decision-making role
which a manager must play?

Under the aegis of Pottinger, the efforts of the department to
upgrade the staff and improve the organization of its Title VI program
have continued. By April of 1975 the Federal Programs Section (FPS),
which had the Title VI coordinating functions in the Civil Rights Division,
had increased its staff to about 32 professionals consisting of 14 attorneys, four research analysts, and ten coordination analysts. This
increase represented a significant philosophical and managerial change
in DOJ thinking. For the first time non-lawyers were employed and
given responsibilities separate from and possibly complementary to
the roles traditionally played by the lawyer-dominated staff of the
past. In addition the Federal Programs Section had other staff changes:
two deputy chiefs were made responsible for the coordination of the
Title VI activities of the 25 grant-administering agencies. Also added
was a lead coordinator who reported directly to the deputy chiefs, or
to the FPS chiefs when appropriate. Most important, these coordinators
who were working with their counterparts in the Title VI agencies were
equal opportunity specialists, not lawyers. While it may be too early
to appraise the results of this managerial innovation and its apparent
break with the past, it appears that the Justice Department is beginning
to assemble a staff with the array of skills needed to achieve its
managerial responsibilities as Title VI coordinator. The question is
whether the department will also revise its unduly narrow and legalistic
interpretations of the Title VI enabling orders. These practices of the
Justice Department have created a weak link in the enforcement chain
at a critical place—the level of intermediate management which deals
directly with the line managers for Title VI.

NOTES

1. Code of Federal Regulations: Title III - The President,
1964-65 Compilation (Washington, D. C. , Federal Register, National
Archives and Record Service, General Services Administration, 1967),
pp. 348-49.

2. Ibid. , pp. 339-48.

3. U. S. Congress, Senate Subcommittee on Labor, Committee
on Labor and Public Welfare, The Equal Employment Opportunity
Act of 1972, 92nd Congress, 2nd Session, 1972, p. 17.

4. Interview by author with David Norman, Assistant Attorney General, Civil Rights Division, Department of Justice, December 1972.

5. United States Commission on Civil Rights, The Federal Civil Rights Enforcement Effort (Washington, D. C. : Government Printing Office, 1971), pp. 249-50.

6. Interview by author with David Norman, Assistant Attorney General, Civil Rights Division, Department of Justice, December 1972.

7. Ibid.

8. Civil Rights Division, Department of Justice, 1972 Annual Report, xeroxed (Washington, D. C.), pp. 30-31.

9. Ibid.

10. United States Commission on Civil Rights, The Federal Civil Rights Enforcement Effort—A Reassessment (Washington, D. C. : Government Printing Office, 1973), pp. 236-37.

11. United States Commission on Civil Rights, The Federal Civil Rights Enforcement Effort—1974, Vol. 6, To Extend Federal Financial Assistance (Washington, D. C. : Government Printing Office, 1975).

12. United States Commission on Civil Rights, The Federal Civil Rights Enforcement Effort—A Reassessment, op. cit. , pp. 233-34, including footnotes 6, 7, 9, 10.

3

THE GAP ON THE LINE: THE TITLE VI GRANTING AGENCIES

Federal departments and agencies were required by Title VI of the Civil Rights Act of 1964 to eliminate discrimination in making grants and loans to state and local agencies and private organizations for social and economic programs. Through the statutory mandate of Title VI, supplemented by executive orders and court decisions, the federal government's obligation to prevent discrimination in all financial assistance programs was established. According to Section 601 of the Civil Rights Act of 1964, no person "shall, on the ground of race, color, or national origin, be excluded from participation in, be denied the benefits of, or be subjected to discrimination under any program or activity receiving Federal financial assistance." As operating managers, the departments and agencies made the actual decisions about federal grants and loans and the equal opportunity conditions under which they were granted. They were the line agencies who administered the government's vast financial assistance programs, while the White House, the top budget agencies (BOB and OMB), and the Department of Justice had staff responsibilities in the execution of the Title VI.

In enacting Title VI, Congress directed each of the federal departments and agencies extending federal financial assistance to issue rules and regulations to put the provisions of the statute into effect. Congress also intended that the federal agencies adopt uniform regulations as far as possible. In the months immediately following the passage of the law, a task force made up of representatives from the White House, the Commission on Civil Rights, the Department of Justice, and the Bureau of the Budget worked with HEW to develop regulations for that agency, regulations which were then used as a model for other departments and agencies. In July 1967, after about three years of experience with the administration of Title VI, an interagency committee was formed, with the Department of Justice serving as chairman, to consider the adoption of uniform amendments to the Title VI regulations of agencies. The proposed uniform amendments contained several substantive provisions not found in the original regulations, and some agencies redrafted their regulations to take into account the proposed amendments. However, they were not submitted for presidential approval until the last days of the Johnson administration and were not approved.

Since that time, procrastination in the issuing of uniform amendments has continued apace. Proposed amendments to Title VI regulations of 20 agencies were printed in the Federal Register for " a proposed rule making" on December 9, 1971. The Civil Rights Division of the Justice Department reviewed comments from interested parties and recommended that 11 of the agencies further alter their drafts. By August 28, 1972, seven of these agencies had made additional changes and sent them to the Department of Justice for submission to the president. In addition, there remained other agencies with major Title VI obligations which had not even proposed regulations, among them the Equal Employment Opportunity Commission and the Appalachian Regional Commission. [1] Despite all this activity recognizing the need for uniform regulations, the decisions and interpretations of the proper jurisdiction and coverage of Title VI of the Civil Rights Act have been made on an agency by agency basis, not according to government-wide guidelines. Although the Department of Justice was given the responsibility for coordinating the Title VI activities of all departments and agencies, it failed to develop a uniform policy and guidelines for agencies to use when applying Title VI to giving financial assistance.

The failure of the executive to establish definitive guidelines on the applicability of Title VI had deleterious effects on the administration of the anti-discrimination ban on federal financial assistance programs. There was confusion over the scope and coverage of Title VI. Meanwhile, there were procedures adopted for protecting the government and private agencies receiving the grants. Although minorities who were supposed to benefit from the programs received haphazard and negligent treatment, the state and local agencies getting the federal money for their programs were amply protected against irresponsible and ill advised actions of the grant-administering departments and agencies. [2]

TITLE VI COVERAGE: NO GOVERNMENT-WIDE GUIDELINES

The lack of government-wide guidelines for Title VI had negative consequences of many kinds. Two of the difficult questions of jurisdiction were whether Title VI covered membership by minorities on planning, advisory, and supervisory boards receiving federal funds,

and membership in federally assisted private organizations. Due to
lack of government-wide guidelines, these matters of coverage were
handled agency by agency. Some planning, advisory, and supervisory
boards supported or assisted by money from federal agencies acted in
a planning or advisory capacity to state and local governments. Others
administered federal grants made directly to state and local governments. There was little question that the plans developed by such
boards were subject to the requirements of Title VI. To the extent
that the plans excluded areas with heavy minority group concentrations
or otherwise discriminated against minority group members, they
would have been in violation of Title VI.

The knottier jurisdictional issue was whether Title VI required
that minorities be members of these boards. The agencies were left
to deal with this problem virtually on their own. The Law Enforcement
Assistance Administration (LEAA) of the Department of Justice, for
instance, made planning grants to states for setting up and operating
state law enforcement planning agencies (SPAs) to develop statewide
law enforcement plans and establish law enforcement priorities. The
Economic Development Administration (EDA) of the Commerce Department (DOC) offered planning grants to county and district communities
to develop Overall Economic Development Programs (OEDPs) which
were required before an area or district could receive EDA funds for
the construction of public work facilities. The Department of Housing
and Urban Development (HUD) also operated programs that involved
planning boards. For example, under its program of planning grants
for metropolitan development, known as the 701 Planning Grant Program, the plans were developed by state, metropolitan, and regional
planning agencies.

Neither LEAA, EDA, nor HUD has yet determined that Title VI
applies to the membership on the boards of these planning agencies.
Operating with federal funds under LEAA program guidelines, state
planning agencies were required to have balanced representation,
including representation of community or citizen interests. Yet,
LEAA has not determined that these guidelines required adequate
minority representation, nor has it determined that Title VI applies.

In April 1969, the Lawyers Committee for Civil Rights Under
Law filed a complaint with LEAA alleging that blacks had been systematically excluded from membership on the board of the Mississippi
State Planning Agency. Of the 34 members of the board only one was
a black, although blacks comprised approximately 42 percent of the
state's population. LEAA requested an opinion from the Department
of Justice's Civil Rights Division regarding the applicability of Title
VI to membership on the Mississippi SPA. The response from the
Civil Rights Division suggested that board membership was subject
to Title VI. The response also suggested that exclusion of blacks
from SPA membership was a violation of LEAA's own guidelines:

> Even apart from the question whether or not there is a
> violation of Title VI, it is possible that exclusion of
> Negroes in the instant case is violative of that provision
> of the guidelines promulgated by your agency . . .
> In Mississippi, where Negroes represent over
> 42 percent of the total population, it is difficult to en-
> vision a "representative" group from which Negroes
> have been systematically excluded. [3]

In June 1969 the Lawyers Committee for Civil Rights Under Law
brought suit against the Mississippi Commission on Law Enforcement,
seeking a judgment which would enjoin the defendants from excluding
blacks from being represented on the state planning board. The lower
court refused to grant an injunction, holding that the plaintiffs had
failed to show discrimination in the governor's appointments to the
SPA board and had failed to offer proof that the plaintiffs or the class
they represented—blacks residing in Mississippi—were more qualified
than the present members of the commission. The court nevertheless
recommended that more blacks be appointed to these posts. The decision was appealed to the U. S. Court of Appeals of the Fifth Circuit.
In 1972 LEAA issued a proposed guideline relating to the Title VI
implications of minority representation on SPA supervisory boards
and Regional Planning Units. Title VI violation would be presumed if
minority membership was proportionately low.

In the Commerce Department the EDA took the position that
Title VI did not apply despite the fact that, under existing EDA policy,
all applicants for planning grants had to comply with Title VI with
respect to employment practices and the conduct of their operations.
Although both deputy assistant general counsel for the Commerce
Department and the special assistant for equal opportunity recognized
that Title VI applied to minority representation on Overall Economic
Development Program committees, the special assistant for equal
opportunity felt that coverage could be better provided under EDA's
own regulations. Nevertheless, no procedures had been established
by EDA concerning this matter by late 1970.

Two years later, DOC-EDA issued a directive requiring minority
representation in membership and employment in Development District Organizations, County and Multi-County Planning Organizations,
and Overall Economic Development Program committees. The directive established minimum minority representation, implementation
procedures for selection and approval of minority representatives,
and affirmative action requirements for staff employment of minority
persons. Organizations requesting EDA funds for the first time had
to be in compliance before assistance could be approved. Organizations
receiving assistance prior to June 1, 1971, were required to be in
compliance by December 1972. Only about 30 percent of the districts

were in full compliance with regard to both staffs and boards by the end of 1972.

In a survey of 701 planning agencies receiving HUD grants in 1969, HUD found that of the 23 states having planning boards that furnished data on the racial composition of these boards, only one had a black member and no other minorities were represented. Nevertheless, no action to assure greater minority representation was considered by the HUD at that time.

Other departments which have issued regulations or policies related to Title VI aspects of planning and advisory boards were the Departments of Agriculture (DOA), Labor (DOL), Health, Education, and Welfare (HEW), and the Environmental Protection Agency (EPA). *

Department of Agriculture

The DOA organized a number of advisory groups to help develop and implement agricultural programs. In many of these bodies, minority groups were under-represented—for example, in the Rural Development Committee supported by the Rural Electrification Commission established at the national, state, and county levels. The national and state committees developed general policies, programs, and priorities pertaining to rural development, while the county or other local committees were responsible for details of the development process. In a recent study DOA revealed that membership on county committees was a better measure of community involvement than representation on state or district committees. But in the 16 southern states where county committee memberships were examined by DOA, only 10 percent of the county committee membership was black, while blacks constituted more than 23 percent of the rural population. In Arkansas, where the rural population was about 16 percent black, the membership of blacks on county committees was less than 2 percent. The situation in Louisiana, Maryland, Mississippi and South Carolina was equally bad or worse. These committees were recipients of DOA assistance, so that Title VI requirements should have applied to them.

Department of Labor

The Manpower Administration of DOL established a policy implying some racial and ethnic requirements for the Cooperative

---

* In order to describe how this law has been implemented by the various federal departments and agencies, I relied heavily upon the research of the U. S. Commission on Civil Rights on the enforcement of Title VI by government agencies. CCR studies were made in late 1970, in the second half of 1972, and again in 1975.

Area Manpower Planning System (CAMPS), but has not formulated a policy on the applicability of Title VI to all planning and advisory bodies. These area and manpower councils funded mainly by DOL served in an advisory capacity, identifying manpower needs, setting priorities, and developing comprehensive manpower plans. Although the council members must be selected from three representative groups (clients, business-labor, and agency-sponsored), minority group representation as a requirements was implied but not spelled out in the selection of client representatives. In the choice of the latter, however, Title VI required a parity between the proportion of council members from a particular minority group and the proportion of clients from that minority group. If this situation did not exist, a Title VI violation should have been presumed by DOL.

Department of Health, Education, and Welfare

In the Health and Social Services Division of HEW, Title VI was considered applicable to the selection and tenure of members of the planning, advisory, and governing bodies of the recipients of HEW grants (state advisory committees and boards for individual projects). The minority group membership of these boards was reviewed and made a part of the assessment of reports on state compliance status. To date, no statistics have been compiled on the racial/ethnic composition of these boards and no comprehensive studies to measure the influence of these boards on the general policies or actions of state agencies have been made.

Environmental Protection Agency

The proposed Title VI regulations for EPA prohibited denying a person the opportunity to participate in a program's planning and advisory body because of race, color, or national origin. However, there appeared to be no method to insure minority group participation.

Another issue concerning the coverage of Title VI was connected with minority membership in federally assisted organizations. A variety of federal programs gave assistance to private groups and organizations in the course of carrying out their functions. Policy and practice related to minority group membership in these groups differed widely. For example, the Department of Medicine and Surgery of the Veterans Administration (VA) administered a program which provided space in VA hospitals to national service organizations that helped disabled veterans mainly by assisting them to fill out forms for government assistance. Such organizations included veterans organizations, the Masons, and the American Red Cross. In late 1970 there were 495 office spaces made available to these organizations in 165 VA hospitals. While the VA considered the services being provided in the hospitals to be subject to Title VI—that is, services had to be dispensed in a nondiscriminatory manner—it did not believe that the membership policies of these service organizations were covered by Title VI.

The Department of Housing and Urban Development took a position contrary to that of the VA with respect to fraternal organizations participating in its urban renewal program. HUD's rationale seemed to be the more compelling.

> While . . . the owner-participation agreement must contain appropriate nondiscrimination covenants, a question remains as to whether these covenants must preclude discrimination on the basis of race, color, or national origin in the owner-participant's membership policies and practices. . . . The Department has determined that the fraternal organization must use and operate their property without discrimination, and that a membership . . . would be incompatible with the commitments in the required covenant. [4]

The Small Business Administration (SBA) also required an assurance of open membership policies from any social, civic, or fraternal organization which sought assistance under its programs. The SBA position was stated in one of its directives concerning its direct loan program.

> . . . that consideration of race, color, or national origin of applicants for membership in the organization during the term of the loan would be inconsistent with its commitment as set forth in the execution of the "Assurance" which is deemed to override any membership policies to the contrary required by either the local or national charter or constitution and bylaws. [5]

Decisions and interpretations concerning issues of Title VI scope and coverage have tended to be accomplished on an agency by agency basis rather than government-wide. Sometimes failure to provide coverage has not resulted from a conscious decision to exclude it, but from the lack of any decision at all. Despite the need for uniform federal policy on these important civil rights issues, neither the Department of Justice nor any other authority has attempted to develop definitive guidelines on the applicability of Title VI up to late 1970.

TITLE VI SANCTIONS

There were ample penalties provided in Title VI and its related regulations for assuring that minorities were protected from discrimination had these sanctions been applied fairly, fully, and, above all, promptly, but these sanctions were not applied. Experience to date has indicated, however, that with rare exceptions the bias in implementation procedures of this act has been in favor of the recipient agency or organization, and only secondarily in favor of the protection of the rights of beneficiaries. The stringent procedural requirements for using Title VI sanctions against recipient bodies made a travesty of the idea that federal departments and agencies were arbitrarily denying states, localities, and private organizations the needed federal funds because of Title VI violations. Before sanctions could be invoked several steps had to be taken. First, the agencies were required to try to secure voluntary compliance. Second, under the terms of Title VI, agencies had "to consider alternative courses of action consistent with achievement of the objectives of the statutes authorizing the particular financial assistance."[6] Before cutting off financial assistance they could take other action, including referral to the DOJ for legal action. Moreover, if an agency chose to terminate funds it had to take several additional procedural steps.

The specific penalties provided and the steps by which sanctions should have been applied under Title VI were carefully summarized in the Civil Rights Commission's Report as follows:

> It is important to distinguish between the procedural requirements for refusing or terminating Federal financial assistance as compared to deferral of such assistance. In order to refuse to provide or to terminate Federal assistance, there must be an express finding of discrimination on the record after the recipient is afforded an opportunity for hearing, and a full report must be filed with the appropriate congressional committees. According to Department of Justice guidelines for enforcement of Title VI, however, an agency may defer action on an application without providing the above safeguards. The guidelines provide that deferral is appropriate only in the case of applications for noncontinuing assistance or initial applications for programs of continuing assistance. Moreover, deferral cannot be continued indefinitely.[7]

Sanctions as a tool of enforcement have been used most sparingly. This has occurred despite ample legal basis for them. Increased resources, additional time for refining and institutionalizing the techniques of implementing Title VI, and obvious awareness that voluntary methods without the use of mandatory enforcement actions have historically not proved sufficient to the task.

The shortfall in progress toward effective implementation of Title VI by departments and agencies with major Title VI responsibilities who reported to the Commission in late 1972 has been summarized and updated through late 1975 wherever new information was available.

Department of Health, Education, and Welfare

The higher education enforcement program of HEW received low priority, the evidences of which were inadequate staff, a correspondingly small number of compliance reviews, and the fact that it had never invoked the enforcement mechanism for state systems or private institutions failing to meet their responsibilities under Title VI. This was the case despite lengthy negotiations seeking elusive voluntary compliance.

There were three methods of enforcement available to the Office for Civil Rights (OCR) of HEW in seeking Title VI compliance by elementary and secondary school districts: voluntary negotiations, referral to the Justice Department for possible litigation, and the use of sanctions. During 1972, the three methods were applied by OCR:

First, voluntary negotiations (such as protracted conferences and discussion, and telephone calls) were conducted 185 times in the southern and border states. OCR gave no indication of the number of these negotiation efforts which resulted in compliance.

Second, the OCR referred 73 school systems to DOJ for possible litigation. There was usually no follow-up by OCR to see what action, if any, DOJ had taken. OCR obtained no reports from DOJ on the status of matters referred to the department. When DOJ failed to institute litigation, no further action generally was taken by DOJ or OCR.

Third, when sanctions were used and Title VI enforcement proceedings were brought against three school districts in the southern and border states, the proceedings were characterized by inordinate delay.

A review of OCR activity indicated that, even where school systems were found in noncompliance, the enforcement sanction—termination of federal financial assistance—was only rarely used. In the Elementary and Secondary Education Program, HEW's jurisdiction was increased to include the Emergency School Aid Act and sex discrimination. HEW has also de-emphasized use of the Title VI enforcement sanction in favor of voluntary negotiations, but there is no indication that this approach is succeeding. The compliance and enforcement effort has been blunted by Nixon administration policies on school desegregation, which have lowered the standard of compliance and effectively eliminated administrative enforcement from the arsenal of enforcement weapons. This reluctance on the part of OCR to enforce compliance persisted even after it was under court order because of its apparent negligence in taking such action. This same reluctance to apply mandatory enforcement procedures was evidenced in OCR's dealings with institutions of higher learning at the end of 1974. OCR has repeatedly permitted civil rights violations by colleges and universities to continue without imposing sanctions.

The Health and Social Services Division of HEW found six recipients in noncompliance, five of which were referred to the Office of General Counsel (OGC) for review and determination of enforcement . action. Since the Health and Social Services Division and the Contract Compliance Division shared the services of only four lawyers in OGC, there were serious enforcement delays. Only those problems which could not be resolved by regional staff were forwarded to the headquarters office in Washington as indicating noncompliance.

Department of Labor

Action was initiated by DOL in February 1972 to terminate two of the nineteen recipients found in noncompliance during 1972. No such action was taken in the other seventeen cases. Besides these, there were other cases of noncompliance in various stages of negotiations. No administrative sanctions such as grant deferrals or fund terminations were invoked during 1972. Negotiation was the only strategy DOL used with noncomplying recipients.

Office of Economic Opportunity

No action was taken by OEO to terminate grants because of noncompliance with Title VI. Grants were terminated because of violations of program requirements, though some of these grantees were also in violation of Title VI. In some cases, Title VI termination procedures were intentionally avoided because of their cumbersome nature.

Department of Agriculture

When DOA conducted about 23,000 onsite post-award compliance reviews among its more than 213,000 Title VI recipients, it did not

find that even one recipient was in noncompliance. Of the 974 pre-
approval reviews made by the Farmers Home Administration (FHA)
and the Rural Electrification Administration (REA), only one applicant
was barred. DOA has been dragging its feet in making efforts to
obtain compliance. Its actions against recipients have been limited
to civil litigation. Beginning in April 1973, the Office of the Inspector
General was to have made a series of civil rights audits in selected
areas to ascertain the level of compliance. It has now reached the
point where there are no more excuses for delays in terminating
assistance to recipients if discrimination is found in either their
employment or service.

Department of Commerce

There were no details on enforcement mechanisms used in DOC
when the Economic Development Administration found a recipient in
noncompliance.

Environmental Protection Agency (EPA)

At EPA, simultaneous conciliation and investigation were the
major enforcement tools. Though EPA has not barred any prospective
recipients from any program, there was evidence that grants were
not made when an investigation of an alleged Title VI violation was
pending. Apparently voluntary compliance has been secured in every
case where there was a violation of Title VI. EPA is still a young
agency and perhaps has not been faced with a situation where satis-
factory accommodation could not be made, but its performance in the
future warrants close and careful scrutiny as challenges to its
authority increase.

Department of Interior (DOI)

The DOI has not provided its recipients adequate notification of
what constitutes full compliance with Title VI. Administrative procedures and regulations need to be developed. It is no wonder that,
of the 330 onsite reviews performed in 1972, no recipient was found
in noncompliance.

Department of Justice

The LEAA has reported no findings of noncompliance. While a suit was pending against one LEAA recipient the agency continued to fund the defendant. LEAA has never initiated a suit and has intervened in three suits. Yet LEAA officials have preferred achieving compliance through the courts rather than applying administrative sanctions.

Department of Transportation (DOT)

Only three of DOT's more than 2,000 recipients were found in noncompliance during 1972. No administrative or judicial action was initiated nor was there discussion of DOT's usual procedure when a recipient was found in noncompliance.

Department of Housing and Urban Development

HUD's greatest failing in its enforcement of Title VI has been its failure to use its authority to the fullest extent. When a recipient was found in noncompliance HUD's actions were directed almost exclusively toward achieving voluntary compliance. Although it has the power to defer funding until compliance is obtained, HUD estimated that only 13 deferral status letters were issued during 1972. HUD has never terminated funding when actual discrimination was found. Instead, it has allowed recipients to remain in noncompliance, relying on negotiations in an effort to obtain compliance through voluntary action. Apart from negotiation, HUD had no formal mechanism for encouraging recipients to take affirmative action to further the purpose of Title VI. The overall effectiveness of HUD's enforcement program did not appear to improve significantly between the Civil Rights Commission's report of 1973 and the 1974 assessments. It still had not employed the sanctions available to it under Title VI and it was inclined to permit negotiations with recalcitrant recipients to continue indefinitely without apparent improvement.

Department of the Treasury

The Internal Revenue Service has been a significant force in limiting discriminatory practices in nonpublic schools through the use of its power to set rules governing the tax-exempt status granted to such schools. However, the limitations in the sanction rules which

it established and the scope of coverage of such rules have left the
way open for continuing inequality of opportunity in nonpublic educational institutions. It has not banned discrimination against faculties
of private schools on the basis of race, although HEW has such a ban
in federally funded public school systems and the Title VI regulations
of most government agencies prohibits discrimination in employment.

The administration of Title VI programs has been heavily
weighted with procedural safeguards protecting the thousands of
agencies receiving federal funds, while minorities who are supposed
to benefit from the programs have been neglected or ignored. In
virtually every Title VI program the rights of minority group members with legitimate complaints about discriminatory delivery of
services have been subordinated to those of the funded agencies. Lack
of government-wide guidelines for Title VI enforcement has resulted
in haphazard and negligent management of civil rights and equal opportunity responsibilities by the federal funding agencies. Minorities
need some fair and efficient ways to restore the balance between the
treatment accorded them and the agencies receiving the grants-in-aid
money.

NOTES

1. U. S. Commission on Civil Rights, The Federal Civil Rights
Enforcement Effort—A Reassessment (Washington, D. C.: Government Printing Office, 1973), pp. 236-38.

2. U. S. Commission on Civil Rights, The Federal Civil Rights
Enforcement Effort (Washington, D. C.: Government Printing Office,
1971), pp. 179-81.

3. Law Enforcement Assistance Administration, Guide for
State Planning Agency Grants: Grants for Comprehensive Law Enforcement Planning (November 8, 1968). Pamphlet.

4. U. S. Commission on Civil Rights, The Federal Civil Rights
Enforcement Effort (Washington, D. C.: Government Printing Office,
1971), pp. 192-94.

5. Ibid.

6. Ibid., pp. 194-95.

7. Ibid.

4

**THE GAP ON THE LINE:
MAJOR TITLE VI
COMPLIANCE MECHANISMS**

The discrepancies between the goals espoused by the laws and regulations and the actual achievement of equal access by minorities to the services provided by federally funded agencies were caused by many factors and various major agents. However, the first line of responsibility rested with the federal agency making the grant to a recipient. As granting agency it had the duty to insure that such assistance was dispensed to beneficiaries by the governmental bodies and private organizations receiving the funds without discrimination because of race, color, or national origin. As the administrator of the grant the granting agency thus had the obligation first to satisfy itself that the recipient was complying with Title VI and second to engage in periodic monitoring of the recipient's activities to insure the continuing nondiscriminatory use of federal grant monies by all recipients under its supervision. The grant-administering agencies pursued a variety of activities to insure compliance by their recipients, ranging from merely issuing explanatory pamphlets and educational materials to conducting hearings leading to grant termination.

There were four major procedures by which agencies tried to achieve and maintain Title VI compliance: assurances, compliance reports, compliance reviews, and complaint-processing. The following is a review of these procedures and the experience of key federal departments and agencies in applying each one:

ASSURANCES

In order to insure that recipients have met with requirements of Title VI and its regulations, agencies have developed assurance of compliance forms which are to be filled out by their recipients. Generally, the applicant for federal financial assistance promises to comply with Title VI and all requirements imposed by the corresponding regulations. He also expressly recognizes that federal financial assistance will be given on the basis of this assurance of compliance, and that the government has the right to seek judicial enforcement of it.

Shortly after the passage of Title VI, there was the belief that a well drafted, legally sound assurance would provide the principal tool for Title VI enforcement. According to this belief, assurances would serve several purposes. In the first place, recipients would be put on notice that they were liable to forfeit federal financial assistance if they violated Title VI enforcement. Second, the act of signing the assurance would, in itself, induce recipients to make bona fide efforts to comply with the act. Third, the assurance would provide a clear legal basis upon which action would be taken to terminate funds if the recipient signed and then violated the agreement.

Such optimism was not destined to be justified by subsequent experience. During the summer and fall of 1965 the Commission on Civil Rights conducted a survey of health and welfare services in the South. On the basis of this survey the commission concluded that it appeared that the mere act of obtaining assurances provided no guarantee of full compliance with Title VI. Subsequent reviews and studies have furnished additional evidence that submission of assurance forms did not, in fact, assure compliance with Title VI.

The process by which these assurances were obtained varied widely from one administering agency to another. The procedures for gathering such assurances raised many questions which were answered in different ways by various federal agencies: Of whom would assurances be required? Who should secure the assurances? Should the assurances be contained in the application or incorporated by references? Should the assurance attempt to set forth all of the types of conduct proscribed by Title VI and the agency's Title VI regulations? What procedures should be followed upon a recipient's refusal to execute an assurance?

Treatment of any of these issues was not dictated by Title VI or the agency's regulations. In fact, since there was no effort made to achieve uniformity of interpretation and coordination of practices, there was a good deal of variation in the way agencies responded to these questions. In most of the agencies with Title VI responsibilities assurances were obtained by program or service personnel, the latter being a part of the contract division of the granting office. The usual practice was for an agency to use one basic form, but in some agencies minor revisions were introduced.

This form of implementation procedure has not been highly effective, and the extent to which it has been misused or even

completely ignored, though probably unknown, is undoubtedly significant. For example, file cabinets at HEW's Office for Civil Rights
were filled with 441 assurances from southern local school systems
whose practices were patently in violation of Title VI of the Civil
Rights Act years before desegregation was accomplished. The experience of the Department of Agriculture was another illustration of the
nature of the problem and the dilemmas involved. The Department of
Agriculture was somewhat unique in its approach to obtaining Title VI
assurances from recipients. Of the more than 7,500 assurances
required by DOA by mid-1968, 165 incidents of refusal to file were
under negotiation. By the end of March 1969, 23 refusals to file were
still under negotiation for more than 30 days. Eleven of these refusals
were by land grant universities which were grant recipients under the
Federal Extension Service program. In April 1970, Title VI assurances had not been certified by the presidents of eleven recipient land
grant universities or by the directors of the corresponding Cooperative
Extension Services. A U. S. Commission on Civil Rights report
stated:

> Department of Agriculture officials have indicated that
> they have discouraged recipients from signing assurances
> until they are in full compliance. Agriculture's point is
> well-taken; it would be a travesty of Title VI to accept
> an assurance from a recipient who is clearly in noncom-
> pliance.
>
> Commendable as is Agriculture's refusal to engage
> in this sham exercise, the fact remains that a substantial
> number of Agriculture recipients are still in noncompli-
> ance and continue to receive financial assistance from
> the Department. [1]

COMPLIANCE REPORTS

One of the most, if not the most, important obstacles to the
enforcement of Title VI of the Civil Rights Act was the failure and
inadequacy of administering agencies to obtain periodic compliance
reports from recipients of federal grants. It was the experience of
such agencies in this aspect of their Title VI responsibilities that
raised serious questions not only about the adequacy of their implementation of Title VI, but also about their good faith in the pursuit of
their statutory responsibilities. In fact, it was in this area that
experience to date bordered on the scandalous.

The following statement from the Civil Rights Commission
Report of 1971 is revealing:

The most compelling method of monitoring Title VI compliance undoubtedly is to conduct periodic, onsite inspec-
tions of each of the hundreds of thousands of recipients
of Federal aid who dispense services and other benefits
to the millions of Americans whom Title VI is designed
to protect. Such an undertaking, however, is impractical.
A well-developed system of compliance reports, utilizing
data collection and analysis, can provide an adequate
basis for identifying actual or possible discrimination,
thereby pinpointing programs, facilities, and services
which require more intensive scrutiny and/or enforcement action.

But very few Federal agencies have attained . . .
these objectives, and data collection and analysis have
rarely been utilized to evaluate the extent to which benefits of federally assisted programs are reaching minority
groups. 2

A review of the development of the compliance report technique
during 1971 and 1972 revealed the following: first, the development
of reporting systems was spotty from agency to agency, ranging from
nothing at all to rather sophisticated systems of collection of data;
second, evidence that compliance reporting systems have reached
the analysis stage was meager; third, indication of the specific purposes served by the reports collected was generally either vague or
completely missing.

The status of the compliance report as a tool for compliance
in selected departments and agencies with major Title VI obligations
is summarized in the following section.

Department of Health, Education, and Welfare

In HEW, the responsibility for Title VI rested with the Office
for Civil Rights. Within OCR, there were three areas for which
reporting systems had been developed: the Elementary and Secondary
Education, Higher Education, and Health and Social Services Divisions. The Elementary and Secondary Education Division conducted
a detailed annual survey of enrollment by race and ethnicity which
covered the nation's public school systems. The data covered faculty
and pupil assignments within schools; there were also questions in
the survey which related to bilingual education, new school construction, and the acquisition of sites. OCR had an effective method of
using these data as a basis for determining compliance. It has continued to expand and develop its rather extensive elementary and

secondary education compliance reporting system, and its effectiveness has improved, but with significant limitations.

In the Higher Education Division, information was requested from public and private institutions concerning the racial and ethnic breakdown of part time and full time students according to their academic year. Enrollment statistics which indicated progress or lack of progress in serving minorities supplied one of the primary bases for selecting institutions for compliance reviews. OCR viewed increased minority attendance as an indication of successful implementation of the Higher Education program, but there was some question as to the validity of this view.

The data on enrollment by race and ethnicity were gathered and published every two years as a basis for setting compliance targets for the institutions covered and making comparative analyses of colleges and universities on the level of compliance achieved. Its principal weakness was the time lag between the collection of the data and its availability for analysis, which to date has been much too long for effective use by management as a compliance tool. There was a four year lag in publishing the 1970 data, and almost a three year delay before the 1972 data emerged.

The Health and Social Services Division had a state agency reporting system which was not comprehensive, and OCR was therefore unable to determine the number of reviews conducted by state health and social service agencies. When in 1972, for example, a sampling of ten states using the system showed mixed results, revisions were made to produce more accurate records. Subsequently this division underwent major reorganization, and one hopes that it now includes a more adequate reporting system.

Department of Labor

The DOL instituted a reporting system which yielded an extensive amount of racial and ethnic data on services provided to program beneficiaries as well as on employment practices of some recipients. For instance, each State Employment Security Agency was required to submit a monthly statistical report on the race of each person served. The Employment Service Automated Reporting System constituted an integral part of DOL's Title VI process since it was supposed to give an indication of state agencies that might be in violation of Title VI. But with the data required only on a statewide basis, and local agency summaries only at the discretion of the state agency, the ability of DOL to determine whether discrimination existed at the local level could be impaired.

Sponsors of the manpower programs of DOL were also required to submit racial and ethnic data. An attempt was being made by DOL to develop what it called a Universe of Need profile for each program area in order to insure parity between the race of the participants and the eligible population. Though the reporting system appeared to be somewhat elaborate, there was a question as to whether or not the system was being utilized to its fullest extent. In fact, there was little evidence that any meaningful analysis or evaluation was being done after all of the data were collected.

The Employment Service Automated Reporting System was used until mid-1974, when DOL put its new Manpower Operating Data (MOD) system into operation. MOD differed from the earlier system primarily in the methods of collecting data and probably in the quality of the data collected, but it has also proved to be a disappointment in its application to civil rights and equal opportunity issues. The civil rights staff expressed great hope that MOD would be of use to them, but these hopes have not yet come to fruition.

Department of Agriculture

The Secretary of Agriculture has directed each of the agencies or services of the department to establish a reporting system for collecting and reporting racial data on participation. The operating services, about eleven of which had Title VI responsibilities, differed in the way they met their reporting requirements. The Farmers Home Administration (FHA), for example, had been collecting data on its loan programs for more than five years. Although the data were collected by county offices and aggregated on a statewide basis, which might obscure discrimination in a county office, the FHA, according to the Commission on Civil Rights, made the best use of eligibility data of any agency in the department.

The Extension Service (ES) first resisted collecting data and then finally began to collect information on employment and beneficiaries in major areas, but to date has not evaluated it. There was, however, a national evaluation under way to assess the ability of ES programs to reach, service, and meet the needs of various racial and ethnic groups and to measure the quality and quantity of services provided.

The Food and Nutrition Service of DOA used a sampling technique which included the collection of racial and ethnic data from the National School Lunch Program. In addition, it has had a semi-annual reporting requirement for the Commodity Distribution and Food Stamp Programs. There were two reports in 1971: one was

inaccurate and the other provided no eligibility data. A quality control
system similar to that of HEW was also instituted, based on a sampling of participants who were not public assistance recipients. Racial
and ethnic statistics collected on food stamp and food distribution
programs revealed a high rate of minority participation, but were
meaningless without eligibility data.

Department of Commerce

The Economic Development Administration of DOC was preparing
a data processing system designed to do three things: first, to match
the number of projected jobs and the race and ethnicity of prospective
employees submitted by grant applications with information from an
Equal Employment Opportunity Commission form which reported
actual employment; second, to provide background information for
pre-approval reviews and general information on an area's equal
opportunity position; and third, to improve the ability of EDA's Civil
Rights Office to set priorities for compliance reviews.

Environmental Protection Agency

This new agency used racial/ethnic data supplied on its report
forms from applicants and maps to determine whether disproportionate
numbers of the unserved population were minorities.

Department of Justice

The Law Enforcement Assistance Administration (LEAA) has
distributed compliance report forms covering law enforcement
agencies and developed a tentative system for analyzing the results.
It was in the process of developing similar forms for correctional
institutions and court systems, but by the end of 1975, the survey
forms had not been distributed.

Department of Transportation

In 1971, the Secretary of Transportation gave the collection of
racial/ethnic data a high priority in order to evaluate Title VI compliance, but the procedures have not materialized even though efforts
to upgrade the collection of these data have been made by some
agencies and bureaus within the department.

In its 1974 assessment of Title VI enforcement, the Commission on Civil Rights found that the DOT had made little progress in identifying the long range implications of its massive grants-in-aid programs in terms of their impact on racial and ethnic groups.

Department of the Interior

There was no reporting system requiring recipients to file information on the use of facilities operated by the Bureau of Outdoor Recreation or any of its grant programs covered by Title VI.

Department of Housing and Urban Development

Although HUD has been collecting racial and ethnic data in its housing programs, complete tabulations were not available in 1975. Publication of data on single family housing programs was expected by the end of 1972. Except for data on public housing, which have been collected since that program's inception, data on multifamily housing programs were incomplete and invalid for meaningful analysis. Comprehensive racial and ethnic data were not collected on participants in HUD community development programs, except in conjunction with relocation.

HUD data analysis was restricted by the absence of meaningful comparison data. For example, HUD did not collect data on the racial and ethnic composition of neighborhoods in which single family housing sales were made, or on the racial and ethnic composition of the population for which its own programs were targeted.

A further serious weakness was that housing data were to be tabulated only by Standard Metropolitan Statistical Area (SMSA) and county but not by smaller areas such as cities or communities, greatly limiting the usefullness of the data. This weakness might be mitigated to some extent by the fact that the affirmative marketing plans now required of builders and developers include racial and ethnic data by subdivision and project, data which could be useful in detecting residential patterns of segregation. To assist in overall planning of its projects, HUD has planned to map 268 metropolitan areas to show areas of racial and ethnic concentration. Important planning tools have been designed to include subdivision data and SMSA and county tabulations of mortgage insurance data.

Except for these maps, HUD data collection and use have been restricted to statistics on participants in HUD programs. HUD has not regularly collected data on private housing or made systematic use of census data to survey the nation's patterns. This collection of

uncoordinated, incomplete, and sometimes confusing racial and ethnic
data could not be called a system, and it is not readily apparent how
such data can serve as an effective management tool. The apparent
lack of progress up to 1975 in the face of mounting needs for effective
civil rights and equal opportunity management activities was even
more distressing. At the end of 1974, the U. S. Commission on Civil
Rights summarized its findings on HUD's activities as follows:

> HUD's system for racial and ethnic data collection and
> use continues to be poor, making it difficult, if not
> impossible to determine the extent to which HUD
> programs are reaching minorities and women.
> a. HUD's racial/ethnic data are not generally cross-
>   classified by sex.
> b. HUD does not collect racial and ethnic data on
>   private housing, neighborhood composition, or
>   the population for which HUD's programs are
>   targeted.
> c. Equal opportunity field staff rarely utilize the
>   limited data which are available. [3]

Thus it must be concluded that not only was the HUD collection inadequate (though voluminous) but that which was available was inadequately
analyzed and very much underused for management purposes.

Veterans Administration

The Veterans Administration began its collection of racial and
ethnic data in the fall of 1968 for its housing programs, and its collection has grown since that time to include information on the property locations and the racial and ethnic backgrounds of buyers.
According to these data sales to minorities have been generally high
but have tended to be concentrated in segregated situations, particularly in the case of blacks. The VA initiated the gathering of data on
the racial/ethnic origin of applicants for guaranteed and direct loans
in 1971. In 1973 it added the collection of properly location data for
these loans and data that would show whether veterans were buying
homes with VA help on a segregated or an integrated basis.
   In 1974 the central office of this agency broadened its data
system so that the VA could identify monthly trends in minority participation in VA's acquired property, loan guarantee, and direct loan
programs. It is expected that with the use of this system the VA will
be able to correlate race and ethnic identification with other significant factors such as down payment size, time lapse between appli-

cation and loan approval, and discrepancies in price paid by minority and white nonminority buyers. It is also expected that the system will include racial/ethnic data having to do not only with participants, but also with applicants and/or with persons eligible to participate in the VA housing programs. Through this system the agency could find out the relative participation rate by various racial and ethnic groups. When the system is fully operative it should improve the extent to which the racial and ethnic data collections are actually used for management purposes.

A major criticism of VA's system to date is that its rather extensive body of racial and ethnic data is notably underused. For instance, while the amount of such data on purchases made with the assistance of VA loans is sizeable, the use of such data is limited. The central office has failed to do more than investigate the activities of a field station in conjunction with the routinely scheduled evaluation of that office when the data indicate that discrimination exists. The field stations have assumed only a minor role in using these data. Acquired property data are tabulated by hand in the field stations and sent directly to Washington without analysis by field personnel. Raw data from the loan guarantee applications are sent to the field stations to VA's Data Processing Center, which in turn forwards the tabulations to the central office. Again no field analysis is made. None of the field stations reviewed showed any inclination to use the data as a basis for investigation of the operation of its programs or as a means of measuring its own progress in increasing minority participation in VA housing programs. Further, field stations have not been provided with instructions as to the use of the racial/ethnic data to which they have access. [4]

COMPLIANCE REVIEWS

Compliance reviews include a variety of activities conducted by agencies to determine whether recipients were following nondiscrim-inatory practices. All agencies with Title VI responsibilities were required to perform compliance reviews based on the regulations in the particular agency. The language was generally identical in all agencies, conforming almost word for word to the HEW regulation: "The responsible Department official or his designee shall from time to time review the practices of recipients to determine whether they are complying with this part." Agency reviews of compliance with Title VI by recipients of federal financial assistance ranged all the way from an investigation of a single complaint to a rather compre-hensive and detailed examination of many aspects of a recipient's program. The most effective means of conducting such reviews, though probably the most costly in time, money, and energy, was an on-site investigation of a recipient's operations.

Although these regulations requiring reviews were clear and unambiguous, several agencies had never performed a Title VI compliance review of any of their recipients as late as mid-1970. Moreover, when such reviews were performed, they were generally post-approval reviews, administered after the federal assistance had been extended and the recipient's program had been in operation for some time. In addition, they left much to be desired in the way they were conducted by administering agencies in terms of timeliness, extent of coverage, quality, and comprehensiveness. According to the findings of the U. S. Civil Rights Commission published in 1971:

> Those agencies that do perform compliance reviews rarely reach more than a small percentage of their recipients each year. For many agencies, a large number of recipients have never been subject to an onsite compliance review, e. g. , HEW, HUD, DOC, DOT, OEO, and VA.
>
> Several factors have caused the limited number of compliance reviews by Federal agencies. Foremost has been the shortage of equal opportunity manpower (e. g. , HEW, OEO, VA, HUD, DOT, and Department of Labor). A second factor has been the low priority accorded Title VI activity by many civil rights staffs (e. g. , FHWA, HUD, and the Department of the Interior). A third cause has been the complaint orientation of some agencies, which assumes that their recipients are in compliance if no complaints are filed or, alternatively, the practice of some agencies of placing priority on investigation of complaints over conducting compliance reviews.
>
> The compliance reviews that are conducted by many agencies are, as a rule, of poor quality and grossly inadequate in scope. There are many reasons for these deficiencies including: (1) lack of criteria for selecting candidates for review; (2) failure to develop and/or issue adequate guidelines for reviewers; (3) no training or poor training for civil rights staff involved in Title VI; (4) insufficient and, at times, incompetent or insensitive Title VI staff; (5) reliance on agency program or on State personnel with no civil rights training or sensitivity to perform the reviews as part of their other duties; (6) reliance on contract compliance personnel to do Title VI reviews while conducting their own reviews under Executive Order 11246; (7) failure by the civil rights office or the responsible program adminis-

trator to recommend corrective action to recipients who
engage in questionable practices or (8) if recommendations
are made, failure to conduct follow-up reviews to ascertain if the recipient has taken adequate corrective action. [5]

Post-Approval Reviews

The shortcomings in the post-approval compliance reviews conducted by Title VI grant agencies in 1971 still remained at the beginning of 1973, though it was apparent that positive efforts were being
made by some agencies to correct the weaknesses of their procedures.
The nature and extent of such efforts to improve compliance with
Title VI are indicated in the following review of the stages of development of post-compliance review activities reached by grant-administering agencies at the end of 1972 and in mid-1975 where information
was available.

Department of Health, Education, and Welfare

The Elementary and Secondary Education Reports and Recommendations resulting from onsite reviews were of generally high
quality. From the standpoint of the structure of the monitoring process, HEW was ahead of all other Title VI agencies. Compliance
standards, however, were lowered, and enforcement mechanisms
were not being put to full use to eliminate discrimination within
school systems by the end of 1972.

Since 1972 HEW compliance review operations in elementary
and secondary schools have improved, but important weaknesses
remain. Although the department finally began to review the compliance status of big city school systems and gave greater attention to
in-school discrimination against all minority students, the Office for
Civil Rights did not conduct a sufficient number of compliance reviews
to convince school districts that the federal government meant business
in its commitment to enforce Title VI. The long lag between the investigation, analysis, and probable cause determination and negotiation
tended to undermine the effectiveness of the enforcement plan. Negotiated agreements were made less effective by weaknesses in OCR's
follow-up system.

In the Higher Education Division of HEW's civil rights division,
99 field investigations were conducted in fiscal year 1972, as contrasted with 212 in 1969 and about 150 man-hours spent. Since there
were more than 2,600 institutions receiving financial assistance 99
reviews seemed less than adequate, particularly in view of the fact
that deficiencies in compliance were found in a substantial number of

the 99 educational institutions reviewed. The decline in the number of
reviews was attributed by OCR to the limited size of the staff and to
higher priorities put on other programs. At the end of 1974, HEW had
covered only a small part of the total number of colleges and universities that it was supposed to monitor. The U. S. Commission on
Civil Rights concluded that "HEW has failed to conduct in-depth and
regular compliance reviews of colleges and universities receiving
Federal funds . . . and has repeatedly permitted civil rights violations by colleges and universities to continue without imposing sanctions. " It stated further:

> In the 10 years since Title VI was passed, HEW has con-
> ducted only 803 Title VI compliance reviews, which
> means that less than 30 percent of the 2, 900 campuses
> covered by the Act have ever been reviewed. Further,
> it conducted fewer reviews in Fiscal Year 1974 than it
> had in Fiscal Year 1969, and some of its regional offices,
> such as those in New York and Chicago, have conducted
> no reviews in the last two years. HEW's instructions
> for conducting Title VI compliance reviews are too broad
> in nature, and do not require an adequate amount of
> record examination and data analysis. HEW's ability to
> conduct adequate reviews has been seriously impaired
> by its failure to require colleges and universities to
> compile and analyze pertinent statistics and to maintain
> written affirmative action programs.
>
> Although 60 percent of the Higher Education
> Division's resources have been devoted to its contract
> compliance program, the Division has not reviewed a
> significant number of colleges and universities to
> determine whether they maintain and follow affirmative
> action plans which comply with the Executive Orders.
> As of September 1974, HED had approved affirmative
> action plans of 20 colleges and universities, 2. 2 per-
> cent of the total, and HED recognized that seven of the
> accepted plans did not conform with Executive Order
> regulations. During Fiscal Year 1974, HED conducted
> complete compliance reviews of only 60 colleges and
> universities, or six percent of the total number of which
> the agency is responsible. Furthermore, HEW failed
> to conduct its compliance reviews according to Execu-
> tive Order regulations. [6]

In the Health and Social Services Division, state agencies
carried the major responsibility for Title VI compliance, with on-

site reviews conducted by regional OCR staff in addition to those done,
by state agencies. OCR emphasized reviews of state agencies to
insure equal services for all people. The regional offices determined
what facilities were to be reviewed; 450 on-site reviews were conducted in the first three quarters of fiscal year 1972, some of them
as a part of the monitoring of state agencies. Other reviews were
performed on a preselection or on an area basis, as a part of special
Title VI studies.

Department of the Treasury

The IRS program of compliance reviews of nonpublic schools
under Revenue Ruling 71-447 was highly deficient. According to the
Civil Rights Commission, "The agency has so loosely defined what is
expected of private schools that enforcement action is unlikely except
where discrimination is overt. "[7] Despite an increasing number of
segregated academies established to avoid desegregation, the IRS's
national office required that field offices review only 2 to 4 percent of
the private schools within their jurisdiction during the fiscal years
1973 and 1974. During 1973 the Southeast region failed to review even
this minimum number of schools. Furthermore, no guidelines for the
selection of schools for review were established by the IRS national
office, so that the standards for choice of targets differed among the
key district offices. Nor were formal guidelines set up by the IRS for
its reviewers.

A random sample of reports of compliance reviews by the Commission on Civil Rights showed that they were generally inadequate.
Generally they did not contain any analysis of the fund solicitation
letters, mailing list, or recruitment sources of schools to determine
whether they were discriminatorily constituted or utilized. While
nearly 100 private schools have had their tax exempt status revoked,
very few of the revocations resulted from actual reviews by the IRS.

Department of Labor

In fiscal year 1972 there were 2, 825 state Employment Service
(ES) and Unemployment Insurance Service (UIS) offices and 10, 613
program sponsors, as compared with a total of 160 post-award
reviews made by the Department of Labor. This amounted to an
average of 14. 5 reviews per region. Nineteen recipients were found
in noncompliance. Yet DOL's guidelines for conducting compliance
reviews were well organized and comprehensive. The reviews examined by the DOL Office for Civil Rights were found to be incomplete
in terms of noting whether recommendations for corrective action
were actually being implemented.

Department of Agriculture

Most on-site compliance reviews were conducted by DOA agency program staff and cooperating state personnel, but a considerable amount of monitoring was performed by DOA units such as the Office of Equal Opportunity and the Office of the Inspector General. The number and quality of Title VI compliance reviews varied from agency to agency within the department. In some agencies, documentation of answers on review forms was not required.

Office of Economic Opportunity (OEO)

In fiscal year 1972 OEO conducted 44 on-site compliance reviews, which was 33 fewer than the number conducted in 1971. The number of reviews per regional office ranged from zero in San Francisco to 18 in Atlanta; the average number of reviews per region was four. The number of compliance reviews was inadequate for an agency with over 1,800 grantees. OEO continued to lack a system for determining compliance review priorities and conducting periodic reviews until the time of its demise.

Department of the Interior

The DOI compliance reviews were limited to recipients of grants from the Land and Water Conservation Fund administered by the Bureau of Outdoor Recreation, with 330 on-site reviews conducted in 25 states. Though none of the recipients was found to be in noncompliance, all recipients were asked to take some affirmative steps to acquaint minorities with the programs, to involve minorities in recreation planning and development, and to increase minority employment. Specific time limits were not given for taking these steps, and follow-up reviews were not planned. Compliance reviews were conducted without relating to a larger plan of action.

Department of Transportation

In DOT, the Federal Highway Administration (FHWA) performed a limited number of post-award reviews. By August 1972 nine reviews had been conducted, but final evaluations had not been made of some of them. Reviews were conducted by the FHWA general staff, with the regional civil rights staff supplying the general coordination and guidance. The civil rights staff of the Urban Mass Transportation Administration (UMTA) made 120 post-awards reviews during fiscal year 1972. Where Title VI matters were considered there often was inadequate documentation. UMTA had 566 recipients, and over one-third of them had neither a post-award nor a pre-award review during 1972.

Department of Commerce

The Economic Development Administration of DOC did a poor job of monitoring, performing only 26 post-award on-site compliance reviews in fiscal 1972, while new projects involving 1,156 recipients were being approved. But for the following quarter the director of the Office for Civil Rights required a quarterly report of compliance reviews in an effort to improve the compliance review activity of the field staff. The purpose of the report was to measure the number of reviews planned against the number conducted in order to determine if the scheduled reviews were in accordance with priorities.

Department of Justice

LEAA designated eight so-called impact cities as subjects of its first comprehensive, on-site compliance reviews. Two of these, Dallas and St. Louis, were completed. Requiring about 100 man-days per city, these reviews were supposed to focus on employment and Title VI matters in the police departments. As it turned out, only limited attention was paid to Title VI matters, while the major focus was on employment practices and operational procedures. LEAA denied the Commission on Civil Rights access to the actual review reports, but gave them a copy of its proposed Compliance Review Manual. According to CCR, the Title VI questions needed refining.

Environmental Protection Agency

This agency conducted only one on-site post-award Title VI review in 1972.

Department of Housing and Urban Development

HUD conducted 186 on-site, post-award Title VI compliance reviews during fiscal year 1972, an increase of about 60 over the previous year. But this represented only a small percentage of the recipients needing review, since there were approximately 12,000 locally-funded agencies with Title VI responsibilities. In addition there were developers, builders, and sponsors of HUD-assisted housing subject to review under both Title VI and Executive Order 11063, but HUD did not estimate the number of the latter under its jurisdiction.

The average number of reviews conducted by each HUD regional office for the entire year was only 18.6. While 70 man-hours were spent on an average review, the period between initiation of a review and completion of an investigative report varied from three months to almost a year. Work-load assignments pertaining to compliance reviews in each regional office were not, in general, set forth by the assistant secretary. These assignments should be based on an analysis of conditions in the region, and should require that all recipients be reviewed once during a specific time period, for example, once every five years.

The Title VI Handbook prepared by HUD contained checklists for compliance reviews of housing authorities, urban renewal and relocation agencies, and community development agencies. A large number of other recipients, however, were not covered by these checklists. For example, the Handbook failed to include checklists for reviews of developers, builders, and sponsors of subsidized housing. The U. S. Commission on Civil Rights summarized the situation at HUD at the end of 1974:

> Compliance Reviews because they include all aspects of operation of a HUD-funded agency program, are a far more effective and systematic way of assuring the non-discriminatory operation of the programs than Complaint Investigations, which may address only one aspect. However, many Regional Equal Opportunity Officers report that they are so under-staffed that they are generally able to conduct Title VI Compliance Reviews only as a by-product of Title VI Complaint Investigations. HUD conducted 80 Title VI Compliance Reviews between July 1972 and March 1973. Forty-nine of the Reviews originated from Title VI Complaints. HUD reviews have focused principally on local housing authorities, despite evidence of discrimination by other recipients, especially developers of subsidized housing.
>
> In FY-72, HUD determined that it would first focus on local housing authorities and conduct Title VI community-wide Compliance Reviews during the third and fourth quarters. HUD set no goals for the number of reviews conducted. In fact, few offices conducted community-wide reviews because of their heavy workloads and the length of time and size of staff needed to do such a review. The only office visited by the Commission staff which did a community-wide Title VI Compliance survey was San Francisco.

Shortly after the reorganization of the Equal Opportunity program in April 1972, the central office instructed Regional Equal Opportunity staff to identify Title VI problems with 'remedy potential' and to use these to establish priority areas for Title VI compliance activities. Regional staff interviewed by the Commission, however, were apparently often unaware of this directive and stated that the central office had not given them any direction.

In January 1974, six months into Fiscal Year 1974, HUD formally established Title VI Compliance Review goals for that fiscal year. Up to that time goals had been set only for Regional offices to continue to identify 'remedy potential' cases. Regional offices themselves did not set rigorous schedules for Title VI Compliance Reviews. Regional office time, according to the central office, is being used for training. The Regional offices thus have very little time left for establishing their own Compliance Review goals. HUD's central office, which could issue guidelines for the establishment of goals, admits that complaints will undoubtedly continue to play the major role in Regional office decisions. [8]

The shortcomings of HUD's Title VI compliance review activities which were apparent at the end of 1972 were even clearer at the beginning of 1975 despite sincere though inadequate efforts to the contrary. It appeared that the Title VI deficiencies in HUD were deep-rooted, arising from policy and strategy considerations of the past. The HUD experience may have reflected the consequences of the lack of line authority of its assistant secretary for civil rights over civil rights enforcement staff at the field level. Since priority on staff time was set by the regional director, the agency-wide predominance of complaint processing and ad hoc compliance techniques and strategies tended to relegate compliance methods (particularly compliance reviews) to a secondary, if not peripheral, position as an enforcement tool.

Title VI compliance review approaches have historically been secondary to the Title VIII (housing) complaint techniques in seeking civil rights and equal opportunity compliance in the housing field. As a result, the affirmative use of the compliance review as a primary enforcement tool has been slow to emerge at HUD. Consequently, the crucial importance of compliance reviews was largely unrecognized and the scope of their use in terms of proportion of eligible recipients reached and the types of programs covered remained spotty and limited in application.

Pre-Approval Reviews

While most agencies that conducted compliance reviews did so after a grant had been awarded and the project completed, there are a few that conducted pre-approval reviews. According to the U.S. Commission on Civil Rights:

> A problem inherent in this approach [post-approval reviews] is well illustrated in the field of housing. Once a site for a public housing project is selected and the project is completed, a post-review finding that the site has been discriminatorily located is of little value. The same problem arises in connection with the construction of a sewer line which discriminatorily by-passes the minority community of the city. To assure that this does not occur, each project proposal must be examined before approval. Information which will enable the agency to determine whether or not the project as contemplated will discriminate against some persons on the basis of race or ethnicity should be requested before the project is approved. [9]

Among the agencies for whom the pre-approval compliance review procedure was peculiarly important were HUD, EDA, and various divisions of DOT including the FHWA and the UMTA.

An examination of major Title VI agencies between the years 1970 and 1972 gives the impression that some of these agencies were trying vigorously to improve their preventive stance through increased investment in pre-approval reviews, but there was also the feeling that others were not. Regrettably, the data available were not sufficient to support a firm judgment on this matter. The status of pre-approval reviews in selected agencies as of 1972 has been summarized and updated through 1975, when information was available, in the following section.

Environmental Protection Agency

The EPA emphasized pre-approval reviews. During fiscal year 1972 EPA staff performed 767 pre-award reviews, which represented at least a paper review of every recipient of a construction grant for treatment facilities. There were some on-site reviews, which consisted of interviews with local government officials and members of the minority community, but there were no guidelines for these reviews. The EPA on-site review procedures were greatly lacking in uniformity and comprehensiveness.

Department of Labor

In DOL, pre-award reviews were either conducted on-site or at the desk. In the second half of fiscal year 1971, 295 pre-award reviews of contractual programs were made by regional Equal Employment Opportunity personnel. In contrast, only three reviews were made in all of the following fiscal year. No reason was given for this sharp decline in 1972, when more than 10,000 Manpower Administration program sponsors were either re-funded or funded for the first time.

Department of Agriculture

Only two of the eleven DOA agencies with civil rights responsibilities conducted pre-approval reviews during fiscal year 1972. They were the FHA, which conducted 242 reviews, and the Rural Electrification Administration (REA), which conducted 732 reviews. Of this number, only one prospective recipient was barried, in an action taken by FHA.

Department of Commerce

The Economic Development Administration's (EDA) pre-approval procedures were being improved, as a result of computer operations and experience, to yield a more thorough analysis of projects, project areas, and beneficiaries. All applications were reviewed by civil rights staff in the field before being forwarded to the Washington office for final approval and authorization.

Department of Health, Education, and Welfare

Pre-approval reviews were not conducted by the Higher Education and Elementary and Secondary Education Divisions in the Office for Civil Rights. The Health and Social Services Division limited their pre-approval screening to Medicare compliance activity. Once cleared, facilities were considered in compliance until there was a change of ownership or some indication of noncompliance.

The one exception to the absence of pre-approval reviews by the Elementary and Secondary Education Division was the pre- and post-grant reviews of programs operating under the Emergency School Assistance Program (ESAP) and the Emergency School Aid Act (ESAA). These reviews were generally useful, prompting school districts to correct discriminatory practices expeditiously despite the fact that these reviews did not take as much time to conduct as the usual Title VI review. Under its ESAA program, OCR for the

first time reviewed large city districts such as San Francisco and
Dallas, which were under court order to desegregate. In cases where
pre-grant reviews revealed violations, OCR was generally able to
secure compliance from districts through post-grant reviews under
both ESAA and ESAP. When voluntary compliance was not forthcoming,
OCR terminated funds of programs financed under these two programs.
On the negative side, however, OCR has not instituted administrative
sanction proceedings under Title VI against such districts. As a
result, other federal funds have been received by such recipients
during the time when they had prima facie Title VI violations.[10]

Department of Transportation

No pre-approval reviews were made in connection with the
Federal Aid Highway Program during 1972 unless reviews that were
conducted as a part of the overall project reviews are construed as
Title VI reviews. If that was the case, the review process did not
involve pre-approval examination of a project by civil rights personnel.

The Urban Mass Transportation Administration, on the other
hand, performed 92 pre-approval compliance reviews in 1972. One
person was responsible for checking all grant applications in terms
of their potential impact on minority communities. The UMTA Office
of Civil Rights and Service Development was given sign-off authority,
which consisted of the right to hold up construction because of civil
rights non-compliance in all grant applications by the administrator
of UMTA. The reviewer of the civil rights aspects of the grant concentrated on projects exceeding one million dollars. This official
also had responsibility for formulating a more comprehensive review
procedure to supplement or replace the checklist in use.

Office of Economic Opportunity

OEO grant proposals were examined jointly by program and
human rights officials in OEO's regional offices. The review consisted
of an examination of documents submitted to justify funding or re-
funding. These documents included affirmative action plans and racial
and ethnic data on minority groups in the target area. OEO grantees
were primarily community groups organized for the purpose of
receiving OEO funds, and did not exist as separate entities before
receiving OEO funding.

Department of Justice

LEAA conducted no pre-award reviews. The administrator of
LEAA expressed doubts about the feasibility of performing pre-award

reviews because of the block-grant nature of its assistance program. This view was not shared by the Civil Rights Commission. In the cases of certain discretionary grants which LEAA allocated for special projects, there were plans to conduct pre-approval reviews but the scope of these plans has not been determined.

Department of the Interior

No pre-approval reviews were conducted by DOI.

Department of Housing and Urban Development

HUD stated that 6,600 pre-approval application reviews and a minimum of the same number of pre-award on-site reviews were conducted. However, performing these reviews did not obviate the need for post-award reviews on a regular basis. All direct compliance activities were reviewed by equal opportunity staff in the HUD regional offices; pre-approval application reviews were handled by area and FHA insuring offices within each region as part of the funding process.

COMPLAINT PROCESSING

Complaint processing was the fourth of the major ways used by fund-granting agencies to monitor Title VI compliance efforts of state and local government and private institutions. It differed from the other three procedures in that the initiative necessary to trigger it had to come from an aggrieved party, usually the beneficiary or his representative, while the other three approaches were characteristically initiated and directed by management, presumably to aid the beneficiary of the grant. Consequently, complaint processing was by far the weakest of the compliance tools; it depended on the courage, knowledge, and unusual motivation of an individual or group to seek redress of a grievance which was usually against a larger and much more formidable foe. The Civil Rights Commission reports:

Although Title VI does not specifically mention complaint procedures, methods for handling them are outlined in general terms in each agency's Title VI regulations. All agencies provide the right to file a written complaint with the appropriate agency to any person who believes he has been subjected to discrimination.
The regulations also provide that the "responsible department or agency official" or his designee will launch

a "prompt [underlining supplied] investigation whenever
a compliance review, report, complaint, or any other
information indicates a possible failure to comply . . ."
This same provision outlines in general terms what the
scope of the investigations include.

All agencies also require the responsible agency
official to apprise the recipient of any instances of noncompliance that may have been revealed in the course of
an investigation and then to attempt to resolve these
informally. If the noncompliance cannot be corrected by
informal means, the agency can proceed to effect compliance by termination of assistance or other means authorized by law. Conversely, if an investigation discloses
compliance, the responsible agency official is obligated
to inform the recipient and complainant of the fact in
writing. Since the regulations provide the complainant
with no right of appeal if the complaint is found to be
invalid, the complainant's only recourse is private
litigation.

Agencies also prohibit intimidatory or retaliatory
acts against complainants. The provision is not limited
to persons who file complaints but also applies to any
person who testifies, assists, or in any way participates
in an investigation, review, or hearing. The provision
also requires that the identity of the complainant be kept
confidential except under certain circumstances.

Finally, Title VI regulations require recipients
to inform beneficiaries of their right to file a complaint. 11

In spite of these rather specific provisions in Title VI for the
processing of complaints, there have been serious shortcomings in
the ways that federal agencies have responded to complaints of discrimination in federally funded programs. According to the same
report quoted above:

Inordinate delays, and in many instances, actual failure
to conduct investigations, are not uncommon. In some
instances the quality of the investigation has been found
wanting and in other instances agencies have failed to
take effective remedial measures after alleged Title VI
violations have been substantiated. A widespread short-
coming has been the failure on the part of recipients to
inform beneficiaries and applicants of their right to com-
plain. Another pervasive problem has been the absence
or inadequacy of agency procedures for responding to

complaints, including delineation of responsibility, investigation, and followup. [12]

The character of the complaint processing by selected agencies with large Title VI obligations was gleaned from the brief reports of their activities since 1970 submitted to the Commission on Civil Rights for its 1973 report, [13] updated when information was available, and described in the following section.

Department of Health, Education, and Welfare

In the Elementary and Secondary Education Division, investigating complaints made by individuals within school districts was one method of monitoring used by the Office for Civil Rights. Complaints might trigger a full scale on-site review, be referred to another agency, investigated on-site, or negotiated by letter. Thorough comprehensive reports were prepared, including recommendations.

At the end of 1974, according to the Commission on Civil Rights, the HEW Elementary and Secondary Education Division was still inadequate in its complaints handling process, through progress was being made in various regional offices in coping with their caseloads more effectively. While OCR received hundreds of complaints per year, its investigation program had serious weaknesses. Because OCR failed to set a maximum time limit on investigations of complaints, there was a tendency for delay in processing them. Regional offices carried large backlogs of complaints. This, in turn, sometimes resulted in negative effects on complainants. [14]

In the Higher Education Division during fiscal year 1972, the number of complaints received at headquarters was 84, though there might have been other complaints which were resolved at the regional level. In some cases on-site investigations were made, while others were handled by letter and telephone. In the view of the Civil Rights Commission, the Higher Education Division of the Office for Civil Rights still had an inadequate process for handling complaints in late 1974.

In the Health and Social Services Division a great deal of time was often taken to resolve a complaint or negotiate voluntary compliance.

Department of Labor

DOL reported that 168 Title VI complaints were received during fiscal year 1972. However, since the DOL system for handling complaints was rather confusing, with many complaints included that were not Title VI related, there was a question as to whether all 168 complaints were related to Title VI.

Department of Commerce

EDA received four complaints, two of which were found to be valid. Complaints pertaining to employment were easier to deal with than those concerning services, which generally required more individualized remedies.

Environmental Protection Agency

EPA processed 23 Title VI matters during fiscal year 1972, some of which resulted from complaints and others from compliance reviews. No action has been taken on some of these cases, pending establishment of EPA policy. No complaint investigation guidelines have been established.

Office of Economic Opportunity

OEO required that each grantee be assigned an EO officer who received and resolved Title VI complaints. Complaints that were not resolved at the grantee level were sent to the regional office. The complaints which involved grantee employment practices and other other complaints which could not be resolved at the regional level were forwarded to the Inspection Division, which had three investigators working full time on civil rights complaints. The promptness of resolving Title VI complaints improved, and the complaints investigation reports were comprehensive and well documented.

Department of Transportation

The handling of complaints was centralized in DOT's Office of Civil Rights. Of the 13 complaints received in fiscal year 1972, five involved highway-related programs. Three of these had been received late in 1971 but had not been resolved by August 1972.

Department of Justice

During fiscal year 1972 there were 42 complaints received by LEAA. Fifteen of these were resolved, two because LEAA did not give financial assistance to the party against whom the complaint was made. Eight investigations had been completed but their status was unresolved. Of the 19 cases remaining, 17 were under investigation.

LEAA was not very prompt at resolving complaints. The one complaint investigation report which the Commission on Civil Rights was allowed by LEAA to review was of good quality, but this may have been the exception to the rule as far as LEAA reports were concerned. The reluctance of LEAA to provide the CCR all complaint investigations necessary for a competent appraisal of its grant administration functions reflected the confusion in the Justice Department over its litigative and coordinative functions.

Department of Agriculture

Title VI complaints were received in the departmental Office of Equal Opportunity, which sent the complaint to the agency involved. The agency then sent the complaint to the Office of the Inspector General (OIG) which either investigated the complaint or returned it to the agency for the necessary information which would enable OIG to make a full investigation. In addition to performing a fact-finding task, OIG also evaluated complaints. After OIG established the facts concerning discrimination, the DOA Office of Equal Opportunity advised the agency of the steps to take to remedy the situation. Of the 20 Title VI complaints received in fiscal year 1972, 16 involved the Food and Nutrition Service, two the Farmers' Home Administration, and two Extension Service programs. There appeared to be a great delay between the investigation and settlement of the cases; some cases were still pending one year after the case had been investigated. When there was a disagreement between the individual agency and the OEO division as to the remedies needed to resolve the discrimination complaint the case was taken through several departmental levels, sometimes going to the Secretary of Agriculture before appropriate action was agreed upon.

Department of the Interior

No complaint procedures had been established in DOI. No instructions to inform the public of the procedures in filing a complaint about discriminatory practices by a DOI recipient had been issued.

Department of Housing and Urban Development

In conducting compliance activities under Title VI, HUD placed greater emphasis on compliance reviews than on dealing with complaints. In fact, HUD received fewer than 400 complaints in fiscal year 1972. Voluntary compliance was achieved in only 57 cases. HUD did not indicate the status of the remaining 337 cases.

An examination of HUD's complaint-processing experience during the approximately three year period through 1974 revealed that the agency still had serious problems of complaint backlogs, rather vague and varying kinds of communication between regional offices and headquarters, and differing degrees of involvement in complaint processing from region to region. [15]

The preceding review of the experience of various agencies with both the compliance-review technique and the complaint technique of implementing Title VI of the Civil Rights Act demonstrates their serious difficulties and deficiencies in securing Title VI compliance, especially when complaints have constituted a significant part of the workload. This no doubt motivated the Office for Civil Rights to take the step in June 1975 of proposing to the Congress a new set of procedural regulations for civil rights enforcement. The OCR requested rules that would subordinate complaint-processing techniques to more affirmative approaches, thus allowing the agency to take the initiative in enforcement through assurances, compliance reports, and compliance reviews.

The means of assuring compliance with Title VI by government departments and agencies have been fundamentally remedial in character rather than preventive. Although the compliance report and the compliance review provided two potent weapons for insuring compliance with Title VI, unfortunately fund-granting agencies have concentrated instead on using post-approval techniques of a limited scope. Strangely enough, there has been little indication of how sampling techniques might be applied to make these compliance actions produce results for more programs under an agency's jurisdiction. Moreover, while all officials in an administering federal agency have the ultimate responsibility for compliance, this obligation has in reality been delegated to specialized civil rights units and personnel in most cases. In effect, the program administrator who made the grants has assumed no active responsibility for civil rights compliance. Civil rights functions must become an integral part of overall management. Attention to Title VI enforcement should be drawn inward from the peripheral and elective aspects of management toward the central core of its decision making. If an administering agency is to make an accurate and comprehensive plan for a program and fully evaluate it, the agency must understand its equal opportunity and civil rights objectives, and evaluate program activities on the basis of effectiveness in meeting equal opportunity goals as well as program goals.

NOTES

1. U. S. Commission on Civil Rights, The Federal Civil Rights Enforcement Effort (Washington, D. C.: Government Printing Office, 1971), p. 215.

2. Ibid., pp. 215-16.

3. U. S. Commission on Civil Rights, The Federal Civil Rights Enforcement Effort—1974, Vol. II, To Provide For Fair Housing (Washington, D. C.: Government Printing Office, 1974), p. 333.

4. Ibid., p. 249.

5. U. S. Commission on Civil Rights, The Federal Civil Rights Enforcement Effort (Washington, D. C.: Government Printing Office, 1971), p. 220.

6. U. S. Commission on Civil Rights, The Federal Civil Rights Enforcement Effort—1974, Vol. III, To Ensure Equal Educational Opportunity (Washington, D. C.: Government Printing Office, 1975), pp. 368-70.

7. Ibid., p. 365, Item 3.

8. U. S. Commission on Civil Rights, The Federal Civil Rights Enforcement Effort—1974, Vol. II (Washington, D. C.: Government Printing Office, 1974), pp. 56-60.

9. U. S. Commission on Civil Rights, The Federal Civil Rights Enforcement Effort (Washington, D. C.: Government Printing Office, 1971), p. 228.

10. U. S. Commission on Civil Rights, The Federal Civil Rights Enforcement Effort—1974, Vol. III (Washington, D. C. Government Printing Office, 1975), pp. 360-61. For a detailed description, see also pp. 87-101.

11. U. S. Commission on Civil Rights, The Federal Civil Rights Enforcement Effort (Washington, D. C.: Government Printing Office, 1971), pp. 230-31.

12. Ibid., p. 231.

13. U. S. Commission on Civil Rights, The Federal Civil Rights Enforcement Effort—A Reassessment (Washington, D. C.: Government Printing Office, 1973).

14. U. S. Commission on Civil Rights, The Federal Civil Rights Enforcement Effort—1974, Vol. III (Washington, D. C.: Government Printing Office, 1975), pp. 118-27, 361-62, Item 10.

15. Ibid., Vol. II, pp. 52-55 for a detailed description of complaint-processing by HUD during this period.

PART

II

**ADMINISTRATION OF
CIVIL RIGHTS/EQUAL
OPPORTUNITY POLICIES
IN GRANT PROGRAMS**

**PUSHED TO THE SIDE:
THE FEDERAL
CIVIL RIGHTS UNITS**

Every executive in the federal bureaucracy who is the administrator of a program sets substantive program goals for his agency to achieve. He is required by law and departmental regulations to see that these goals are met in compliance with Title VI of the Civil Rights Act of 1964. Unfortunately, most administrators operate on the assumption that all civil rights and equal opportunity responsibilities should be taken by a separate civil rights staff. Unless such a civil rights staff finds evidence that this grant manager's program is not in compliance with Title VI, he usually assumes he has no responsibility for demanding compliance from recipients of federal funds. This misconception—if not overt denial—of his own civil rights obligations has caused the grant administrator to contribute substantially to the current wide gap between policy statements and compliance practices under Title VI.

The organization of equal opportunity activities in separate civil rights units within departments and agencies of the government has, in most instances, worked to allow grant managers to avoid their duty to include equal opportunity as an integral part of the administration of financial assistance. Moreover, the frequent practice of placing civil rights staff members in a status subordinate to their counterparts in program management appears to have seriously hampered the implementation of Title VI in the major departments and agencies of the federal government. Civil rights have been sealed off and downgraded to the point where they are seldom considered relevant issues when the federal monies are being handed out.

The organization of the management put in charge of implementing Title VI has varied from department to department, but in general it has been set up in separate civil rights and equal opportunity

units within departments and agencies with Title VI responsibilities.
From this sequestered position in the various departments, these
units have attempted to use their resources, such as they are, to
bring about compliance by the public and private bodies receiving
grants from the program managers in their agencies with the Title VI
section of the Civil Rights Act of 1964.

Sound management principles dictate that the civil rights managers should establish objectives and then use their resources in such
a way as to meet their goals, to find out the reasons for their shortfalls, if any, and then to reset their goals more realistically. It has
been an uphill fight for the civil rights managers in most instances.
Some have been more successful than others at setting firm goals
and establishing specific periods of time for achieving them. Some
civil rights managers have taken firm positions on Title VI, others
have not, and the rest fall at various points in between. The euphem-
istic phrase "goals and timetables"—from the "management by objective" system used by the Office of Management and Budget for the
federal government bureaucracy—meant different things to different
managers. But whatever management technique was used, the real
measure of whether civil rights executives were effective as managers
lay in their success at achieving their goals. This success was a
function of many variables, some of which were directly within their
control, but many of which were not.

CIVIL RIGHTS MANAGEMENT IN TITLE VI AGENCIES

The stage of development reached by the civil rights/equal opportunity units (CR/EO units) in the adoption of "management by
objective" techniques was evident partly in the extent to which they
used goal-oriented systems of organizing and managing their work.
In 1973 a personal interview study was conducted for the purpose of
exploring, among other things, the management practices of the civil
rights executives in all the federal agencies with major civil rights
responsibilities. At that time most of the managers were beginning
to develop systems for collecting racial and ethnic data that could, in
some way, provide objective measurements of the civil rights performance of their agencies. However, most of these efforts were in
early if not embryonic stages of development. Where data were regularly collected, they were seldom organized for systematic and
regular analysis. No systems were found that had reached the stage
at which data could be used by agencies for decision making. Eleven
of the 12 civil rights managers had developed some type of reporting
system. One manager reported that his office was in the process of
developing a reporting system. None of the executives were specific

about what they sought to accomplish by using their system, and only
one executive had a unit under his direction to analyze the data being
collected. *

The progress toward instituting management by objective systems is reviewed department by department in the subsequent discussion. While most of the civil rights executives professed having
established goals for their activities, it was not clear whether the
goals were objective and viable tools capable of being used for effective management. Too often the goals referred to expected results
over a given period of time, and not to the output or results per
unit of investment or input of resources of all kinds. The examination of the way Title VI activities were administered in the departments and agencies with major Title VI responsibilities revealed wide
differences in management postures and many variables affecting the
administration of Title VI throughout the bureaucracy. They reveal
that rather low state of the art of management in these units during
this period.

Department of Health, Education, and Welfare

During a period when the systems of racial and ethnic data
collection and use in other divisions of the Office for Civil Rights in
HEW were developing in effectiveness and sophistication, most
notably in the Elementary and Secondary Education Division, the
Health and Social Services Division made little progress in instituting
such a system. Without question this failure has been a significant
factor in the managerial ineffectiveness of this division. Effective
monitoring of the division's programs has not been achieved, particularly in those involving hospitals and nursing homes, and even though
in 1973 all recipients of HEW funds were required to collect racial
and ethnic data on beneficiaries, state agencies administering funds
granted by the Health and Social Services Division were not collected
nationwide.

OCR has experienced resistance by various states to its efforts
to collect information for this and other programs—for example, for
its Elementary and Secondary Education Division. The reasons given
for this seem to be rationalizations for weak and indecisive manage-

---

* The personal interview study of the perceptions of civil rights
managers of the organizational structure, the managerial practices,
and the power and authority they possess in the federal bureaucracy
was conducted by the author in 1973. The findings of the study are
presented in Chapter 6.

ment rather than justifiable causes for the failure to implement
Title VI adequately. [1]

The Higher Education Division of the Office for Civil Rights in
HEW has failed to compel the recipients of funds to set goals and
establish timetables for meeting their Title VI responsibilities. Moreover, the OCR has made known no long range plans for upgrading
Title VI enforcement in higher education. But the OCR turned the
corner in management capability in 1972, when it was finally brought
into the department's Operational Planning System (OPS). OCR has
adopted its own OPS, which requires that all of its divisions and
offices make annual enforcement plans which the OCR tracks to
appraise how well its own subunits are reaching their goals.

Department of Labor

Each State Employment Security Agency has been required to
submit an annual report to DOL giving the racial and ethnic composition of its staff at all occupational levels of the population it serves
and of its applicants. Instructions concerning minority representation
on Employment Service (ES) staffs required all agencies to submit a
minority staffing plan showing goals for each employment service and
unemployment insurance office as part of the state's Plan of Service
which constituted justification for the agency's budget request. Each
state agency's minority staffing was evaluated to ascertain whether
its staff was at least in proportion, at all levels, to the racial and
ethnic composition of the state's population and, ideally, to the applicants it served. The state plans projected during 1972 did not seem
sufficient to overcome the effects of past discrimination, and it was
not clear how much time DOL would give the states to achieve representative levels. Once the State Employment Agencies came under
the jurisdiction of the Equal Employment Opportunity Commission by
the EEO Act of 1972, improvements were expected.

The Manpower Administration has been in the forefront among
agencies in its effort to develop rather sophisticated systems for
collecting racial and ethnic data, and it appears to have gone farther
than most agencies in the systematic analysis of these data. However,
its efforts to assure that both civil rights and program staff are willing
and able to utilize the findings of these periodic surveys as a tool for
managing the civil rights aspects of the Manpower Administration's
mission have not been successful. The 1974 civil rights enforcement
report states:

The Department of Labor has one of the more comprehensive systems for collecting nationwide data on a

federal program, called the Manpower Operating Data
(MOD) System . . . . The data are submitted by each
local office to the State Employment Security Offices
which process the data and submit them on computer
tape to DOL's Regional Offices on a monthly basis. . . .
Such a system could be useful in measuring the civil
rights compliance status of the local offices. Indeed,
data on the number of referrals and placements for
various fields of employment are maintained by race
and ethnic origin cross-tabulated by sex. In theory,
such information could be tabulated to show, at a glance,
the status of minority and female participation in ES
programs, information that it may take a civil rights
review team several days to determine on site.

In mid-1974 the DEEO Director expressed disappointment with the MOD system. He noted that, moreover, because of different ways of counting from state
to state, the data are not comparable enough to enable
nationwide use. He observed, too, that the employment
categories used are too general to be used to determine
whether applicants are being placed according to their
qualifications.

The DEEO also noted that the MOD data are four
or five months out of date by the time they are tabulated
in computer print-out form. [2]

Department of Agriculture

The Department of Agriculture has had a policy aimed at
achieving a good racial and ethnic data system since 1970, but its
application continues to fall far short of this policy. The DOA has
one of the most comprehensive data collection requirements relative
to program participation, but the process of collecting, the frequency
of collection and analysis, and the reliance on faulty methods used by
state and local Extension Service offices have limited the quality of
the results and thus restricted its usefulness as a management tool.

The Secretary's memorandum of May 18, 1972, directed all
agencies to establish a system for targeting benefits to prospective
minority participants, beginning in fiscal year 1973. The directive
gave the individual agencies responsibility for setting their own
targets, including setting goals to improve minority participation.
The DOA Office of Equal Opportunity was given the responsibility for
assessing the reasonableness of the definitions of parity participation

and participation targets. Though August 15, 1972 was set as the due date for goals for 1973, the deadline was flexible.

Department of Commerce

The Economic Development Administration required its recipients to file affirmative action plans ensuring equal opportunity. The minimum goal for minority participation in its programs was to equal the minority percentage in the project area's population. But departmental civil rights officials believed that EDA was accepting plans which did not fully conform to the model requirements and which continued to allow under use of minorities in white collar employment. All plans were subject to future review in the field and in Washington in order to improve compliance with affirmative action requirements.

Environmental Protection Agency

Goals and timetables for minority participation in the EPA's grant program have not been established.

Department of the Interior

There has been no discussion of goals and timetables or any other management technique in DOI. This was consistent with the rest of DOI's Title VI program, which has been characterized by a lack of urgency, poor planning, and underutilization of manpower resources.

According to the CCR report, the Department of the Interior "requires that applicants and recipients collect and maintain ethnic data showing the extent to which minority groups and women participate in federally assisted programs. This data may be estimates or actual counts and are required to be done on a visual basis only . . . the data are to be available to USDI only on demand with no requirement that they be forwarded on a regular basis. If data are not submitted to OEO and used, the recipients may lose interest in keeping it accurately and the process is likely to deteriorate."[3] It is readily apparent that DOI has no periodic reporting system which can be used for decision making by managers. There appears to be modest and not very accurate collection of some racial and ethnic data, but a virtual absence of analysis and no basis for use as a management tool.

Department of Justice

The Law Enforcement Assistance Administration provides an example of the experience of a relatively young agency in making grants to state and local governments covered by Title VI. It initiated several racial and ethnic data surveys covering various phases of its programs, but was singularly unsuccessful in bringing any of them to completion. Consequently, these surveys were not available for effective civil rights management in this agency. It attempted its first ethnic and racial survey in 1972, but after two years it had received responses from only about one-half of the police departments receiving the questionnaires. Yet it took no action to get responses from the remaining departments, and later cancelled plans for a second racial and ethnic survey, choosing instead to use the EEOC Public Agency Form, which provides much less adequate information for Title VI enforcement purposes. A similar type of survey to cover community-based and correctional facilities was planned for mid-1972, but procrastination continued and, as late as 1975, it had not been distributed.

Several omissions from the survey forms could be enumerated, but further detail is unnecessary in concluding that the LEAA has not successfully collected, analyzed, and used for managerial purposes racial and ethnic data. LEAA made an ambitious start in a period when it could have built effectively on what other agencies had done. However, it appears to have progressively abdicated its equal opportunity responsibilities and, therefore, to have rendered its reporting quite ineffective as a management tool. It appears to have knuckled under to its more recalcitrant recipients rather than to have led them as it should as a granting agency.

Department of Transportation

No recent administration has been particularly innovative in identifying the long range civil rights implications of DOT programs and the coverage afforded by Title VI. Title VI issues have not even been identified in some programs. The Federal Highway Administration (FHWA), for instance, has not determined the extent to which Title VI applies to opportunities generated or facilitated by highway construction. Even where Title VI issues have been identified—for example, in the selection of contractors—a uniform method for dealing with these matters has not always been spelled out. There has been no discussion of goals and timetables. [4]

While DOT made massive grants-in-aid to state and local governments and other government entities and to private non-profit agencies and institutions, it did not adopt a periodic system of assessing the benefits of these grants in terms of their impact on the racial and ethnic groups involved. The departmental Office of Civil Rights appeared to have little power to direct actions of the various administrations in DOT. It served primarily in an advisory and technical assistance capacity. According to the CCR report:

> The FHWA has instituted no comprehensive system for collecting racial and ethnic data although a pilot data collection project was influential in altering a proposed route after it demonstrated that a proposed interstate route would have a disproportionate negative impact on the minority community. [5]

There is no evidence that the Urban Mass Transportation Administration (UMTA) made any effort in this direction.

ORGANIZATION AND STAFFING
OF CIVIL RIGHTS UNITS

While the status of the civil rights executive varied from agency to agency, he was generally in a subordinate status in terms of his title, grade level, position in the administrative hierarchy, and authority, particularly his authority to enforce Title VI. His position was also circumscribed by fragmentation of responsibility or lack of authority to implement Title VI, and by the inability—in cases of departmental decentralization—to command the performance of civil rights staffs in the bureaus. Among the seven large federal departments having heavy involvement in civil rights activities, none except HUD had a civil rights administrator at the assistant secretary level. In three of these agencies (Commerce, Interior, and Labor), the departmental civil rights officer was a GS-15, which did not give him a supergrade status. In four of the smaller agencies (LEAA, OEO, SBA, and VA) with important Title VI responsibilities, only one of them—the Veterans Administration—had a civil rights administrator in the supergrade category.

In agencies whose civil rights functions were divided into separate civil rights offices within the component bureaus (for example, Commerce, Transportation, and Interior) the civil rights administrator generally had a lower grade and a position subordinate to his program management counterpart. The inferior status of the civil rights office in most departments was defined by the administrative layers interposed between the secretary and his top civil rights officers. In only three of the seven large agencies with important civil rights activities (HEW, HUD, and Transportation) did the civil rights director report directly to the secretary, while in three others (Agriculture, Commerce, and Labor), he reported to an assistant secretary. In the Department of the Interior he reported to the deputy undersecretary. Only in VA did the civil rights executive report directly to the administrator.

Title VI civil rights operations and authority were marked by decentralization and fragmentation. In only two out of seven of the large agencies with major Title VI programs were these activities centralized in department-wide civil rights offices. At HUD and HEW, enforcement operations were centralized in single departmental offices, the Office of the Assistant Secretary for Equal Opportunity and the Office for Civil Rights, respectively. On the other hand, of these seven agencies only HEW also had centralized authority for the decision making regarding Title VI.

In the remaining agencies various patterns of segmentation existed. Responsibility was divided between the departmental civil rights offices and the civil rights offices of the operating bureaus in the Department of Commerce and the Department of Transportation; at Interior and Agriculture, it was divided between the department office and designated civil rights staff in the bureaus and at the Labor Department, among various staff components.

No single pattern was adopted in the small agencies; LEAA had no organization for putting Title VI regulations into effect; OEO and SBA had centralized operations. According to the CCR report, VA "shared Title VI enforcement with the program divisions." The report also stated that in the eleven federal agencies without major Title VI programs, "the emphasis tends to be perfunctory, sporadic, and centralized. Usually only one person in the headquarters office has a Title VI function and, since almost no staff time is devoted to Title VI activity, the relative advantages of centralization cannot be evaluated."[6]

The Commission on Civil Rights described the cardinal weakness of departmental civil rights executives in the severe limitation of their line authority in the following terms:

> The influence and leverage of the departmental civil
> rights head and of his counterpart in the operating
> bureaus are also lessened by his inability to exercise
> line authority over Equal Opportunity staff in the field
> offices, generally responsible to a Regional Director.
>
> Title VI functions such as Compliance Reviews
> and Complaint Investigations generally have been
> decentralized to the agencies' field offices.[7]

Among the eleven federal agencies with Title VI programs, only two (VA and LEAA) "anticipate centralized operations in which compliance activities will be conducted by headquarters personnel. At the Department of the Interior, compliance activities are divided between field staff and headquarters staff. Most agencies which have decentralized compliance enforcement to the field have designated the full-time civil rights specialists to perform the functions of review and investigations."[8]

The specific organizational structure, position in the departmental hierarchy, and the staffing of the Title VI operations, differed from agency to agency as demonstrated in the descriptions of some selected departments that follow.

Department of Health, Education, and Welfare

The Office for Civil Rights, which was given the responsibility for Title VI matters in HEW, was a part of the Office of the Secretary of HEW, and had a staff of 708 members in the Washington headquarters offices as of June 1972. In addition to the director, deputy director, and a number of special assistants, there were also assistant directors for management, planning, public affairs, congressional affairs, and special programs. The major divisions of the Office for Civil Rights were the Divisions of Elementary and Secondary Education, Higher Education, Health and Social Services, and Contract Compliance. The heads of these four divisions reported through the deputy director to the director for civil rights.

The Higher Education Division of OCR was created in July 1972 with a staff of 13 members: eight worked exclusively on Title VI matters, and five divided time between Title VI and Health Manpower. In ten regional offices of OCR, there were 31 professionals who divided their time between Title VI and Health Manpower and 55 professionals who devoted full time to the administration of Title VI.

As of June 1972, the Elementary and Secondary Education Division of OCR had 177 professional staff members who spent more than 50 percent of their time on Title VI matters. Ninety-four of 177 staff members were distributed among the ten regional offices. Of these, Seattle, Boston, Kansas City, and Denver had fewer than four professional staff members each to deal with elementary and secondary education matters, while the number in the remaining regions ranged from nine to 19.

In the Health and Social Services Division of OCR, 55 professionals devoted full time to Title VI matters. The headquarters office had a director, deputy director, two operations officers, and three regional coordinators. Some regions (Atlantic, Chicago, and Dallas) were identified as Health and Social Services trouble spots in which additional staff was added to take care of the heavier workload.

The division providing legal services to OCR was in HEW's overall Office of General Counsel—not a part of OCR. Supervised by an assistant general counsel and his deputy, the Civil Rights Division of the Office of General Counsel (OGS) was composed of three branches: first, the Emergency School Assistance Program (ESAP), Vocational Education, and Educational TV; second, Elementary and Secondary Education and Special Projects; and third, Contract Compliance, Health and Social Services, and Higher Education.

The size of the legal staff of the Civil Rights Division of the Office of General Counsel did not keep pace with the growth of the OCR staff working in all of these areas. For example, in 1967, when OCR had a staff of 278 the Civil Rights Division of OGS had 32 staff members, 15 of whom were professionals. By June 1972, although the OCR staff had increased to 708, the legal responsibilities still rested with a staff of only 33 members, 19 of whom were attorneys, and 14 clerical staff.

Once the Office for Civil Rights began moving away from its heavy traditional involvement in the dual school structure of the South and started attacking the more subtle forms of discrimination such as testing, ability grouping, and the assignment and treatment of students within schools, the workload of the legal services division was greatly increased. More time was required to prepare for administrative enforcement hearings—for example, the Boston hearings required six months of preparation time—and the duration of hearings was longer. In 1972, the number of attorneys engaged in Elementary and Secondary Education issues increased from three to seven. Since then, responsibilities have continued to increase without a corresponding increase in the size of the legal staff.

Department of Labor

The prime unit of the DOL giving financial assistance to state and local governments was the Manpower Administration, which had a small Division of Equal Employment Opportunity (DEEO) at the Washington headquarters. In the late 1960s, the director of DEEO had official access to the assistant secretary for manpower and, through past associations, could reach the secretary of labor by telephone. But in 1974 the office was downgraded in the managerial hierarchy to the level of a division of the Office of Investigation and Compliance and had to report through that office instead of having direct access to higher officials.

Moreover, the policies, regulations, and procedures governing elimination of discrimination in operating programs were carried out by the ten assistant regional directors for manpower who conducted all the negotiations for securing voluntary compliance with the agency's civil rights requirements. The director of the DEEO in Washington had no line authority over the CR/EO activities carried out by personnel in the regional offices and, at the regional level as at headquarters, the specialized civil rights staffs served purely in staff capacities.

As to the composition of the staff, the Manpower Administration had 37 full time equal opportunity specialists with Title VI responsibilities in the spring of 1975, 12 of whom worked in the DEEO overseeing and monitoring regional operations and developing training and technical assistance programs. In the regions, there were 25 positions for full-time equal opportunity specialists, which was an average of only 2.5 per region.

Environmental Protection Agency

At EPA the director of the Office of Civil Rights and Urban Affairs reported directly to the EPA administrator and had overall responsibility for contract compliance, minority economic development, and women's programs, as well as Title VI enforcement. Within the office were the Equal Opportunity Division, with branches for EEO and Contract Compliance, the Women's Program, and Minority Economic Development. The Title VI headquarters staff provided technical assistance and guidance to the field civil rights staff, who were under the immediate direction and supervision of their respective regional administrators. There was no counterpart to the headquarters Title VI chief in any region. Only one region, Atlanta, had even one person who devoted more than 50 percent of his time to Title VI enforcement. There were 18 full time professional civil rights staff members in the Washington office and 20 in the field. Of the 38 staff members, only three in the Washington office and one in the field devoted more than half time to Title VI matters, even though there was a Title VI function in each region. Moreover, the person charged with providing day-to-day guidance on Title VI matters was relegated to a subordinate position in the organizational hierarchy. The limited size of EPA's staff, in CCR's view, was the most discouraging aspect of its Title VI enforcement mechanism. Ideally, EPA saw a need for about 60 full time professionals, 50 of whom would be in the field to meet Title VI responsibilities.

Department of Commerce

The assistant secretary for administration has had the overall responsibility for Title VI activities and enforcement within the Department of Commerce. However, the primary operational responsibility has been delegated to the department's Office of the Special Assistant for Civil Rights, which performed coordinative and guidance functions. The department's office periodically conducted studies of EDA's Office of Civil Rights and its field operations. The deputy assistant secretary for economic development made the final decision in all matters upon which there was disagreement between the director of civil rights and regional directors.

As of July 1972, the professional full time staff of EDA's Office of Civil Rights increased in number from 15 to 20. With EDA's major workload in the Southeast and Southwest, assigning only three full time professionals to the Atlanta region and two to the Austin region left those offices very much understaffed. The reasons for the poor staffing, according to EDA and DOC's civil rights offices, were the shortages of staff and its poor quality. As of August 1971, sex discrimination was included in EDA/DOC legislation. Should the compliance program be kept at its present staffing level and, at the same time, be given responsibility for compliance in the area of sex discrimination, the attention given to other problems must be reduced.

Department of the Interior

The Office for Equal Opportunity at DOI had six full time professionals working on Title VI enforcement; all were located in the headquarters of the Office for Equal Opportunity in Washington, D.C. The priority assignment of that staff, after it had become familiar with programs and compliance mechanisms, should have been the development of a Title VI program with priorities, goals, administrative procedures, and regulations. No attempts have been made, however, to involve program and state officials in the task of insuring an acceptable standard of compliance with Title VI, nor have efforts been made to require that civil rights considerations be included in all phases of DOI programs. Although the civil rights office recognized a need for additional staff, it has not taken advantage of available resources.

Department of Justice

In DOJ, the director of the Office of Civil Rights Compliance (OCRC) reported directly to the LEAA administrator. Eight full time professionals were on the staff, seven of whom devoted more than half time to Title VI-EEO matters, while the eighth was a contract compliance specialist. Each OCRC staff member was responsible for a specific staff function, such as complaint processing or compliance reviews. Other responsibilities were assigned when necessary on an ad hoc basis. In addition, other LEAA personnel contributed to civil rights operations. For example, a computer system analyst for the Information Systems Division was assigned full time to work with OCRC in data gathering and tabulation to expedite fact finding.

LEAA's civil rights operation was entirely centralized, and the director (OCRC) did not envision that any significant compliance responsibilities would be delegated to regional staff. The staffing level was inadequate for the workload, according to CCR, and LEAA's plan to delay the hiring of authorized professionals was unjustified by the LEAA contention that an increase in staff would seriously interfere with the work flow in OCRC.

Department of Housing and Urban Development

In April 1972, HUD created four offices within the Office of the Assistant Secretary for Equal Opportunity, each responsible to the assistant secretary and his personal staff. In one of these offices, the Office of Compliance and Enforcement, Title VI and Title VIII compliance activities were consolidated. A second, the Office of Voluntary Compliance, was formed to conduct such efforts as the development of large-scale affirmative action plans to promote equal housing opportunity activity by state and local agencies and by all sectors of the real estate industry. The third, the Office of Program Standards and Data Analysis, was created to carry out programs in line with HUD's emphasis on the development of program standards and on systematizing the collection and use of racial and ethnic data. The fourth office, Management and Field Coordination, was made responsible for field staff training and technical assistance.

In reorganizing its central office for equal opportunity, HUD appeared to have recognized the need for more effective fair housing enforcement and for widespread affirmative action to promote equal housing opportunity. Ten regional offices handled all equal opportunity complaints and conducted all compliance reviews. They also trained and evaluated area and FHA insuring officers. Within regional offices there has been a reorganization parallel to that in the Washington office, consolidating Title VI and Title VIII compliance activity and adding the responsibility of monitoring equal opportunity activities of the area and insuring offices.

Under the regional offices there were 39 area offices which had direct funding responsibility for HUD programs in their areas. Equal opportunity personnel in these offices were responsible for reviewing affirmative marketing plans submitted by builders and sponsors of HUD-assisted housing and for overseeing the implementation of other equal opportunity standards by HUD's program staff.

The FHA insuring offices, which were responsible to the area offices, had no specific units with equal opportunity functions, but since they processed applications for participation in FHA programs, they were responsible for implementing equal opportunity standards for housing programs.

The Office of the Assistant Secretary for Equal Opportunity at HUD has long been hampered by inadequate staff in meeting its fair housing responsibilities and insuring nondiscrimination in HUD's programs of assistance. When HUD greatly increased the scope of its activities in the reorganization of its equal opportunity offices, the staffing problem became even more critical. Despite requests for additional staffing, HUD had only 347 positions allocated for civil rights in fiscal year 1972, and about 43 percent of that staff time was assigned to activities other than fair housing and nondiscrimination in HUD programs. Seventy-two positions were assigned to the central office, 134 to regional offices, and 141 to area offices. The FHA insuring offices had no equal opportunity staff at all.

For fiscal year 1973, 80 new positions were requested, making a total of 427, 77 for the central office, 128 for the regional offices, 147 for area offices, and 75 for the FHA insuring offices. Additional staff would have increased HUD's ability to improve the fair housing efforts of its program participants, but HUD would not provide any additional staff for the already overextended regional programs for compliance review and complaint-processing. Overall, the anticipated increase in staffing would have provided only a small portion of what was necessary for adequate staffing of HUD's Equal Opportunity Office.

Department of Transportation

The Federal Highway Administration appointed a special assistant to FHWA's director of civil rights to devote full time to Title VI and Title VIII matters. FHWA also had in its OCR 35 full time professional positions, 14 at headquarters and 21 in the field. Only three of the 35 devoted more than 50 percent of their time to Title VI matters.

The Urban Mass Transportation Administration had ten full time professional civil rights staff members, but only one devoted more

than half time to Title VI. Within UMTA's Office of Civil Rights and
Service Development there was one urban planner who carried the full
responsibility for pre-award reviews. A substantial increase in the
number of persons assigned this pre-award responsibility was greatly
needed. The External Program Division had primary responsibility
for Title VI enforcement efforts other than pre-approval reviews.
Although some personnel in the division were supposed to be involved
in varying degrees in Title VI activities, their actual involvement
seemed minimal. In addition, UMTA has experienced a drastic reduc-
tion in staffing—a retrenchment which has cut back both program and
civil rights operations. [9]

There was strong evidence to suggest that the power to make
decisions and the occupational status of civil rights executives in the
federal bureaucracy have declined since 1972. This was discernible
in the structural changes in the organization. Other signs of decline
were not so readily verifiable because of the limited access to relevant information, but close observation and conversations with present
and past civil rights managers reinforced the impression of their
deteriorating position.

The second-rate position to which Title VI matters have been
consigned in federal agencies has guaranteed second-rate results or
worse. The Commission on Civil Rights described the organizational
position and status needed for the effective administration of Title VI
and contrasted them with the pitiably insufficient resources and priorities devoted to safeguarding minority access to federal assistance
programs:

> In view of the scope and complexity of civil rights
> problems and their crucial importance to the future
> well-being of the Nation, effective administration,
> coordination, and enforcement of the laws aimed at
> resolving them deserve high priority attention.
> Title VI is among the most important of these laws.
> If it is to be enforced effectively, those who carry
> out the civil rights responsibility of federal agencies
> must be in a position to affect agency policy and to
> make decisions concerning program operation.
> Accordingly, the chief civil rights official should be at
> the highest administrative level and his office should
> be comparably situated within the agency's structure.
> His status and organizational position within the
> bureaucracy should be at a level which affords the
> opportunity to participate fully in key agency policy
> decisions. In addition, he must have sufficient staff

to conduct the kind of comprehensive compliance program that is necessary.

In none of the federal departments and agencies that operate Title VI programs is the civil rights office organized and staffed adequately. In most cases, the civil rights chief is of low status and his position in the agency hierarchy is subordinate to those who operate programs; his authority to affect agency policy is limited and, in some cases, nonexistent; and his staff is hopelessly insufficient. [10]

NOTES

1. United States Commission on Civil Rights, The Federal Civil Rights Enforcement Effort—1974, Vol. VI, To Extend Federal Financial Assistance (Washington, D. C. : Government Printing Office, 1975), pp. 190-97. For further information on agency reviews, see pp. 162-63.

2. Ibid. , pp. 435-38.

3. Ibid. , pp. 252-54.

4. United States Commission on Civil Rights, The Federal Civil Rights Enforcement Effort—A Reassessment (Washington, D. C. : Government Printing Office, 1973), p. 362.

5. U. S. Commission on Civil Rights, The Federal Civil Rights Enforcement Effort—1974, Vol. VI, To Extend Federal Financial Assistance, op. cit. , p. 789. For more details, see pp. 509-10.

6. United States Commission on Civil Rights, The Federal Civil Rights Enforcement Effort (Washington, D. C. : Government Printing Office, 1971), p. 198.

7. Ibid.

8. Ibid. , pp. 196-98.

9. United States Commission on Civil Rights, The Federal Civil Rights Enforcement Effort—A Reassessment, op. cit. , pp. 403-404.

10. United States Commission on Civil Rights, The Federal Civil Rights Enforcement Effort, op. cit. , p. 196.

6

SPECIALISTS AT BAY: THE CIVIL RIGHTS EXECUTIVES AND THEIR STAFFS

The executives who head the civil rights and equal opportunity activities in the departments and agencies of the federal bureaucracy have specific responsibilities for the administration of the policies of the nation in this area, but they do not bear those responsibilities alone. The enforcement of the civil rights and equal opportunity laws requires the participation of many other levels of management. With respect to Title VI of the Civil Rights Act of 1964, for example, numerous other management units participate either partially or fully in setting policy for or administering the programs that distribute the benefits of federal grants-in-aid amounting to billions of dollars annually. The other managements involved to a greater or lesser extent are the state and local governments and private organizations which are the recipients of federal funding, the departments and agencies of the federal government administering the grant programs, the Department of Justice, which is the coordinating agency for Title VI programs, the Office of Management and Budget, which is the budgeting and monitoring agency of the executive branch of the federal government, and, at the top, the Office of the President itself. At some point in the administration of Title VI funds, each one of these entities is engaged in making decisions which either directly or indirectly affect the amount of consumer services and so-called free goods received by the beneficiaries of the subsidized programs. Decisions made by each layer of the managerial hierarchy also determine whether these services financed by federal grants-in-aid are allocated according to the laws banning racial and ethnic discrimination.

The civil rights executives and their staffs are wholly involved in implementing public policy related to civil rights and equal opportunity for minorities. The effectiveness of the individual CR/EO

manager depends on his ability to devise and carry out activites that
will maximize the objectives of his mission. It also depends on his
ability to minimize the use of his resources for activities that do not
clearly contribute to that end, and to avoid altogether those that tend
to foster either a continuing or growing differentiation in the delivery
of services based on minority status. The test of the CR/EO executive's managerial effectiveness is whether he can influence the distribution of the benefits of federally assisted programs in such a way
that minorities receive a more equitable share of goods and services
relative to their numbers in the population than they have in the past.
In other words, although success is related to the way the CR/EO
executive uses his resources as a manager, it is measured in the
final analysis by the extent to which all of his activities, individually
and collectively, work to close the gap between the promise of equal
access to assistance by minorities and the actual fulfillment of this
promise.

The civil rights executive would have a better chance of making
public policy a reality if he were given a position and status in the
organizational structure of the bureaucracy that would allow him to
fulfill his mission. Effective management of CR/EO goals requires
that the civil rights unit be an integral part of the management echelon
that makes policy decisions. If a civil rights unit is to accomplish its
objectives, it cannot be a peripheral and secondary appendage without
peer status among the major divisions of a department or agency.
This means that the civil rights executive must participate regularly
and fully in the formulation of the overall management policies of his
department. Without his presence at and participation in senior staff
meetings, the CR/EO aspects of overall policy are not likely to be
fully and effectively considered when plans are made for programs
and for management of the department affairs. If the civil rights
executive is not included in policy and planning meetings regularly,
but is only called in when the senior staff think they need his special
expertise, he is unable to draw their attention to the less obvious
implications of their policies and practices for civil rights and equal
opportunities matters.

The administration of civil rights and equal opportunity statutes
can no longer be thought of in terms of merely remedying wrongs that
come to the attention of management in the form of complaints. The
use of affirmative action techniques as the only element in the machinery of civil rights enforcement is not sufficient, contrary to what is
so often assumed. Affirmative action aims only at correcting deficiencies where they are found. By law, affirmative action is required
only when it is necessary to redress a discriminatory act, so tech-
nically there is no affirmative action mandated until there is a
violation of the law. Using only affirmative action techniques is thus

merely patching up past wrongs while neglecting the larger responsibility management has for running its current operation in such a way that discrimination on the basis of race and ethnic origin never occurs. After a management has in fact carried out its responsibility not to discriminate for a period of years, affirmative action will not be needed because no violations will occur. The more management reduces the gap between the inequitable minority and majority benefits, the less remedial action will be necessary. Such a situation would be promoted by including the civil rights manager in making all major policy decisions so that he might be able to alert top managers to the civil rights implications of all aspects of their plans and decisions.

The full participation of the civil rights manager in departmental affairs also requires that he have direct access to the head of his department or agency. This should not be merely nominal access through an undersecretary, assistant secretary, or executive assistant to the head of the department or agency. Besides having this access to the head, the civil rights manager needs to be in a position equal to the other top managers, including program managers, to compete for adequate resources to carry out his job effectively. This enables him to fight for his rightful share of the departmental budget without facing the obstacles of status inadequacy and unduly circumscribed support personnel and technical resources. He should also have control over the recruitment, selection, hiring, promotion, and termination of his staff.

Unfortunately, the civil rights executives in the federal government have rarely been accorded the position and status in the bureaucratic hierarchy that would allow them to enforce the civil rights and equal opportunity laws effectively. They have always faced major obstacles. Besides the organizational limitations placed in their way, they have had to contend with the extremely negative effects of the social climate of racial and ethnic prejudice. The institutional forms and personal attitudes that divide Americans pervasively on the basis of racial and ethnic identity, and especially on the basis of color, create resistance to almost everything the civil rights executives try to accomplish. [1] The social milieu of racial division and bigotry is also characterized by a situation in which it can be assumed that "a rational discriminator (for example, a monopolist named 'whites') is trying to maximize his gains from discrimination, including economic gains and increases in social distance."[2] In other words, the civil rights executive faces resistance to the implementation of the civil rights and equal opportunity laws not only from the irrational forces of personal bigotry and racism, but also from the self interest of the rational discriminator who stands to gain economically from getting an unfair share of the benefits of federally assisted programs.

In appraising the CR/EO executive as a manager, then, it is important to keep in mind the environment in which he and his staff must operate from day-to-day and the organizational restrictions on his effectiveness. Of course the manager himself is painfully aware of these limitations and finds them frustrating and discouraging. But his continued efforts are necessarily based on the premise that if he and other such managers collectively pursue their goals diligently and efficiently over a sustained period of time, the long-range consequences will be to close the gap between the promise of equality of opportunity and the actual achievement of it. The premise on which he works may very well be false. A persistent and disturbing question is whether the civil rights staffs in the federal bureaucracy are working against impossible odds. A great many forces come into play that stand in the way of changing discriminatory practices outlawed by the Civil Rights Act of 1964. Most of these forces are undoubtedly beyond the control or influence of civil rights managers and their staffs. The nature of these forces and their implications for CR/EO policy and efforts have both philosophical and practical meaning for the federal civil rights effort. But their treatment is outside the scope of this book, though critically important.

Conscious of the larger context within which they operate, the civil rights managers who are working in the federal bureaucracy or have worked there in the past try to achieve their goals despite all the impediments. The performance of the federal civil rights executives as managers is of course critical to the achievement of the nation's commitments in this area. In order to understand their perception of their efforts as managers, decision makers, and policy makers, the author conducted personal interviews with the top civil rights executives in the federal bureaucracy to explore, among other things, how they perceived their policy mission, how they went about discharging it, what tools of management they used and planned to use in the future, and what relationships they had with executives in positions affecting achievements of their goals, such as the heads of their departments and agencies, the program managers of the fund-granting agencies, the civil rights staffs at headquarters and in the field, the regional directors in their respective agencies, and the coordinating and budgeting officers in the Department of Justice and the Office of Management and Budget.

In all, I interviewed 40 high level civil rights executives, twelve of whom were the directors of the various civil rights/equal opportunity activities in departments and agencies with major Title VI programs. The interviews lasted from one to three hours, and were somewhat structured by an interview guide which was submitted to

each executive in advance.* Although the interviews did not follow
the guide slavishly, the issues included in the guide were discussed
in each case whenever the topics were pertinent to the executive's
particular sphere of management, and to whatever extent he would
permit. Because many of the executives who supervised the administration of Title VI programs were also the directors of department-
wide civil rights units including other grant programs and equal opportunity programs, the discussions included the consideration of broader
civil rights issues and of the organization of the entire civil rights
unit within any department or agency in cases where Title VI and
other programs were directed by the same individual. The interviews
stressed three areas of the federal civil rights and equal opportunities
programs: first, the organizational structure of the CR/EO units;
second, the management techniques used by departmental and agency
CR/EO executives; and third, the power and authority of the top CR/
EO executive as an administrator, decision maker, and policy maker.
The report which follows gives the views of the top civil rights administrators in the eight departments and four agencies with major
responsibilities for enforcing Title VI of the Civil Rights Act of 1964.†

CR/EO UNITS: ORGANIZATIONAL STRUCTURE

At the time of the interviews with the civil rights executives,
all twelve of the departments and agencies in which the CR/EO units
were located were at various stages of decentralizing management
decision making, in keeping with the policy established by the Nixon
Administration. However, five of the eight managers of department-
wide civil rights units reported that policy and administrative matters
in their areas continued to be developed and monitored from their
headquarter offices and then filtered down to the civil rights personnel

---

*See Appendix 6 and 7 for interview guide, "Guide for Inter-
views with Equal Opportunity Program Heads," and a list of the civil
rights executives who were interviewed. Chapter 6 is based on this
personal interview study.

†The findings of this analysis are tentative. Research in much
greater depth and more comprehensive in scope is needed in order to
fully understand and appreciate the role, contributions, limitations,
and personal frustrations of this important type of executive officer
in the implementation of the civil rights and equal opportunity policies
of the nation.

located in regional offices. The remaining three executives of this type of CR/EO unit had partially decentralized operations. One executive said, "I'm beginning to delegate more authority to the field. " Two of his programs had become decentralized, but his Title VI program remained centralized. He pointed out, however, that he did not have final decision-making power with respect to Title VI inasmuch as he could only make recommendations about civil rights matters to the program director responsible for dispensing federal assistance.

Another CR/EO executive explained that within his department each agency had its own civil rights staff which was directly responsible to the head of that particular agency. However, this same CR/EO manager said that he had continuous relationships with his civil rights counterparts in all of the agencies in his department, and that he provided them with program direction and evaluation. The remaining CR/EO director of an umbrella-type civil rights operation thought that his operation "was somewhat decentralized in the sense that each region has to determine its own priorities based on the peculiar needs of that region. " Concerning the relationship between the central CR/EO office and the personnel in each of these regions, he commented, "We give them policy guidance and procedures and support and all of this, but the civil rights employee is actually hired, fired, promoted and all of that by the regional administrator, so it is the regional administrator's program. "

Of the four Title VI program directors who headed CR/EO activities in a single agency and not an entire department-wide CR/EO unit, only one said that civil rights decisions in his agency were made at the headquarters level rather than in the field: "The field civil rights employee might be domiciled there in the region and the regional staff might give him administrative support such as housekeeping, travel, etc. We have people in posts of duty offices sometimes in geographical areas that don't conform to our regions because the civil rights workload does not necessarily conform to the general workload of the agency. " In this agency, in other words, the civil rights staff in the field were under the supervision of the Title VI director in Washington.

Another Title VI civil rights head explained that the two larger agencies within his department had their own offices for civil rights, and he served them in a kind of coordinating relationship. In one of the agencies of this department the Title VI civil rights staff reported directly to the assistant secretary of the agency, while in the other agency the regional directors for that agency exercised administrative control. Technical and functional control was exercised at the headquarters' civil rights level, however.

The third Title VI CR/EO executive said that the regional CR/EO field staffs in his department reported directly to their respective departmental regional directors. He emphasized, however, that the field personnel's report had to come to him for final approval. The other civil rights manager in this group referred to himself as a staff officer, and explained that his office did only the investigative part of the Title VI program, while another organization in his department actually administered the Title VI program. It was not clear whether the functions that his office performed were or were not decentralized.

THE CIVIL RIGHTS EXECUTIVE AS MANAGER

Although there were a variety of factors interfering with the ability of civil rights managers to conduct their programs, none of the managers gave the impression or overtly indicated that the operations of their units were crisis-oriented or that anything prevented them from planning their programs. Eleven of the twelve civil rights managers had developed some type of reporting system, and the other one said that his office was in the process of developing one. However, none of the executives was specific about what he sought to accomplish from using his system, and only one said that he had organized a unit under his direction to analyze the data being collected by the reporting system.

Five of the eight civil rights managers who were responsible for all civil rights activities in their departments said that they were using the data from their reporting system for management purposes, but only one of them gave any indication as to how his office did this. In explaining the reasons for not using the data this way, one executive remarked, "I depend on my own judgment." Each one of the civil rights directors in the remaining departments and agencies with centralized programs explained that he was in the process of developing his "own system."

Of the four agencies with decentralized civil rights offices, one of the Title VI directors claimed he used the data from the reporting system for internal management; another spoke of his electronic monitoring system as being in the developmental stage, and the remaining two gave no indication that they used their reporting systems for management purposes. One of the latter commented: "Reporting systems are as good as the people that make the reports, and one of the things we have here in Washington is professional bureaucrats who write well. I wouldn't give a dime for reports." When the topic of reporting systems for management purposes was discussed during the interviews, the civil rights executives talked more about being required to prepare reports to submit to other offices than about using them for their own work. The impetus for developing reporting systems seemed to come mainly from external sources such as the Office of Federal Contract Compliance and the Civil Service Commission, and not from a perception of their own management needs or on the instructions of the Department of Justice, which was the coordinating agency for Title VI programs. Explaining that there was no impetus from a higher managerial level to develop and use reporting systems for internal management in the Title VI area, one civil rights executive said:

> Part of it is because the Justice Department has not given the kind of guidance that we have gotten from the Office of Federal Contract Compliance in contracts and the Civil Service Commission for in-house employment. There is no particular system by which compliance reviews are made. It's up to the administrator of a particular Title VI program or region. Now we are beginning to get eligibility data, but the program is too new to make a management tool.

> There will never be any substitute for human judgment, particularly in programs of this type. Even the best statistical methods, as I have been taught, only establish a basis for probability for occurrence or lack of occurrence of some particular actions, and it's still a matter of human judgment of each case, certainly in this field.

When goals were imposed by a higher authority, however, the civil rights manager was able to use them as a basis for measuring effectiveness in applying the equal opportunity policy. According to one manager, the reporting system for the Office of Federal Contract Compliance had enabled him to measure what he had done according to the national norm for a particular industry. It had also enabled him to look at the quarterly reports required by the Civil Service Commission and ascertain the number of opportunities that various units in his department had had to make progress under the affirmative action programs.

While all of the CR/EO executives reported that they had set goals, definitions of these goals were absent from their interviews. In fact, there was no evidence that any CR/EO executive had established well formulated written goals for his Title VI programs. None of the civil rights managers spoke of goals in relation to Title VI. In civil rights programs where goal setting was required by a higher authority such as the OFCC and the CSC, on the other hand, efforts at setting formal goals in written form were made systematically. One of the managers made the following observation: "You can always set goals, but whether or not they are realistic—there are too many factors over which the civil rights manager has no control. I feel that it can't be done to track the efficiency and effectiveness of his staff. "

On the subject of their staffs, the managers felt that they had difficulty recruiting people with the needed qualifications, though they had some good and dedicated people. There was the ever present pressure of people in other agencies within the department trying to get unqualified staff out of their own programs. One executive observed that it is unfortunately true that CR/EO personnel in government agencies are not uniformly well qualified, and that in some cases people are given jobs in the EO programs when they cannot do good work elsewhere. There was also some employment of people as a means of payment of political debts. According to one manager, "The most serious obstacle right now is the lack of the ability to go out in the open market and procure trained people." Another manager had the following to say about the problem of maintaining a staff of high quality: "You often find yourself in the position of having very inferior quality people at very high levels in some instances. Every priest who wanted to get out of being a priest in the Catholic church was sent to me for an interview as a possibility in the office. I have people working in the program who are not effective for many reasons. We have inherited people who were brought on for various reasons. They are here to draw a paycheck." On the other side of the coin, this comment: "We have a good reputation in the field. We always get a tremendous number of people. They feel frustrated where they are and they think they will be less frustrated here."

As for staff development in civil rights units, according to the executives there were generally no systematic training programs for their staffs, and training was not an item in the budget. New staff members were usually paired with experienced staff in a kind of informal on-the-job training situation. Some of the managers were doubtful that their staffs could get the kinds of formal training they needed, in any case. One said "No place else including the Civil Service Commission can give us the kind of training we need for our people, so we have to train them ourselves. There aren't many qualified people around." On the specific type of skills that need development, another manager commented, "I find that I'm going to have to train people to do negotiating."

CIVIL RIGHTS EXECUTIVES: POWER AND AUTHORITY

The eight civil rights managers with responsibility for all of the civil rights and equal opportunity activities in their departments said that they reported to the heads of their departments on all policy matters relating to civil rights. Half of this group stated that they reported to their department heads on day-to-day operations as well, while two of them said that they reported to a deputy department head, and one reported to an assistant secretary for administration. One manager did not provide any information on this point.

Seven of the eight CR/EO managers reported that they were members of the executive staff of their departments and participated in the regularly scheduled meetings with all the other top officials in their departments. The other manager did not claim to be a member of the executive staff, but stated that he had easy access to the head of his department directly by telephone.

In the four departments where there were individual managers for each type of civil rights program, the civil rights director who was responsible for the Title VI program was the person interviewed. In this category, all four of the Title VI directors were at lower levels organizationally than the eight managers who were in charge of overall departmental civil rights units. Three of the Title VI directors had only indirect access to the department head or his designee in civil rights matters. This meant that they had access to the department head only through the person they reported to, who in turn had access to the department head or his designee. The other Title VI executive said that he had direct access to the administrator of his agency "if and when I need him," though he expressed an acute awareness of his agency head's heavy schedule and used this prerogative sparingly and as a last resort. Ordinarily, then, these Title VI managers reported to a person who was at least two levels below the head of the department. Two of them reported to an assistant secretary, one to an associate deputy administrator, and one to a special assistant.

Where there was a civil rights component in the field, it was expected that the decision-making power of the departmental civil rights executive would be weakened. While there was neither overwhelming support nor disavowal of the proposition by the civil rights executives, it is conceivable that they would have no way of knowing whether this was true or not. In situations where regional civil rights personnel reported directly to the regional director of the department and where decisions about civil rights matters were made by the regional director, the departmental or agency-wide civil rights executive serving in a staff capacity in Washington might be unaware of what decisions were made unless his advice was requested or a crisis brought an issue to his attention.

When a disagreement over a civil rights matter occurred between a departmental civil rights executive in Washington and a departmental or agency regional director, there were various ways of settling it. One manager reported that he was required to put his case before a higher authority, since he did not have the power to make the final decision: "I have had occasions to, let us say, lock horns with the regional administrator and again I have been fortunate in the support that I got from the administrator and deputy administrator at headquarters. I pick my battles, of course." Another CR/EO executive, on the other hand, pointed out that while authority for implementing the equal opportunity aspects of programs was delegated to the program administrators, particularly to the regional program administrators and assistant secretaries in program areas, he himself had full authority to make direct contact with the regional administrator or the assistant regional administrator for equal opportunity in order to seek corrective action and more effective performance. He indicated that he and others of his staff dealt routinely and directly with the assistant regional administrators for equal opportunity, and that this did not lead to any complications for the regional administrator. This CR/EO executive said that he also had the right to pull a case out of a regional or area office and have his headquarters staff process it directly if he believed that the regional administrator was not handling it effectively.

The discussions of the status of the civil rights executives in relation to program managers brought a variety of responses. None of the civil rights executives reported having a continuous relationship with program managers. Among those departments with centralized civil rights offices, two of the eight executives had no relationship at all with the program managers. One of these executives stated "The equal opportunity director has no policy or administrative authority with reference to departmental program managers and activities at any level." The status of another civil rights executive, on the other hand, appeared to be superior to the program manager's, as suggested by a comment made by his deputy: "Our civil rights executive makes the civil rights decisions and they are only subject to change by the agency administrator."

Three of the managers said that they had peer relationships with the program managers in their departments. "We are structurally co-equal," was the way one manager put it. However, another executive who said "All of my line communication is directly with the head of the bureau and he is below the assistant secretary," implied that his status was subordinate to that of the program manager. One of the department-wide managers did not discuss his relationship with the program managers in his department.

In the decentralized civil rights programs, two of the four Title VI CR/EO directors stated that they had no dealings with program executives. The other two seemed to have a status subordinate to the program managers in that they were far removed from the

level of the program executives organizationally. The remark
"The assistant secretary for administration is on the same level with
the assistant secretaries in charge of programs" indicated that the
civil rights manager was below that level, and therefore was not an
equal of the program administrator.

The civil rights executives who purportedly had a peer relationship with program managers were nevertheless on the defensive when
a civil rights issue arose because it was referred to a higher authority
for a decision. One civil rights executive gave an example, "Now this
actually happened to us. Where I found probable cause, the associate
director overruled me." One of the other civil rights directors
reported that he, on the other hand, had had three confrontations with
program managers and that, in each instance, the agency head had
ruled in his favor.

The civil rights managers did not adequately explain their
common feeling of managerial subordination despite their nominal
peer status with program managers. In five of the departments the
CR/EO executives were members of the executive group which met
regularly, often weekly, with their agency heads. Why was a decision-
making official interposed between the agency heads and the CR/EO
executives under these circumstances? Were there real or assumed
restrictions on bringing civil rights issues before this executive
group?

On the issue of whether the civil rights executives controlled
their own budgets, it appeared that an increasing number of them
were preparing and even defending these budgets because of recent
pressure from the Office of Management and Budget for departments
to obtain budgets from their civil rights people. Eight of the twelve
civil rights managers reported that they prepared and defended their
own budgets. Three executives did not discuss budgetary matters
with the interviewer, and one executive reported that he did not prepare and defend his budget, although he had influence on its preparation through his superior.

In six of the twelve departments and agencies civil rights appropriations were a line item in the departmental budget. This meant
that the civil rights executive had a definite amount of money that he
could plan to spend during the fiscal year. Without this he could not
count on having a specific amount to support the activities of his unit.
In five instances, I could not determine from the remarks of the
executives whether or not civil rights was a line item in the budget.
The remaining manager said that he budget was not a line item but a
"specified letter order" from the OMB in his department head's
overall budget. Under this budget arrangement, the civil rights manager might get another letter cutting the amount he could spend.

Seven of the eight executives who prepared and defended their own budgets were in centralized civil rights settings with positions as directors of all the departmental civil rights activities. The remaining executive in this group was responsible for Title VI and contract compliance activities in his agency, but it was not clear what level of control he had over his budget. Six of the eight managers were members of their departments' top policy-making executive staff, and could therefore fight for CR/EO budgets at senior staff meetings.

If a CR/EO manager had the status and prestige to prepare and defend his budget, his personal presence at the budget hearings increased his chances of obtaining the resources he needed to manage his program. Of the group of eight civil rights managers who prepared and defended their own budgets, only one of them reported that he had never been requested by his department head to go before a congressional appropriations committee. Another executive explained that he goes to "the Hill" to defend his budget "when the civil rights portion of the budget is questioned." One other executive, who on previous occasions had accompanied top program officials to congressional appropriations committee hearings, was not asked to go to Capitol Hill at the last budget presentation. This change occurred when the head of the agency changed his relationship with the CR/EO unit: instead of receiving reports directly from the civil rights manager he began to get them through an assistant secretary.

At the time of the interview study of the federal civil rights executives there was almost no evidence that they were using racial and ethnic data in any form or fashion to plan or to appraise the quality of their work. Data for decision-making purposes were being collected in some cases but were rarely being analyzed. Certainly whatever analysis there was had not reached the stage where managers could get specialized information for use in the civil rights field. The Department of Health, Education, and Welfare probably came closer to making some management decisions on the basis of racial and ethnic data collection and analysis (in the area of elementary and secondary education) than most if not all other departments and agencies. In the main, however, this was forced on HEW by the pressure of outside groups like the NAACP, the Legal Defense Fund, the American Friends Service Committee, and others, along with some insiders who pointed out that school desegregation efforts had to be based on percentages of black and white school enrollment. But whatever other data were being collected for the enforcement of the Civil Rights Act, no analysis or use of them for systematic management decision making was discernible in the interviews with the executives in charge.

There was much evidence in the interviews of the gradual erosion of the power and authority of the civil rights executives.

Some of these managers had held considerably more power when the
civil rights/equal opportunity programs were first established. But
as the benign neglect policies of the Nixon administration took hold
and spread throughout the system, most of the civil rights executives
were pushed farther from the mainstream of influence and decision
making in their departments and agencies. Their relationships with
members of the managerial hierarchy above them, the policy-making
officials, deteriorated. They were forced increasingly to report to the
heads of their departments through several layers of management
standing between them and the real policy-makers. In many cases
they had to report to an assistant secretary for management, or to an
assistant to the assistant secretary for management, neither of whom
was required under his defined position to have any knowledge, expertise, or concern for the civil rights of minorities. These management
people were often briefed on civil rights issues by another official,
who also knew very little and sometimes cared even less about civil
rights matters. Trying to penetrate these bureaucratic layers with a
message for the head of the department was an almost hopeless task.
The result was that the civil rights executives in the federal government became increasingly powerless to influence policies and to
enforce the civil rights laws of the nation. This was further reinforced
by the widely reported pressure on CR/EO executives to employ
unqualified poor performers and misfits in the civil rights units
because higher level management wanted to move these people out of
other units. This is a serious and sometimes sinister obstacle to
effective CR/EO management.

NOTES

1. Report of the National Advisory Commission on Civil Disorders (New York: Bantam Books, 1968), pp. 1-2, 9-10.
2. Lester C. Thurow, Poverty and Discrimination: Studies in
Social Economics (Washington, D. C.: The Brookings Institution,
1969), p. 118. In Chapter VII, "Discrimination," Thurow provides a
theoretical and empirical analysis of white monetary gains and black
losses from discrimination in seven general categories: employment,
wages, occupation, human capital investment, access to and return
on capital, monopoly power, and price. He states that "many of the
effects of discrimination rest on monopoly and monopsony powers
of whites. Governments and Negroes can attempt to break down these
powers in government, labor, and business institutions" (p. 130).

III

MINORITY MANAGERS IN THE FEDERAL BUREAUCRACY

7

THE SCARCE FEDERAL OFFICIALS: MINORITIES AT HEADQUARTERS

In both the public and the private sectors of the economy, success or failure of the enterprise depends heavily on the quality of the managers in charge. The good executive gets performance from his staff, whether in a private business or a government bureaucracy. Although alike in the need for effective management, the two kinds of enterprises, public and private, are different in a number of significant ways. One of the most important of these differences lies in the nature of the ends sought by the enterprise rather than the means employed to achieve the ends. While in general terms private enterprise seeks profit as its goal, the public enterprise seeks the welfare and security of all the citizens as its goal.

Differing goals aside, both the public and the private business are similar in that the managers of both are expected to secure maximum returns from available resources. The private manager is judged by the bottom line of profits or losses in the annual report to the stockholders. The bottom line of the manager in the public business, in contrast, is the well-being of the people of the nation. The general welfare is undoubtedly a fuzzier goal than profits and possibly a more difficult one, but that is not to say that it cannot be measured and judged in more or less objective terms approaching the effectiveness of the dollars and cents accounting used in private business.

One of the goals mandated by law and policy for the management of every federal program and agency making financial grants from the federal treasury is equal access to the benefits of federally-financed programs regardless of race, color, or national origin. In operational terms, managers of various government agencies and programs have interpreted this goal of their enterprise in widely differing ways. Some managers have considered equal opportunity as an active

immediate objective, while others have envisioned it as a long-range
goal with little connection with their day-to-day operations. Some
have worked on it overtly and directly, while others have considered
covert approaches more effective and palatable. "Watch what I do,
not what I say" was suggested by one administration as a way of
understanding its approach. Still others have given the appearance
of accepting it explicitly by publicizing their commitment to equal
opportunity, but in practice have either underemphasized it, failed
to activate it, or sometimes overtly prohibited its implementation.

But the equal opportunity goals of the federal enterprise were
never merely ones which the public manager had the privilege to
select for inclusion in his program according to personal whim.
Equal opportunity was not a goal to be arbitrarily assigned to some
activities and not to others. Rather it was an overall objective imposed by the Constitution and by statutes and regulations (federal,
state, and local) required of every program manager in the federal
bureaucracy. Under current nondiscrimination laws and policies, all
programs were supposed to be conducted without discrimination, and,
more specifically, in compliance with the Civil Rights Act of 1964.
Yet such goals have generally been applied to the management of
federal programs as sparingly as possible, or ignored and separated
completely from the other more generally accepted functions of management. Civil rights and equal opportunity objectives have usually
been given relatively low priority, and were dealt with if and when
the other more central and generally accepted mission of a program
allowed, or if they were forced to the center of attention by outsiders.

Despite the efforts of CR/EO staffs to make civil rights and
equal opportunity issues of primary rather than secondary concern,
the implementation of Title VI in the management of federal programs
and activities has continued to lag badly. Although heads of government departments have adopted formal civil rights objectives and
made official statements about equal opportunity goals for their
departments, such goals have frequently not been incorporated into
the programs of the operating agencies, bureaus, offices, and sec-
tions down the line in the departments. The secretary of the Department of Health, Education, and Welfare, for example, may have
viewed Title VI as an integral part of program administration for
vocational education grants to various states, but whether the Bureau
of Adult Vocational and Technical Education (BAVTE) of HEW employed such an objective when administering the grants was questionable. It was even less likely that the regional BAVTE staffs thought
that their management responsibilities included insuring that vocational education grants were distributed in compliance with Title VI
and Executive Order 11246, even though this was departmental policy
and the legal duty of all its employees.

When any federal official neglected to set up adequate and appropriate procedures for monitoring the awarding of grants by race and ethnic origin—and procedures for such monitoring were almost never set up—he was mismanaging the public business. Theoretically, of course, every manager of the public business was supposedly supervised by his superiors from his immediate boss all the way up the organizational hierarchy in such a way that all of the goals of the public business were pursued in his day-to-day work. But this has rarely occurred in the case of equal opportunity goals. Program managers have rarely been required by their superiors to institute ways of insuring that their grants to recipients have reached eligible minorities in proportion to their numbers in the population. In respect to Title VI and other equal opportunity laws and rulings, their supervision and enforcement have been shifted from the shoulders of the program managers and their supervisors, where the responsibility initially belonged, to the managers of the separate civil rights units.

As long as these conditions prevailed there was very little movement in the direction of the enforcement of the civil rights and equal opportunity laws as an integral part of program management's responsibility. What the bureaucracy needed was an infusion of employees who were sensitive to the rights of minorities and in a position to influence policy decisions and administration of laws. Staff members of minority background were potential candidates for this role. Their presence in the upper executive levels of management in the civil service would probably result in greater attention being paid to enforcing civil rights and equal opportunity laws and goals. It might be possible for them to use the power and status of their offices to secure equal access by minorities to the benefits of federal programs. Of course an equal opportunity for employment in the federal government at the upper grade levels of the civil service was in itself one of the rights that was guaranteed by law not to be denied on grounds of race, color, or nationality. But in addition to the justice of providing fair employment opportunity to minorities, there was the possibility that managers from various minority backgrounds would bend their energies to putting antidiscrimination laws and policies into effect with special vigor because of their unique knowledge of and experience with the issues involved and their qualifications and motivation to deal effectively and continuously with them.

THE SCARCITY OF BLACK EXECUTIVES

Unfortunately, minority representation in the middle and upper levels of the General Schedule (GS) grades of the civil service in

government agencies has not been extensive enough to bring this
about. In the report of the Civil Service Commission on Minority
Group Employment in the Federal Government for 1970, it was shown
that a relatively small number of blacks, for example, held middle
and upper GS grade positions. [1] Although grades 12-18 were the jobs
in the civil service from which the managers and potential managers
were drawn, only 5 percent of black employees held positions at this
level, whereas 25 percent of all non-black* employees were in GS 12-
18 grade level. † This meant that blacks had about one chance in

----

    *The terms "non-black, " "white, " and "others" have been used
synonymously here since the "Spanish surnamed" and "other minorities" categories used by the Census constituted less than 5 percent
of the total of the GS employees. Referring to them separately is
therefore not necessary to support to broad conclusions of the analysis. By using this definition, the importance of the treatment of
other minorities is not minimized, nor is the seriousness of their
plight denigrated. This investigation was limited to black GS employees because data about this group have been systematically collected
on a comparable basis for a longer period of time and because of
restrictions on research resources and time. This analysis warrants
further refinement and parallel application to each minority group.

    †The regional offices chosen for study had a small percent of
other minorites who were GS employees, with the exception of the
Dallas region, which had a larger percent of Spanish-surnamed GS
employees (8. 2 percent) than black GS employees (5. 2 percent). The
percent of minorities other than blacks who were GS employees in
these Civil Service regions were: 0. 8 percent minorities other than
black in the Atlanta region, 0. 7 percent in the Boston region, 0. 8 percent in the Chicago region, 2. 0 percent in the New York region, and
0. 5 percent in the Philadelphia region.

    Since the Spanish-surnamed employees in the Dallas region
constituted a significant proportion of the total employee population
in the GS grades (8. 2 percent), it is conceivable that this could have
given a significant bias to the conclusions regarding blacks in this
region. However, a review of an analysis using a base of all others
except blacks compared with using a base confined to all others
(excluding Spanish-surnamed, Orientals, and American Indians)
showed that it had little effect on the percent that blacks were of the
total employees at various grade levels. We therefore believe that
the conclusions obtained in this study were not significantly altered
by our failure to make the refinement throughout of using the term
non-black to refer to the majority group.

twenty of being employed at this grade level, while government employees other than blacks had about one chance in five. At the GS 9-11 grade level, only 11. 8 percent of all black employees held such jobs, while 26. 2 percent of the white work force was at this level. Thus more than twice as many non-blacks as blacks held jobs in this category.* On the other hand, blacks were more than twice as heavily represented at the bottom grades of federal employment than whites; 46. 1 percent of the jobs held by blacks and 20. 1 percent of the jobs held by non-blacks were at the GS 1-4 level.

It should be noted that the lower levels of the broad GS 9-18 category included professionals, technicians, and other employees who were not in any way involved in management functions such as policy formulation and decision making. Thus when the above comparisons were made, the potential management role of black employees in comparison with whites was probably overestimated because most of the jobs blacks held were at lower levels. Even at the upper grade levels, where policies and strategies are discussed, black participation in management functions was probably somewhat overstated by the bare statistics; though blacks held top positions, this did not necessarily mean that they actually took part in policy-making activities.

THE BLACK SHARE OF FEDERAL
WHITE-COLLAR EMPLOYMENT

In 1970 black white-collar employment in the federal bureaucracy was 11. 1 percent government-wide, which was virtually identical to the percent of blacks in the total population according to the 1970 census. However, this proportion diminished rapidly as blacks reached higher rungs of the GS grade ladder. According to the Civil Service Commission's <u>Minority Group Employment in the Federal Government</u> of 1970, there were 1,283,991 employees in the general schedule of federal employment, of which 142,466, or 11. 1 percent were black. The black penetration rate† at the top was exceedingly

---

*In 1971, the odds favoring the white employee over the black fell to about 2 to 1 in GS 9-11; that is, 25. 8 of 100 whites were in this category compared to 12. 2 of 100 blacks.

†Penetration rate in this study indicates the share of total federal white-collar employment held by minorities (blacks). It may be calculated for any category, for example, for a particular grade level, for an agency, or for all white-collar employees. It is

small, but grew larger as it reached lower levels. In the GS 16-18
category there were 92 blacks or 1.6 percent; in GS 12-15 there were
7,552 blacks or 2.6 percent; in GS 5-11 there were 69,106 blacks or
10 percent; and in GS 1-4 there were 65,716 blacks or 22.3 percent. *
In summary, while in 1970, 111 of every 1,000 total federal white-
collar employees were blacks, only 16 out of 1,000 of those in grades
16-18 (the super grade level) were black; 19 out of 1,000 were in
GS 14-16, 28 out of 1,000 in GS 12-13; 53 out of 1,000 in GS 9-11;
140 out of 1,000 in GS 5-8; and 223 out of 1,000 in the bottom grades
GS 1-4. †

    Although there was some modest relative as well as numerical
improvement in black high level employment reported at the end of
May 1974, the low penetration of blacks into decision-making positions
has not changed significantly since the 1971 Civil Service Commission
surveys. Commission reports through mid-1975 indicated a continuing trend of extreme underemployment of minorities, and of blacks
in particular, at the upper GS grade levels from which managers,
policy makers, and leaders have been drawn in federal government
agencies. ‡

---

obtained by dividing the number of minority members (blacks) by the
total number of employees in the category under consideration.

    *See Appendix Table A.1 for more detailed figures on grade
levels and numbers of total and black employees. Appendix Table A.2
shows the penetration rate of blacks in government-wide white collar
employment as 11.1 percent, which was the same as the total percent
of the black population in 1970. According to the 1971 edition of
Minority Group Employment in the Federal Government issued by the
Civil Service Commission, there was a total of 1,315,476 employees
in GS employment of which 148,957 were black. The total black penetration rate in 1971 was 11.3 percent. However, in the upper managerial and professional levels blacks were not represented in accordance with their 11.1 percent proportion in the total population: in
GS 16-18 there were 113 black employees, or 2.0 percent; in
GS 12-15 there were 8,725 black employees, or 2.9 percent; in
GS 5-11 there were 76,286 black employees, or 10.7 percent; and at
the lowest level, GS 1-4, there were 63,833 black employees, or
21.18 percent.

    †In 1971, 113 out of each 1,000 federal white collar employees
were black; 20 out of 1,000 of those in grades 16-18 (the supergrade
level); 22 out of 1,000 in GS 14-15; 31 out of 1,000 in GS 12-13; 57 out
of 1,000 in GS 9-11; 148 out of 1,000 in GS 5-8; and 218 out of 1,000
in the bottom grades GS 1-4.

    ‡It is my understanding from information given to me by the
Civil Service Commission (CSC) that it no longer publishes annual

THE BLACK SHARE OF
HEADQUARTERS EMPLOYMENT

Despite some moves towards decentralization of the federal
establishment, the Washington headquarters offices of federal agencies
have continued to play dominant roles in the development and implementation of departmental policy. Therefore, when looking at the
status of blacks at managerial levels of federal departments, the penetration rate of this group at the hub of federal program administration
was important to know. In the Washington central offices in 1970 there
were 228,180 employees in GS occupations, of whom 47,971 or 21
percent were black.* However, this 21 percent was somewhat short
of its proportion in the population; in that year blacks constituted
24.6 percent of the residents of metropolitan Washington, D.C. In
the upper grade categories GS 12-18, black employees constituted
3,198 or 3.8 percent of the 84,775 persons employed at this top level
in Washington, D.C. At the other extreme, blacks comprised about
half of the 35,269 employees in GS 1-4—18,087, or 51.3 percent. Put
another way, out of each 1,000 GS employees at headquarters in the

---

minority employment figures in the form that was used in 1965, 1970,
and 1971. Because of the changes in some definitions in the 1973,
1974, and 1975 reports, it is difficult to make exact comparisons with
the data for the earlier years. However, the CSC releases of 1973,
1974, and 1975 lead me to believe that the substantive findings of this
analysis have not changed significantly, even though some of the figures have changed and the design for collecting data has been altered.
See the U.S. Civil Service Commission, Civil Service News, July 17,
1973 (particularly Table 2-A), May 31, 1974, and June 12, 1975
(particularly Tables 1 and 11), indicating the continuing extreme
underemployment of minorities generally and blacks in particular at
GS grade levels from which managers, policy makers, and leaders
in federal government agencies are usually drawn.

*In 1971, there were 234,475 employees in GS occupations in
the Washington central offices, of whom 50,290 or 21.4 percent were
blacks. In the upper grade categories, GS 12-18, black employees
constituted 3,744 or 4.2 percent of the 87,925 employed. At the other
extreme, blacks comprised about one-half of the 35,268 employees in
the GS 1-4 bottom level grades, that is, 17,415 blacks or 49.4 percent. Out of each 1,000 total employees in the major GS categories
at the Washington headquarters, the following numbers were black:
in GS 16-18, 90 blacks or 21 out of 1,000; in GS 14-15, 985 or 28 per
1,000; in GS 12-13, 2,669, or 55 per 1,000; in GS 9-11, 5,281, or
137 per 1,000; in GS 5-8, 23,850, or 329 per 1,000; and, in the
lowest category, GS 1-4, 17,415, or 494 per 1,000.

major GS categories, the following were black: in GS 16-18, 73 employees or 18 out of 1,000; in GS 14-15, 796 or 24 per 1,000; in GS 12-13, 2,329 or 50 per thousand; in GS 9-11, 6,710 employees or 125 per thousand; in GS 5-8, 21,976 employees or 312 per thousand; and, in the lowest category, GS 1-4, 18,087 or 513 out of 1,000.

VARIATIONS IN BLACK PARTICIPATION IN FEDERAL DEPARTMENTS

The extent and probably the character of the participation of blacks in managerial and professional functions in the federal civil service varied from department to department and also within the bureaus, agencies, and other subunits of individual departments. The distribution of blacks by subunits within departments could not be documented with figures since no information about this has been made public. However, data about the percentage of blacks employed in the various departments were available. Those departments whose programs related primarily to people as consumers or workers had higher levels of black employment than those with other kinds of missions. The more people-oriented the department, the greater the black employment relative to other departments and the higher the level of managerial and professional status. The nature of the clients and the general clientele of the department appeared to be significant for the employment of blacks. Those departments responsible for services to the masses of people were more heavily involved with minorities as clients because minorities were proportionately larger in this segment of the population. Therefore the level of awareness of and sensitivity to equal opportunity and civil rights issues was greater throughout such departments. The departments in this group included Health, Education, and Welfare, Housing and Urban Development, and Labor.

Distinguishing these three departments from other departments whose missions were also people-oriented was the fact that the Department of Commerce and the Department of Agriculture served fewer people, and those they served had higher average incomes and socioeconomic status. Such people were mainly those whose primary income was based on profit making as entrepreneurs (business and farm), executive managerial personnel (whether salaried or owner-managers), and farmers (mainly the non-family and corporate farmer). The masses of the citizens, in contrast, were mainly the manpower resources of these major clients rather than the primary constituency to which the departments responded. In the mainly business-oriented Departments of Commerce and Agriculture the employment of blacks in upper managerial positions was lower than in HEW, HUD, and DOL.

The more deeply the mission of a department was involved in
non-human issues, the lower the amount of significant employment
of blacks and the smaller the number and the lower the grade level
at which those employed in managerial and professional pursuits were
engaged. The departments which were resource- and facility-oriented
rather than people-oriented included the Department of the Interior
and the Department of Transportation.

In addition to the particular mission of a department, the
personal commitment to equal opportunity of departmental leadership
was an important factor in determining how many blacks were hired
to fill managerial positions. The basis on which the chief executive
chose the members of his Cabinet was of course critical to the civil
rights and equal opportunity posture, policies, and program implementation of the government departments. Positive or negative attitudes towards civil rights issues on the part of the secretaries of the
departments would therefore not be determined solely by the missions
of their departments, the policies and priorities of the president who
appointed the secretaries would also be very influential. Within this
context, a department head would probably aim for a level of minority
employment consistent with the civil rights position of the current administration and his own personal commitment to equal opportunity.
The political ambitions of the secretary and of his sponsor, the president, would be influential in determining how much to push for minority
employment. Besides responding to these party pressures and personal political ambitions, the secretary of a department would act on
the basis of his awareness of and sensitivity to the minority problems.

The penetration rates of minorities in the upper managerial
levels varied by departments. According to Table 7.1, they were
highest in the departments whose programs were oriented to the
people as consumers and workers. In the GS 12-18 grade level, HEW
had 5.4 percent blacks, HUD 6.8 percent, and DOL 9.5 percent. In
the business-oriented departments, DOA had only 1.4 percent blacks
in these positions and DOC had 3.7 percent. In the resource- and
facility-oriented departments, DOI had only 0.8 percent blacks at
these grade levels and DOT had 1.9 percent. The other departments'
rates of entrance of blacks into grades 12-18 were DOJ 1.5 percent,
DOD 0.2 percent, State Department 4.3 percent, and Treasury
Department 2.5 percent. *

---

* In 1971 at the GS 12-18 grade level there were the following
black penetration rates: HEW, 6.5 percent; HUD, 7.7 percent; DOL,
10.4 percent; DOA, 1.5 percent; DOC, 4.2 percent; DOJ, 1.6 percent;
DOD, 2.2 percent; State Department, 5.1 percent; and Treasury,
2.7 percent.

TABLE 7.1

Penetration Rates of Black General Schedule (White Collar) Employees Government-Wide and for Selected Major Departments by GS Grade Level, 1970

Area	Total	GS 1-4	GS 5-8	GS 9-11	GS 12-15	GS 16-18	GS 12-18
Government-wide	11.1	22.3	14.0	5.3	2.6	1.6	2.6
Consumer and/or work oriented							
Department of Labor (DOL)	25.7	57.7	39.4	20.8	9.5	6.9	9.5
Department of Health, Education, and Welfare (HEW)	21.3	36.9	24.5	9.7	5.5	3.4	5.4
Department of Housing and Urban Development (HUD)	18.6	39.2	32.5	8.6	6.8	7.8	6.8
Business oriented (with consumer elements)							
Department of Agriculture (DOA)	5.5	12.3	7.0	3.1	1.4	1.7	1.4
Department of Commerce (DOC)	14.5	28.3	21.8	7.5	3.9	0.5	3.7
Resource and facility oriented							
Department of the Interior (DOI)	4.0	6.1	6.4	3.3	0.8	0.5	0.8
Department of Transportation (DOT)	5.4	21.2	12.5	3.0	1.9	4.9	1.9
Other							
Department of Justice (DOJ)	9.6	22.4	10.8	2.9	1.6	1.3	1.5
Department of Defense (DOD)	7.8	14.0	9.6	4.4	2.1	0.3	0.2
Department of State (DOS)	31.5	57.8	46.2	22.2	4.4	0	4.3
Department of Treasury (D/Treas.)	12.3	27.3	14.6	5.0	2.5	0.6	2.5

<u>Note</u>: See Table F.2 for total number of employees.

Source: U.S. Civil Service Commission, Minority Group Employment in the Federal Government (Washington, D.C.: Government Printing Office, 1970).

Assuming that the penetration rate for government-wide employment of blacks at the GS 12-18 level was the norm, the penetration rates for the people-oriented departments (HEW, HUD, and DOL) were above the norm, while the remaining departments fluctuated a little above and below, with the resource- and facility-oriented groups tending to be significantly below the norm.

It was in the lower managerial grades (GS 12-15) that most of the blacks held jobs (see Table 7. 2 and Table 7. 3). Their participation at the supergrade level, where policy decisions are made, was extremely limited. In GS 16-18, blacks held only 92 or 1. 6 percent of the 5, 586 such positions in the entire federal bureaucracy. * The number of blacks in GS 12-15 was much larger (7, 552 out of 292, 942, or 2. 6 percent); the rate of black employment in GS 12-15 was identical to the whole range of GS 12-18 employment, which was also 2. 6 percent (see Table 7.1).

From 1965 to 1970 the departments in the federal government showing the greatest amount of improvement in employment of blacks were the consumer- and worker-oriented ones (see Table 7. 4). The business-oriented departments also showed an increase over the same period, but the increase in the Department of the Interior (a resource- and facility-oriented department) was slight. The DOI went from 43 black employees in GS 12-18 in 1965 to 107 in 1970. The only department to show a decrease in the number of blacks employed at a professional level was the Defense Department, which had 1, 253 blacks in GS 12-18 in 1965, but only 255 in 1970. According to Table 7. 4, the changes in the penetration rate of black employees at the GS 12-18 level in the federal departments from 1965 to 1970 were as follows:† government-wide, 100; Department of Labor, 111. 1; Department of Health, Education, and Welfare, 145. 4; Department of Housing and Urban Development, 142. 8; Department of Agriculture, 133. 3; Department of Commerce, 164. 4; Department of the Interior, 60. 0; Department of Justice, 150. 0; Department of Defense, 85. 7; Department of State, 115. 0; and Treasury Department, 92. 3. The Depart-

---

*In 1971 at the GS 16-18 grade level there were 113 black employees out of 5, 755, or 2. 0 percent, and for GS 12-15 there were 8, 725 black employees out of 299, 839, or 2. 9 percent.

†The rate of change from 1965 to 1971 (the addition of one year) did not show any notable changes except in the Defense Department, where an increase of 57. 1 occurred. Changes from 1965 to 1971 for GS 12-18 were: government-wide, 115. 3; DOL, 131. 1; HEW, 195. 4; HUD, 175. 0; DOA, 150. 0; DOC, 200. 0; DOI, 60. 0; DOJ, 166. 7; DOD, 57. 1; DOS, 155. 0; and Treasury, 107. 6. (DOT had not yet been established in 1965, so no figures are available for comparison.)

TABLE 7.2

Number of Employees (Total and Black) and Black Penetration Rates
in Supergrades (GS 16-18) Government-Wide and by Major Departments, 1970

	Total Number of Employees	Total Number of Black Employees	Penetration Rate
Government-wide	5,586	92	1.6
Consumer and/or work oriented			
DOL	102	7	6.9
HEW	323	11	3.4
HUD	102	7	6.9
Business oriented with consumer elements			
DOA	232	4	1.7
DOC	367	2	0.5
Resource and facility oriented			
DOI	196	1	0.5
DOT	305	15	4.9
Other			
DOJ	313	4	1.3
DOD	1,048	3	0.3
DOS	41	0	0
D/Treas.	343	2	0.6

Source: U. S. Civil Service Commission, Minority Group Employment in the
Federal Government (Washington, D. C. : Government Printing Office, 1970).

TABLE 7.3

Number of Employees (Total and Black) and Black Penetration Rates
in Upper Grades (GS 12-15) Government-Wide and by Major Departments, 1970

	Total Number of Employees	Total Number of Black Employees	Penetration Rate
Government-wide	292,942	7552	2.6
Consumer and/or work oriented			
DOL	4,626	442	9.5
HEW	16,521	905	5.5
HUD	4,922	334	6.8
Business oriented with consumer elements			
DOA	15,915	220	1.4
DOC	8,682	336	3.9
Resource and facility oriented			
DOI	12,867	107	0.8
DOT	25,890	484	1.9
Other			
DOJ	8,343	131	1.6
DOD	120,556	2520	2.1
DOS	1,575	70	4.4
D/Treas.	19,332	492	2.5

Source: U. S. Civil Service Commission, Minority Group Employment in the
Federal Government (Washington, D. C. : Government Printing Office, 1970).

TABLE 7.4

Changes in Penetration Rates of Black General Schedule Employees (White Collar) Government-Wide and in Selected Major Departments by Grade Levels, 1965–70

	Government-Wide	Consumer and/or Work Oriented			Business Oriented		Resource & Facility Oriented		Other			
		DOL	HEW	HUD	DOA	DOC	DOI	DOT	DOJ	DOD	DOS	D/Treas.
Total	16.8	29.8	19.7	53.7	48.6	20.8	37.9		95.9	4.0	35.8	12.8
GS 1–4	15.5	38.4	21.8	36.1	75.7	-8.7	22.0		80.6	6.1	22.4	10.1
GS 5–8	45.8	37.3	31.0	98.8	62.8	42.9	68.4		151.2	12.9	39.1	47.5
GS 9–11	55.9	131.1	73.2	126.3	158.3	59.6	83.3		93.3	33.3	136.2	38.9
GS 12–18	100.0	111.1	145.4	142.8	133.3	164.3	60.0		150.0	-85.7	115.0	92.3

Notes: No 1965 data available for Department of Transportation. Change = penetration rates in 1970 divided by penetration rates in 1965 minus 1.00. See Tables F.3 and F.4 for penetration rates.

Sources: Penetration rates for 1965: U.S. Civil Service Commission, Study of Minority Group Employment in the Federal Government (Washington, D.C.: Government Printing Office, 1966); penetration rates for 1970: U.S. Civil Service Commission, Minority Group Employment in the Federal Government (Washington, D.C.: Government Printing Office, 1971).

TABLE 7.5

Representation of Black GS Employees Relative to the
Black Population of the United States, 1965 and 1970

	Parity Representation Index (PRI) 1965	Parity Representation Index (PRI) 1970	Rate of Change PRI 1965-70
Government-wide	0.88	0.11	1.12
Consumer and/or work oriented			
DOL	1.83	2.29	1.25
HEW	1.65	1.90	1.15
HUD	1.12	1.66	1.48
Business oriented with consumer elements			
DOA	0.34	0.49	1.44
DOC	1.11	1.29	1.16
Resource and facility oriented			
DOI	0.27	0.35	1.29
DOT		0.48	
Other			
DOJ	0.45	0.85	1.88
DOD	0.69	0.69	1.00
DOS	2.15	2.81	1.30
D/Treas.	1.00	1.09	1.09

Notes: PRI = penetration rate divided by black population (U.S.);
1960 population census adjusted to 1965-10.8%; 1970 PRI based on
U.S. Census Bureau Population Census-11.2%. See Appendix Table
F.1 for penetration rates.

Sources: Penetration rates for 1965: U.S. Civil Service Com-
mission, Study of Minority Group Employment in the Federal Govern-
ment (Washington, D.C.: Government Printing Office, 1966); pene-
tration rates for 1970: U.S. Civil Service Commission, Minority
Group Employment in the Federal Government (Washington, D.C.:
Government Printing Office, 1971); 1970 population (U.S.) based on
U.S. Department of Commerce, Bureau of the Census, Statistical
Abstract of the United States 1970, Chart No. 21 (p. 23).

ment of Transportation was not established by 1965, so no comparison between 1965 and 1970 was possible.

Another way of looking at the representation of blacks in the managerial and professional levels of the federal bureaucracy was to relate the penetration rate to the percent of blacks in the population. An examination of Table 7. 5 revealed that the parity representation indexes* of the various departments followed the black penetration rate levels rather closely. The parity representation index for government-wide employment was 1. 00 for 1970, while the indexes for the mass consumer and labor-oriented departments were far above the norm: HEW 1. 90, HUD 1. 66, and DOL 2. 29. The indexes for the departments that were below parity were DOI 0. 35, DOT 0. 48, DOA 0. 49, DOD 0. 69, and DOJ 0. 85. Above parity were the State Department, 2. 81, and the Treasury Department, 1. 09. †

VARIATIONS IN BLACK EMPLOYMENT
IN SUBUNITS OF THE DEPARTMENT OF HEW

These wide differences in the numbers of blacks employed at managerial and professional jobs existed in various departments; within each department there were variations in these patterns according to agencies, bureaus, offices and other subunits. Unfortunately, the Civil Service Commission did not tabulate its information in this form for publication in its annual minority government employment survey. The failure to make such a tabulation was significant, because it made it impossible to determine whether the managers of the individual agencies operating government programs were meeting their equal opportunity responsibilities. This (apparently deliberate) omission has seriously limited the ability of people either inside or outside

---

* The parity representation index is equal to 1. 00 when the penetration rate is the same as the percent of blacks in the total population, indicating that black employment in the area under consideration is proportional to the percent of blacks in the total population in the same area. If the penetration rate is less than the black population percentage, the parity representation index will be less than 1. 00, or less than proportional to the population; if it is greater than 1. 00, it is more than proportional to the population.

†The 1971 parity representation indexes for the departments were: government-wide, 1. 01; HEW, 1. 96; HUD, 1. 73; DOL, 2. 49; DOC, 1. 35; DOI, 0. 33; DOT, 0. 52; DOA, 0. 53; DOD, 0. 69; State, 2. 84; Treasury, 1. 07; and Justice, 0. 84.

TABLE 7.6

Penetration Rates* of Black GS (White Collar) Employees for the Department of HEW and Selected Agencies and Bureaus by GS Grade Levels, 1970

	Total	GS 1–4	GS 5–8	GS 9–11	GS 12–15	GS 16–18	GS 12–18
Department-wide	21.3	36.9	24.5	9.7	5.5	3.4	5.4
Agencies							
Office of the Secretary (OS)	26.5	51.5	41.4	13.7	11.7	6.9	11.5
Office of Education (OE)	24.3	48.5	45.5	17.4	8.0	5.7	7.9
Food and Drug Administration (FDA)	17.4	40.4	28.2	12.6	4.4	0	5.6
Social and Rehabilitation Service (SRS)	22.5	34.9	41.1	14.4	5.6	4.8	5.6
Social Security Administration (SSA)	23.3	40.1	23.6	8.2	4.8	0	4.8
National Institutes of Health (NIH)	22.0	56.8	22.9	12.2	3.4	10.3	3.6
Health Services and Mental Health Administration (HSMHA)	23.3	35.0	27.4	9.9	3.1	6.6	3.1

*Penetration rate = total employees divided by total black employees.
Note: See Table F.4 for number of employees.
Source: HEW, Office of Equal Employment Opportunity.

government to monitor the activities of program managers and hold them accountable for their civil rights and equal opportunity perform- ance.

In order to illustrate the possibilities for monitoring of perform- ance by operating agencies within departments, I took the pattern of black employment in managerial positions in HEW as a whole as the norm against which the agencies within HEW were measured. The Office of the Secretary (OS), which included the Office for Civil Rights (OCR) for HEW, had a penetration rate of 11.5 percent in GS 12-18, a high rate that was partly attributable to its location in the Office of the Secretary of OCR, which had the highest level of black employ- ment in the department. The second largest black penetration rate at the GS 12-18 level was in the Office of Education—7.9 percent. The health-oriented agencies stood in sharp contrast, ranking sixth and seventh among the seven agencies in HEW for which data were available (see Table 7.6).

Taking the overall black penetration rate for HEW as a whole as the norm for GS 12-18 (5.4 percent), two agencies ranked above the norm—the Office of the Secretary (OS), 11.5 percent and the Office of Education (OE), 7.9 percent. Two agencies were virtually on par with the norm—the Social and Rehabilitation Service (SRS) and the Food and Drug Administration (FDA), with 5.6 percent each. Those ranking below the departmental norm were the Social Security Administration (SSA), 4.8 percent, the National Institutes of Health (NIH), 3.6 percent, and the Health Services and Mental Health Admin- istration (HSMHA), 3.1 percent.* In the GS 9-11 category, as shown in Table 7.6, all the agencies were above the department-wide pene- tration rate of 9.7 percent in this category with the exception of SSA, which had 8.2 percent. At this grade level, OE had 17.4 percent, SRS 14.4 percent, OS 13.7 percent, FDA 12.6 percent, NIH 12.2 percent, and HSMHA 9.9 percent. At the lower grade levels of GS 5-8, the penetration level for the department as a whole of 24.5 percent was exceeded in OE (45.5 percent), OS (41.4 percent), SRS (41.1 percent), FDA (28.2 percent), and HSMHA (27.4 percent), while SSA (23.6 percent) and NIH (22.9) fell below the departmental norm of 36.9 in this category. HSMHA and SRS had penetration rates below that of the department as a whole (36.9 percent) at the GS 1-4 level, with 35.0 percent and 34.9 percent respectively. OS (51.5 per- cent), OE (48.5 percent), FDA (40.4 percent), and NIH (56.8 percent) were above the norm.

---

*In 1971 there was a slight increase in black employment in the upper grades of GS, with 90 blacks or 2.1 percent in the super- grades 16-18 and 985 blacks or 2.8 percent in GS 14-15.

TABLE 7.7

Deviation[*] of Penetration Rates of Black GS Employees in Selected Agencies and Bureaus from the Penetration Rate in Total D/HEW Taken as Norm by Grade Levels, 1970

	Total HEW (Norm)	OS	OE	SRS	FDA	SSA	NIH	HSHMA
Total	21.3	124.4	114.0	105.6	81.6	109.3	103.2	109.3
GS 1–4	36.9	139.5	131.4	94.5	109.4	108.6	153.9	94.8
GS 5–8	24.5	168.9	185.7	167.7	115.1	96.3	93.4	111.8
GS 9–11	9.7	141.2	179.3	148.4	129.8	84.5	125.7	102.0
GS 12–13	6.2	222.5	156.4	232.2	203.2	83.8	74.1	40.3
GS 14–15	4.1	221.1	156.0	104.8	92.6	95.1	41.4	60.9
GS 16–18	3.4	202.9	167.6	126.4	0	0	302.9	194.1
GS 12–18	5.4	212.9	146.2	103.7	103.7	88.8	66.6	57.4

*Deviation—agency penetration rate divided by HEW penetration rate; equality (PAR) = 100.0.
Source: Data obtained from Director, Equal Employment Opportunity Staff, HEW.

124

Based on this limited information about minority employment in the various HEW agencies, the equal opportunity and civil rights staff of HEW, and particularly the Office for Civil Rights, could identify where their programs were weakest, where current operations should be intensified, and where new initiatives were needed.

As for changes within agencies, bureaus and divisions of the various government departments, no data were available. This was true for the seven major agencies and divisions before 1970, so no study could be made of the changes in penetration rates broken down by agencies within departments over any period of time. To get around this problem, however, a method of measuring change in penetration rates in the HEW agencies was devised (see Table 7.7). The penetration rates at selected grade levels for the Department of Health, Education, and Welfare as a whole as norms for various grade levels and comparisons of the 1970 black representation in the individual HEW agencies with these department-wide norms could be used to determine how far above or below the norms at various grade levels the agencies within HEW stood. This would at least allow a comparison between the black representation in the divisions of HEW and the department as a whole. At the highest grade level (GS 16-18), the HEW agencies had penetration rates either above the norm (100) to varying extents or had no black representation at all at this level in 1970: Office of the Secretary (OS), 202.9; Office of Education (OE), 167.6; Social and Rehabilitation Service (SRS), 126.4; Food and Drug Administration (FDA), 0; Social Security Administration (SSA), 0; National Institutes of Health (NIH), 302.9; and Health Services and Mental Health Administration (HSMHA), 194.1. In the broader category of the GS 12-18 grade level, deviations from the departmental norm in 1970 by the individual agencies in HEW are shown in Table 7.7 as follows: OS, 212.9; OE, 146.2; SRS, 103.7; FDA, 103.7; SSA, 88.8; NIH, 66.6; and HSMHA, 57.4.

It may be of some significance that between 1970 and 1971 the penetration rate of blacks increased in virtually all grade level categories of federal employment in white collar jobs except in the lowest one, GS 1-4. This apparent stability in the retention of black employees occurred during a period of decreasing federal employment. Some questions about the future of black employment by the federal bureaucracy are raised by the fact that blacks did not lose their government jobs during this period. Is the implementation of antidiscrimination laws and executive orders forestalling the operation of the traditional last hired and first fired pattern of past minority employment? Will minorities expand, hold stationary, or lose their gains if overall federal employment continues to decline from year to year? Does this retention of blacks in federal employment reflect a more vigorous leadership in equal employment goals and activities by the

Civil Service Commission? What will be the effect of the 1972 Equal
Employment Opportunity Act, which amended the Title VII equal employment provisions of the Civil Rights Act of 1964 and gives greater
legal authority to the Civil Service Commission?

If the trends in the growth of black employment in federal white
collar employment continue, future minority surveys of employment
should show continuing improvement in the penetration rates for
blacks. If the federal government cuts back overall employment, on
the other hand, there remains the danger of a reappearance of the
traditional employment practices that militate against equal chances
for minorities to be hired and to keep their jobs. The implications
of the trend in either direction are far-reaching for access by minorities to the benefits of federally funded programs, since minority
employees in management and policy-making positions in the federal
government can make use of their experience, qualifications, and
interest to secure a more equitable delivery of federally funded
services to minorities.

NOTE

1. United States Civil Service Commission, Minority Group
Employment in the Federal Government (Washington, D. C.: Government Printing Office, 1970).

8

THE TOKEN FEDERAL
OFFICIALS: MINORITIES
IN FIELD OFFICES

The moves to decentralize many government operations, which were accelerated by the passage of the State and Local Fiscal Assistance Act of 1972 and other revenue-sharing programs, have disturbing implications for the administration of civil rights and equal opportunity laws. Giving more power to state, regional, and local officials does not bode well for the access of minorities to their fair share of the benefits of federally funded programs. Unhappily, there has been little indication to date that the Treasury Department's administration of the revenue-sharing programs has done anything to dissipate the fears and apprehensions about the negative consequences for equal opportunity and civil rights matters of general revenue sharing and other steps to decentralize the management of federal assistance to local agencies of government.

In order for decentralization to work equitably and efficiently for minorities, a number of changes must occur in the staffing of federal agencies. First, minority discrimination in overall federal employment must be promptly decreased. Second, there must be an emphasis on increasing minority employment at policy-making and administrative levels of management. Third, minority management officials must be distributed among strategic types of positions and in various geographic locations so that minorities hold positions at critical decision-making points in the administration of federal financial assistance. Fourth, minorities must get jobs as federal program managers and not only—as they have so frequently in the past—in jobs that relate specifically to civil rights and equal opportunity compliance programs and to department and agency civil rights units.

The full and strategically placed participation of minorities in upper professional and executive positions in the federal bureaucracy is essential not only for assuring equal opportunity in federal employment itself, but also, and perhaps more important, for improving the equitable delivery of services to minorities. The mere presence of minority staff members at the time and place that critical program decisions are made might have the effect of decreasing the number of discriminatory practices employed in the management of grants-in-aid programs. Their presence might help stop both the inadvertent and conscious personal bias entering into decisions of administrators of Title VI funds and counteract the effects of systemic discrimination. It would undoubtedly give minorities a greater sense of confidence that their interests were being fairly handled by agency officials.

DECENTRALIZATION: AN OBSTACLE TO MINORITY ROLE IN MANAGEMENT

Decentralization increases the authority of regional officials to make policy decisions. It enhances the responsibilities delegated to regional offices and upgrades the importance of the management function of regional departmental executives. It also decreases the involvement of headquarters level officials in the day-to-day administration of agency-wide programs. In other words, it tends to roll back the management responsibility and authority for specific program administration from the Washington headquarters level to the region, area, or state level in each department and agency.

In addition, decentralization increases the discretionary power of regional departmental executives and program managers in the specific interpretation and operation of department-wide objectives and program activities. This has particular importance for minorities, who have learned to be suspicious of the peculiar implications of red tape for their well-being. This is not an unfounded suspicion, since decentralization often complicates the complaint procedures and lengthens the channels through which grievances and objections must move before getting to the attention of policy-makers at the national level. As a result, decentralization often lessens the probability that prompt action will be taken in response to the problems encountered by members of minority groups in getting access to programs and services.

Historically, the rights of minorities have not been protected when left in the hands of state and local government. The responsibility for enforcing the civil rights and equal opportunity laws has fallen most heavily upon the federal government rather than state or local government. Under the new federalism, and more specifically under the State and Local Fiscal Assistance Act of 1972, it remains to be seen whether the mantle of federal protection will effectively

shield minorities as well as the dominant elements of the population. *
The new philosophy underlying this law is that power should be shifted
from the central government to state and local levels for achievement
of the action needed by the people. It supports the theory that the
government bureaucracies closest to the people can serve them most
effectively. Such a theory might be realistic in a society with a homogeneous population, but it is unrealistic in a nation with sizable groups
of people of different race, color, and national origin, especially in a
country beset by prejudice, discrimination, and racism throughout
its history. Such an assumption about local responsiveness to the
needs of all the people, including minorities, is unduly optimistic at
best.

In a speech given in 1973, John A. Buggs, the staff director of
the U. S. Commission on Civil Rights, expressed the misgivings felt
by minorities concerning their prospects for equal opportunity under
revenue sharing. He reviewed the dire consequences of the federal
government's retreat from its national obligation to minorities about
a century ago:

> The history of the exercise of power by the units of
> government "closest to the people" has not been one that
> conjures up feelings of joy by those who in years past,
> were handed over to the tender mercies of many state
> and local governments. While our national government
> has not always been in the forefront when the protection
> of the rights, liberties and welfare of the people were
> at issue, it is a fact that in our history of the last quarter
> of a century it has been in the vanguard more frequently
> than has any other element of government.

---

*
   The civil rights responsibilities, implementation practices,
and problems emerging from the administration of the State and Local
Fiscal Assistance Act of 1972 have come under close scrutiny from
various sources. Included among these are the U. S. Commission on
Civil Rights Clearinghouse Report 50, February 1975, Making Civil
Rights Sense Out of Revenue Sharing Dollars (Washington, D. C. :
Government Printing Office, 1975); and Morton H. Sklar and William L.
Taylor's Civil Rights under General Revenue Sharing (Washington,
D. C. : Center for National Policy Review, Catholic University Law
School, July 1975). Revenue Sharing Clearinghouse is published bi-
monthly by the National Clearinghouse on Revenue Sharing at the
Center for National Policy Review, Catholic University of America,
Washington, D. C. 20017.

All over the Nation the members of minority groups
and the poor are fearful of what the New Federalism por-
tends for them. Chicanos, blacks, Puerto Ricans and
other visible minorities are concerned that in clothing
state and local governments with the primary responsibility for dealing with the social and economic problems
of their groups the Federal Government may be handing
them over to a dismal future.

We might well remember the lesson of about one
hundred years ago when the central government turned
over the fate of the newly freed slave to the governments
that had previously defended the institution that had kept
them in bondage. [1]

Federal laws (statutes and judicial decisions) and the federal
agencies enforcing them have been more effective than state and local
laws and agencies in protecting the rights of all racial and ethnic
minorities. Discrimination has always been a practice which denied
civil rights and equal opportunities to minorities throughout the nation.
However, there have been wide differences in the regional and sec-
tional manifestations of discrimination and in the intensity of biased
attitudes; some regions have been more blatant in their discrimination
than others.

The closer federal executives are to line administration, that
is, to dealing directly with recipients and perhaps with beneficiaries
and applicants, the more sensitive they are likely to be to local, sec-
tional, or state interests, and the more prone they may be to administering the law and the federal programs in such a way as to make
them palatable to the immediate constituency by taking into account
their regional practices, local traditions, and racial and ethnic biases.
Because of the nature of the relationship between a regional administrator and the local constituency, there is a reasonable prospect and
a real danger that the responsibility and role of the federal executive
in administering federal programs and seeking national goals may be
diluted to the point of ineffectiveness. In some situations the responsibilities and authority of the federal manager could be distorted and
compromised to the point that his actions would be actively contrary
to the national civil rights and equal opportunity objectives sought by
his department.

Some of the steps that could be taken to avoid the negative
effects upon minorities of the decentralization of management in
government are: first, that departments and agencies place well qualified blacks and members of other minority groups in policy decision
making and program administering positions in regional offices;
second, that such minority managers and executives in regional

offices be given the kind of headquarters-level backing that would
allow them to monitor programs in such a way as to assure that civil
rights and equal opportunity policies are faithfully and fully applied
to each departmental program; and third, that departments and agencies emphasize at headquarters (to the secretary and the agency
director) the nature and scope of the program manager's role in and
responsibility for compliance with civil rights and equal opportunity
laws and regulations in all programs as an integral part of his management responsibilities, and make the quality of his performance of
this function a regular and significant factor in ranking his overall
performance rating as a program administrator. Obviously, a necessary basis for making an objective judgment requires specific reporting on civil rights and equal opportunity activities in as tangible and
measurable a form as possible. [2]

THE SCARCITY OF BLACK EXECUTIVES
IN REGIONAL OFFICES

Black executives who held positions in the upper grade levels of
federal service in regional offices were few and far between. Compared to whites, the chances of a black employee holding a job at the
GS 12-18 level were extremely unfavorable. The odds favoring
whites over blacks at the GS 12-18 grades were 6. 8 to one in the
Washington headquarters office, 6. 9 to one in Atlanta, 5. 4 to one in
Dallas, 5. 7 to one in Philadelphia, 2. 3 to one in Boston, 4. 3 to one
in New York, and 4. 6 to one in Chicago, as shown in the tabulation
on various selected regional offices in Table 8. 1.

In the GS 9-11 grade level, the odds favoring the white employee
over the black fell to about two to one in the regional offices. There
were 26. 2 whites employed at this level out of a total of 100 white
employees, while there were 11. 8 blacks out of a total of 100 blacks.
At the headquarters and regional offices, the odds for employment
for whites and blacks followed the same general trend.

In 1970 the penetration rate of blacks in regional offices was
generally below that for the corresponding grade level in the central
headquarters office. According to Table 8. 2, the penetration rates
by grade level for selected Civil Service Commission regions were
notably lower in the southern regions than in the non-southern. With
few exceptions, the penetration rate by blacks was higher at headquarters than in any of the regions studied. One exception was the
GS 12-18 level in the Chicago region where the penetration rate was

TABLE 8.1

Number of Black and White Employees per Thousand
in GS 12-18 and Their Chances for GS 12-18 Jobs

Civil Service Commission Region	Number of Employees per 1,000 at GS 12-18 White	Black	Number of Chances at GS 12-18 Job for Whites per Chance for Blacks
Central Office (Washington, D.C.)	453	66	6.8
Atlanta	221	32	6.9
Dallas	183	33	5.4
Philadelphia	217	38	5.7
Boston	218	93	2.3
New York	267	62	4.3
Chicago	244	53	4.6

Source: U.S. Civil Service Commission, Minority Group Employment in the Federal Government (Washington, D.C.: Government Printing Office, 1970).

3.9 percent, or 0.1 percent above that for the central office (3.8 percent). *

Indicative of the very small part of the total employment in regional offices in the upper category of management that black employees constituted was their much lower penetration rate in some regional offices than in the central offices in Washington, D.C. The central office penetration rate for GS 12-18, for example, was 2.9 percent higher than for the Atlanta and Dallas regions. And a year

---

* In 1971, exceptions were within the GS 12-18 grade level. For example, at the GS 16-18 level, the rates for the GS 16-18 level for the central office and non-South regions combined were identical at 1.8 percent, and GS 12-15 for the central office and Chicago were the same, 3.9 percent. The Philadelphia region's penetration rate was 2.6 percent, or .5 percent higher, and the New York region's 4.1 percent, or 2.0 percent higher, than the central office's, which was 2.1 percent. However, at the GS 12-18 level which includes the above sub-categories, the penetration rate in the central office was higher than in all the selected regions.

TABLE 8.2

Penetration Rates of Black GS (White Collar) Employees for the
Central Office and Selected Regions by GS Grade Levels, 1970

	Central Office	South		Non-South			
		Atlanta Region	Dallas Region	Philadelphia Region	Boston Region	New York Region	Chicago Region
Total	21.0	6.2	5.2	15.0	3.4	13.0	15.6
GS 1-4	51.3	15.5	11.8	28.8	6.5	26.7	28.5
GS 5-8	31.2	4.8	4.6	16.6	3.6	16.6	18.7
GS 9-11	12.5	3.0	2.5	7.3	1.7	6.1	7.9
GS 12-15	3.9	0.9	0.9	3.0	1.5	3.4	3.9
GS 16-18	1.8	1.3	0	1.0	1.0	3.6	1.7
GS 12-18	3.8	0.9	0.9	3.0	1.5	3.4	3.9

Note: See Table F.4 for numbers of employees.
Source: U.S. Civil Service Commission, Minority Group Employment in the
Federal Government (Washington, D.C.: Government Printing Office, 1970).

later, in 1971, the penetration rate for the central offices had increased
to 3.1 percent more than for the same Southern regions. The penetration rates for the Atlanta and Dallas regions were identical, 0.9 percent for each, while those for non-Southern regions were significantly
higher: for the Boston region, 1.5 percent; for the Philadelphia region,
3.0 percent; for the New York region, 3.4 percent; and for the Chicago
region, 3.9 percent. *

There was only one exception to the finding that the headquarters
rates were generally above the corresponding rates for regional
offices. The exception was the Chicago regional office, where the
penetration rate was 0.1 above the headquarters rate at the GS 12-18
level (see Table 8.2).

---

*Note that the Boston penetration rates tended to be lower than
the other northern regions and sometimes almost as low as the
southern regions. In the following year, 1971, the penetration rates
for both Atlanta and Dallas were 1.1 percent, while those for the
non-southern regions were significantly higher: Boston, 1.6 percent;
Philadelphia, 3.4 percent; New York, 3.5 percent, and Chicago,
4.0 percent.

TABLE 8.3

Number of GS Employees (Total and Black) and Black Penetration Rate
in Supergrades (GS 16-18) by Selected Regions, 1970

| | Government-Wide | Central Office | South | | Non-South | | | |
			Atlanta Region	Dallas Region	Philadelphia Region	Boston Region	New York Region	Chicago Region
Total number of employees	5586	4068	251	116	194	97	138	230
Total number of black employees	92	73	3	3	2	1	5	4
Percent black of total	1.6	1.7	0.8	1.3	1.0	1.0	3.6	1.7

Source: United States Civil Service Commission, Minority Group Employment in the Federal Government (Washington, D.C.: Government Printing Office, 1970).

The extremely limited black share of the total number of
supergrade jobs at the GS 16-18 level, where policy decisions were
made, and at the GS 12-15 level, were documented in Table 8.3 and
Table 8.4. With one exception, the New York region, blacks constituted less than 2.0 percent of all super grade employees in the
regions selected for study and for the United States as a whole. Similarly, blacks in grades GS 12-15 had penetration rates below 4.0 percent in all regions, and in the southern regions, less than 1.0 percent. *
     Another way of judging the entrance of blacks into the mana-
gerial and professional ranks of federal employment in the regional
offices is to compare the penetration rate to the percent of blacks in
the population of each region. This is indicated by means of the
parity representation index† which in Table 8.5 shows the relationship between the overall penetration rate of blacks in selected areas
and their percentage of the total population in these areas in 1965

---

*A year later, blacks still constituted less than 3.0 percent of
all employees at the GS 16-18 level except in the New York region.
New York blacks in grades GS 12-15 had penetration rates below 5.0
percent. In the southern regions rates were less than 2.0 percent.
     †The parity representation index is equal to 1.00 when the
penetration rate is the same as the percent of blacks in the total population and thus indicates that black employment in the area under
consideration is proportional to the percent of blacks in the total pop-

TABLE 8.4

Number of GS Employees (Total and Black) and Black Penetration Rate
in Upper Grades (GS 12-15) by Selected Regions, 1970

	Government-Wide	Central Office	South Atlanta Region	South Dallas Region	Non-South Philadelphia Region	Non-South Boston Region	Non-South New York Region	Non-South Chicago Region
Total number of employees	292,942	80,707	31,054	20,194	27,530	9,832	19,784	32,304
Total number of black employees	7,552	3,125	297	200	832	144	655	1,262
Percent black employees of total	2.6	3.9	0.9	0.9	3.0	1.5	3.4	3.9

Source: U. S. Civil Service Commission, Minority Group Employment in the Federal Government
(Washington, D. C.: Government Printing Office, 1970).

and 1970. Unfortunately there are no data available for the individual
grade levels which precludes the possibility of computing a parity
representation index for each grade level.

The parity representation index provides an indication of the
potential for future expansion of black employment in government
positions. For instance, in 1965 both of the southern regions had
parity representation indexes far below 1.00, indicating the presence
of a sizable underutilized pool of potential employees from which
these regions could draw in the future. On the other hand, each of
the non-southern regions had a parity representation index of 1.00
or above, indicating that the 1965 and 1970 number of black employees in the white collar categories (GS 1-18) was proportionate to or
more than proportionate to the population of each region. It should
be emphasized, however, that this index measured the bottom limits
of proportionality and took no account of the relationship between
population and penetration rate at specific grade levels within the GS
category. In any case, the parity representation index made clear
that a greater potential for large increases in the penetration rate
existed in the South than in other regions of the country. The South
had failed to tap the sources of black manpower for federal employment in proportion to the size of the black population in the area.

---

ulation in the same area. If the penetration rate is less than the
black population percentage, the parity representation index will be
less than 1.00, or less than proportional to the population; if it is
greater than 1.00, it is more than proportional to the population.

TABLE 8.5

Representation of Black GS Employment Relative to the
Black Population of Selected Areas, 1965 and 1970

Area	1965			1970		
	Percent of Black Population	Penetration Rate	Parity Representation Index*	Percent of Black Population	Penetration Rate	Parity Representation Index*
Government-wide	10.8	9.5	0.88	11.2	11.1	0.99
Central office	24.2	17.8	0.73	24.6	21.0	0.85
South						
Atlanta region	24.3	4.1	0.16	22.8	6.2	0.27
Dallas region	16.0	3.8	0.23	15.8	5.2	0.33
Non-South						
Philadelphia region	12.0	12.0	1.00	12.5	15.0	1.20
Boston region	2.8	2.9	1.03	3.3	3.4	1.00
New York region	10.0	11.8	1.18	11.6	13.0	1.10
Chicago region	8.7	14.8	1.70	9.5	15.6	1.60

* Parity Representation Index = penetration rate divided by percent black population of total population.
Rate of change = Parity Representation Index (1970) divided by Parity Representation Index (1965).
  Note: See Tables F.5 and F.6.
  Sources: Department of Commerce, Bureau of Census, Statistical Abstract of the United States (Washington, D.C.: Government Printing Office, 1971), p. 28; Department of Commerce, Bureau of Census, U.S. Census of Population (Washington, D.C.: Government Printing Office, 1960).

The parity representation index also provided evidence that the non-southern regions had done a much better job of achieving equal employment opportunity than the southern regions.

BLACKS IN FEDERAL JOBS IN SMSAs

Since each Civil Service Commission region covers several states and includes populations of various sizes and racial and ethnic mixtures, it is possible that the regional penetration rates may have resulted from a number of interacting factors besides racial discrimination. The racial discrimination factor would also have varied in importance from one area of a region to another. To make a more precise comparison and to limit the number of interacting variables other than racial discrimination, the black penetration rates in the Standard Metropolitan Statistical Areas (SMSAs) were analyzed separately from the regions. This was done on the assumption that the proximity of these SMSAs to their regional offices and the ready accessibility of the respective regional departmental staffs and CSC staffs would make these service areas most amenable to the development of an effective affirmative action program involving minority recruitment, hiring, promotion, and other employment practices. This assumption would be true if the government establishment of the region wished to take such action. Furthermore, since the black population of the nation is, with few exceptions, a predominantly urban one, the size of this group and its level of education and training would probably be somewhat above the average for the group for the region as a whole. In short, if a federal department had the motivation, its chances of achieving equitable utilization of blacks in white collar managerial jobs in the SMSAs were better than in the region as a whole.

Insofar as these assumptions are valid, it is reasonable to expect that on the average, the black penetration rates for the SMSA would be higher than the corresponding rates for the region as a whole. A comparison of Table 8. 6 with Table 8. 2 shows that this was the case in all regions for total employment and for each grade level in 1970. But Table 8. 6 also shows that the penetration rate for all black GS employees in virtually all of the regional host SMSAs was lower than that for the Washington, D. C. headquarters SMSA (which was 21. 0) except for Chicago and Philadelphia, where the rates were 24. 4 percent and 21. 2 percent respectively. However, when the higher grade levels were separated from the broad range of all GS white collar employees, some of the host SMSAs had higher penetration rates in these categories than the central offices. For example, the Philadelphia-New Jersey, New York, and Chicago

TABLE 8.6

Penetration Rates of Black GS (White Collar) Employees
for Selected SMSAs by GS Grade Level, 1970

| | Central Office | South | | Non-South | | | |
		Atlanta SMSA	Dallas SMSA	Philadelphia-New Jersey SMSA	Boston SMSA	New York SMSA	Chicago SMSA
Total	21.0	10.5	6.9	21.2	5.0	19.4	24.4
GS 1-4	51.3	26.6	17.6	37.5	10.0	36.6	46.2
GS 5-8	31.2	7.5	7.2	26.5	6.1	25.0	28.6
GS 9-11	12.5	5.4	3.7	11.8	2.7	9.2	10.9
GS 12-15	3.8	3.3	1.9	4.5	2.0	4.3	5.8
GS 16-18	1.8	4.3	0	2.5	1.4	7.4	1.8
GS 12-18	3.7	3.3	1.9	4.5	2.0	4.3	5.8

Note: See Table F.7 for total numbers of employees.
Source: United States Civil Service Commission, Minority Group Employment in the Federal Government (Washington, D.C.: Government Printing Office, 1970).

SMSAs had penetration rates of 4.5, 4.3, and 5.8 respectively for GS 12-15 jobs; all these figures exceeded the Washington headquarters' 3.8 penetration rate. At the super grade level, GS 16-18, the Atlanta SMSA was 4.3, Philadelphia-New Jersey SMSA, 2.5; Boston SMSA, 1.4; New York SMSA, 7.4; and Chicago SMSA, 1.8 compared with the Washington, D.C. penetration rate of 1.8. There were no black employees at all in the Dallas SMSA at this top grade level in 1970.

BLACK MANAGERS: REGIONAL INCREASES 1965-70

During the period from 1965 to 1970, the regions in the South tended to show greater improvement in the penetration rate than the regions in the non-South. Of course, they increased from an almost minuscule base number. The black participation rate in the middle and upper grade levels of the federal service was extremely small in the South in 1965: 0.3 percent and 0.2 percent at the GS 12-18 level in the Atlanta and Dallas regions, respectively.

The period between 1965 and 1970 produced an increase in the number of black employees at this grade level, from 75 employees to 300 in the Atlanta region and from 27 to 200 in the Dallas region. The penetration rate rose to 0.9 percent in each of these areas in the

TABLE 8.7

Change* in Penetration Rates of Black GS Employees
(White Collar) in the Central Office and
Selected Regions by Grade Levels, 1965-70

	Total	GS 1-4	GS 5-8	GS 9-11	GS 12-18
Central office	17.9	21.2	49.2	64.4	111.1
South					
Atlanta	51.2	66.6	65.5	150.0	200.0
Dallas	36.8	35.6	64.2	127.2	350.0
Non-South					
Philadelphia	25.0	29.7	52.2	46.0	87.5
Boston	17.2	14.0	44.0	30.7	87.5
New York	10.1	10.7	40.6	27.0	70.0
Chicago	5.4	-1.3	32.6	38.5	62.5

*Change = penetration rate 1970 divided by penetration rate
1965 -1.00.

Note: See Tables F.5 and F.6 for penetration rates.

Sources: Penetration rates for 1965: U.S. Civil Service Commission, Study of Minority Group Employment in the Federal Government (Washington, D.C.: Government Printing Office, 1966); penetration rates for 1970: U.S. Civil Service Commission, Minority Group Employment in the Federal Government (Washington, D.C.: Government Printing Office, 1971).

five-year period. The Washington, D.C., Philadelphia, Boston, New York, and Chicago regions had higher penetration rates than the Atlanta and Dallas regions in 1965, and although the non-southern regions showed an increase in black participation by 1970 the percentage of change was not as great as in the Atlanta and Dallas regions. In the New York region, for example, the number of blacks at the GS 12-18 level increased from 341, a penetration rate of 2.0 percent in 1965, to 670, a penetration rate of 3.4 percent in 1970. This percentage of change was small in comparison with that of the Atlanta and Dallas regions during the same years.

These differing regional rates of change in penetration rates of black employees at the GS 12-18 level from 1965 to 1970 were compared in Table 8.7 and are summarized in Table 8.8. The change in penetration rate is calculated by dividing the penetration rate for 1970 by the penetration rate for 1965 minus 1.00.

TABLE 8.8

Changes in Black Penetration Rates in GS 12-18,
1965-70, by Region

Civil Service Commission Region	Changes in Black Penetration Rates in GS 12-18, 1965-70
Central Office (Washington, D. C.)	111. 1
Atlanta	200. 0
Dallas	350. 0
Philadelphia	87. 5
Boston	87. 5
New York	70. 0
Chicago	62. 5

Sources: Penetration rates for 1965: U. S. Civil
Service Commission, Study of Minority Group Employ-
ment in the Federal Government (Washington, D. C. :
Government Printing Office, 1966); penetration rates
for 1970: U. S. Civil Service Commission, Minority
Group Employment in the Federal Government
(Washington, D. C. : Government Printing Office, 1971).

According to Table 8. 7, there was some improvement between
1965 and 1970 at all grade levels in all regions with the exception of
the Chicago region at the GS 1-4 level, where there was a decrease
of 1. 3 percent. With respect to the SMSAs, it was expected that
these urban areas would follow the same pattern of growth rate as
the regions in which they were located. While all of the SMSAs
showed some improvement, the growth rate was larger in the Atlanta
and Dallas areas than in the SMSAs outside of the South (see
Table 8. 9). In 1965 the penetration rate of blacks at the GS 12-18
level was very low in Atlanta (0. 6 percent) and in Dallas (0. 2 percent),
but by the end of 1970 the number of black employees had increased
from 14 to 128 in Atlanta and from 3 to 36 in Dallas, with penetration
rates of 3. 3 percent and 1. 9 percent respectively. *

---

* In 1971 the penetration rate in all regional SMSAs was lower
than that for the Washington, D. C. SMSA for all GS employees except

TABLE 8.9

Changes* in Penetration Rates of Black GS Employees
(White Collar) in Selected SMSAs by Grade Level, 1965-70

SMSA	Total	GS 1-4	GS 5-8	GS 9-11	GS 12-18
Washington	17.9	21.2	49.2	64.4	111.1
South					
Atlanta	138.6	150.9	188.4	285.7	450.0
Dallas	60.4	43.0	213.0	236.3	850.0
Non-South					
Philadelphia-					
New Jersey	7.6	5.6	25.5	43.9	95.6
Boston	31.5	25.0	84.8	28.5	122.2
New York	21.2	13.6	47.0	55.9	95.4
Chicago	12.4	11.0	47.4	37.9	123.0

*Change = penetration rate 1970 divided by penetration rate
1965 - 1.00.

Note: See Tables F.7 and F.8 for penetration rates.

Sources: Penetration rates for 1965: U.S. Civil Service Commission, Study of Minority Group Employment in the Federal Government (Washington, D.C.: Government Printing Office, 1966); penetration rates for 1970: U.S. Civil Service Commission, Minority Group Employment in the Federal Government (Washington, D.C.: Government Printing Office, 1971).

As was the case in the regions of the North, the black penetration rate in SMSAs located in the North was significantly larger than in the southern SMSAs in 1965. The selected SMSAs in the North showed an improvement in the penetration rate for blacks, but the percentage of change from 1965 to 1970 was small compared to the selected SMSAs in the South. The New York SMSA was a rather typical example: in 1965 the number of blacks in the New York SMSA at the GS 12-18 level was 177 and the penetration rate was 2.2 percent, but by 1970 there were 344 blacks at this grade level in New

in Chicago, where the penetration rate was 25.1 percent in 1971 and the headquarters penetration rate for black employees was 21.4 percent. This same pattern was found in all regions at grade levels GS 1-11 and in all SMSAs except Philadelphia, New York, and Chicago in grades GS 12-18.

York and the penetration rate was 4. 3 percent. Table 8. 9 shows the contrast in the growth rates between the southern and northern SMSAs: Atlanta, 450 percent and Dallas, 850 percent between 1965 and 1970 compared with Washington, D. C. , 111. 1 percent; Chicago, 123 percent; Boston, 122. 2 percent; Philadelphia-New Jersey, 95. 6 percent; and New York, 95. 4 percent. *

Although it is encouraging to note the growth in employment of blacks in managerial level jobs in the federal bureaucracy, blacks have been too sparsely represented in the ranks of the decision makers to have had much of an impact on the programs and policies of their departments and agencies. The underemployment of minorities, both at central headquarters and in the regional offices where significant decisions are made, has limited the extent to which blacks have been able to participate meaningfully in the formulation of policies and programs.

At the super grade levels of employees who made or participated in making the major management decisions, only 73 or 1. 8 percent of all the federal employees were black, and 796, or 2. 4 percent, of those in the GS 14-15 positions were black. Furthermore, those individuals were spread over 17 departments and 13 agencies of government in Washington, D. C. and in the field offices of these departments and agencies. In the regional offices, black penetration varied widely from total absence to token presence. The talents of these minority employees were also thinly distributed within the many subunits of the federal departments and agencies. There has been some growth in the rate of entrance of blacks into the federal service at both the headquarters and regional level, but they are still grossly underrepresented and underused in positions of managerial responsibility. When all distributions of blacks in management positions in the federal bureaucracy were reviewed in this study it became abundantly clear that the prospects for blacks to make a significant impact on either overall government policy or on civil rights and equal opportunity policy and practices were minimal.

---

*Changes in the penetration rates from 1965 to 1971 were: central office, 133. 3; Atlanta, 266. 7; Dallas, 450. 0; Philadelphia, 112. 5; Boston, 100. 0; New York, 75. 0; and Chicago, 67. 0.

NOTES

1. John A. Buggs, "The Philosophy and Principles of Revenue Sharing: Progress for Whom?" Speech to An Assembly for Action on Revenue Sharing, Kellogg Center for Continuing Education, Michigan State University, East Lansing, Michigan, June 15, 1973.

2. U. S. Commission on Civil Rights, To Know or Not to Know: Collection and Use of Racial and Ethnic Data in Federal Assistance Programs, February, 1973 (Washington, D. C. : Government Printing Office, 1973), pp. 59-73.

9

COLLECTION OF
RACIAL AND
ETHNIC DATA

The primary and universal role of management, whether in public or private enterprise, is to assemble and combine the various kinds of resources it has available in such a way as to achieve the objectives established for the enterprise. But an effective manager must do more than simply get results. He must always strive for the economic ideal of management, namely, the maximum achievement of the predetermined objectives sought per unit of resources assigned to the production process which he directs. Measured this way, the efficiency of a program in the federal government depends not only on achieving certain results, be they tangible or intangible, but on the number of objectives achieved in relation to the investment of various resources. In short, the size of the output in relation to the amount of input is crucial.

The more tangible, finite, and measurable the objectives, and the more specific the period of time used for comparison, the more accurately the results of the manager's efforts can be monitored, appraised, and evaluated. Many of the broad social objectives of government, however, are not tangible or even clearly observable in some instances. As a consequence, evaluation of the managerial effectiveness of an agency or department of government in reaching social goals cannot always be made in definite, and frequently not in quantifiable, terms. However, if the results of the activities of government agencies with social objectives such as civil rights and equal opportunity are to be rationally planned, appraised, and maximized, it is necessary to develop tools by which the investment of each federal dollar and man-hour of labor can be judged in terms of the best possible results.

To reach this long-range goal, managers of offices, agencies, and departments throughout the government should establish intermediate measurable objectives, even though some of these indicators may not be completely valid or precise. The important thing is first to establish the measures and then to ascertain a margin of error for them, and thus the quality of inferences that can be derived from them. Progress in the measurement of social phenomena depends on persistant, methodical narrowing of the margin of error so that reliability of the measuring device is increased.

Studies of the federal departments and agencies with Title VI grants-in-aid programs show that virtually none of them has devised reliable ways of measuring whether they are delivering services to beneficiaries without discriminating by race and ethnic group. In fact, they cannot provide even a rough indication of their managerial effectiveness in this regard. In cases where agencies have made some attempt to gather relevant data, none has analyzed its information in time for the knowledge and insights derived from it to be used by the managers for making decisions.

For this reason even the limited data collected are relevant to the agency, mainly for public relations and historical purposes rather than for use in decision making by managers. In the discussion of racial and ethnic data collection and use that follows, the major concern will be with the collection, analysis, and use of such information as a tool for effective management. Answers to questions such as the following will be sought:

1. What racial and ethnic data are being collected now?
2. Are they adequate for management purposes?
3. What are the limitations of such information? What is missing that would make the data adequate for managerial purposes?
4. What obstacles to adequacy are apparent?
5. Who should collect such data, and what should this collection include?
6. How often should data be collected?
7. How much data should be collected? Should it be for the total population or for a representative or other type of sample?
8. If samples are used, what should be their characteristics?
9. What is the relationship between the choice of data to be collected and the needs of management in various areas—for example, for compliance, evaluation, and future planning?

COLLECTION OF RACIAL AND ETHNIC DATA: EXPERIENCE OF GOVERNMENT AGENCIES

In order to find out how government agencies have gone about collecting and using racial/ethnic data, the United States Commission on Civil Rights made a study of the data collection systems of the 25

major federal departments and agencies with Title VI grants-in-aid
programs. They found that none of them had established an adequate
system. On the basis of this finding, the Commission made recommendations for developing a nationwide system for collecting racial
and ethnic data in these programs. They suggested that a number of
key decisions had to be made: first, to define clearly what programs
to include in the system; second, to select which aspect of these programs would require collection of data; third, to identify the groups
of people whose racial or ethnic origin should be designated by their
relationship to the program—that is, as eligibles, applicants, or
beneficiaries of the programs; fourth, to decide what racial and ethnic
groups would be specifically identified and what information other
than racial and ethnic origin would be gathered—for example, income,
family size, amount of benefit, and so forth; fifth, to select what
methods should be used for making racial and ethnic identification;
and sixth, to decide on the frequency with which the body of data should
be collected and distributed.

There are no grounds for optimism about prospects for the
creation of such a system in the foreseeable future. Despite the fact
that a policy of nondiscrimination has been required in all federal
programs for many years, according to the Commission on Civil
Rights, "Even where agency-wide policies required the collection of
racial and ethnic data some agencies have made serious omissions
in identifying programs for which these data should be collected.
Moreover, even when programs have been identified for inclusion in
a racial and ethnic data collection system, racial and ethnic data are
sometimes not collected on program aspects which have a significant
effect on the public."[1]

SELECTION OF FEDERAL PROGRAMS
FOR INCLUSION IN THE SYSTEM

Generally speaking, the actual racial and ethnic data requirements of federal agencies have fallen short of the need for racial
and ethnic information. As a rule, such a collection has applied to
federal programs of assistance with particular importance for minority beneficiaries and has been noticeably absent from programs not
traditionally serving minorities.

A case in point is the Department of Agriculture, where the
Civil Rights Evaluation Staff, which is responsible for carrying
out the secretary's directive concerning the collection of racial and
ethnic data, "has interpreted that directive as applying only to those
DOA constituent agencies which, because of their mandates, have a
special responsibility for serving minority beneficiaries. The Secretary's directive, on the other hand, requires that racial and ethnic

data be collected with regard to all Department of Agriculture programs. As a result of this interpretation, only nine agencies, less than half of all DOA agencies, have been identified as providing important assistance to minority beneficiaries."[2]

The scope of racial and ethnic data collection has been similarly limited in the Department of Labor. Its policy was stated by former Secretary of Labor W. Willard Wirtz as referring only to the recording of racial or ethnic identification on employment records. This policy was interpreted in practice to apply to the Manpower Administration, which provides support to State Employment Security Agencies and State Unemployment Insurance Offices and which administers most of the employment programs of the department. As a result, under this policy collection does not include the Labor-Management Relations Services (LMRS) which gives help in the development of effective labor-management relations to industries, organized labor, state and local governments, and other public and private agencies and organizations. Moreover, the department is not required to measure either the extent to which this service is given to minority group organizations or unions or the minority group membership of the organizations receiving such aid.

The LMRS also conducts a Veterans Re-employment Program aimed at assuring that people leaving their jobs for training or active duty in the armed forces, or taking examinations for military service do not lose their jobs and employment benefits. However, because this program is located in the LMRS, where no racial and ethnic data collection is required, it is impossible to determine to what extent the services have been provided to minorities and to what extent minorities need them.

The practice of collecting racial and ethnic data in only those programs having special implications for minorities or those with significant minority participation results in serious omissions in a racial and ethnic data collection system. In programs which provide assistance in areas in which minorities have not traditionally participated, beneficiary data are needed for precisely the reason that they have not been collected. The fact that minorities have not traditionally taken part in these activities has often been the result of deeply entrenched discrimination, and the federal government has an obligation to reverse this trend. Racial and ethnic data are needed to document the extent to which minorities are not included in these activities; they will continue to be necessary to provide direction for improvement in minority participation.

This selection pattern further illustrates the tendency of management officials in government to exclude minorities from the mainstream of their managerial thinking and decision making, and to consider such groups only when it appears that for some reason minorities have unique interests.

Another broadly held misconception of federal officials is suggested in the tendency of agencies to lump minorities and the poor together and to make a single decision covering both groups, despite the fact that the causes of the minority problem and of poverty are different, although the persons involved may be members of minority groups, poor, or both. The Commission on Civil Rights found that to some extent racial and ethnic data collection was limited to programs serving the economically disadvantaged. As a result, many of the programs identified as important for minority group beneficiaries are limited to those aimed at the poor.

Such administrative policy decisions have severely restricted the measurement of equal opportunity, and have tacitly assumed that racial and ethnic discrimination is limited to low income families, whereas in fact it occurs at all levels. A fair managerial approach to the collection of racial and ethnic data requires that it not be confined to programs predominantly oriented to minorities and to the poor, but that it reaches in some appropriate manner all of the program areas (or at least an adequate representative sample) over which management has responsibilities. Granting that the limitations of resources pose difficulties in carrying this out, priorities should be rearranged in such a way that effective gathering of data on programs can be extended over the whole range of activities.

A combination of sampling of information and periodic unannounced on-site visits might increase the effectiveness of the management of the equal opportunity aspects of specific programs. The size of the sample might vary with the type of program, from 100 percent in those of particular importance to minorities to zero percent in those where for some legitimate reason minorities are likely to be either absent or numerically insignificant.

IDENTIFICATION OF PROGRAM ACTIVITIES

Indicative of the comprehensive need for data by management are the many aspects of federal assistance that may be included in any given program. For example, programs often include not only the distribution of goods and services but also research, technical assistance, and training. Participation by minorities should be measured not only in the principal assistance provided by a program but in all of its aspects. Such distinctions are required by HEW in the data submitted to the Office for the Assistant Secretary for Planning and Evaluation.[3]

The Department of Agriculture requires that racial and ethnic data be collected for all significant aspects of program participation including potential participation of people who are not yet participating.

The data collected, however, do not necessarily reflect all the types of assistance provided by a given program. In practice the DOA has often required data on only one aspect of assistance within each program. The Food and Nutrition Service, for example, collects no racial and ethnic data with regard to assistance provided for research. The Forest Service does not collect racial and ethnic data concerning informational assistance supplied; for example, it does not measure the extent of minority participation in civic clubs to which it provides substantial information.

In addition to the direct benefits resulting from grants-in-aid, there are secondary benefits which may accrue to individuals or groups as a result of the distribution of assistance. For instance, land developers who buy land previously improved with assistance from the Soil Conservation Service of the Department of Agriculture are secondary beneficiaries of this service. To cite another case, real estate brokers, bankers, and lending agencies benefit from the growth in business opportunities that may result from housing and mortgage programs administered by HUD. Although these benefits may be of considerable value, no federal agency requires that racial and ethnic data on secondary benefits be gathered, nor has any agency recommended the adoption of such a policy.

Federally assisted programs can at times also have harmful effects on individuals and groups. People or businesses may be negatively affected in terms of financial costs and personal inconvenience. In some instances some victims may be compensated for those effects while others are not. In other cases, no one is given compensation. Examples of the former include the displacement of individuals as a result of construction activity, while the latter include the consequences of air pollution from federal power plants and noise pollution from airports.

It has frequently been alleged that the negative effects of federal programs have not been proportionately distributed between minority groups and the general population. Managers of programs have an obligation to insure that such social costs of federal activity are not greater for one group than for another, and that compensation for the costs of such negative program results is equitably distributed among all groups in the population. Racial and ethnic data capable of detecting such inequities are needed to determine who is bearing the costs. It is doubtful whether the technology of reporting has reached this point however, and even more questionable whether government agencies would be motivated to use it if it were available.

Up to the present such information has been collected only in connection with displacement because of federal activity. A limited amount of information has been collected by the Transportation Department and HUD. On the other hand, other agencies which buy property for federal use on a smaller scale have not collected such information. The National Institutes of Health program for hospital construction, for example, has not gathered racial and ethnic data on persons displaced as a result of hospital construction. Furthermore, no agency to date has gathered such information on projects in advance of project approval and, consequently, even the limited body of information collected has had little value as a management tool.

BENEFICIARY DATA

It is apparent that the selection of government programs that would be required to collect racial and ethnic data systematically and periodically is discriminatorily determined as well as limited in scope and content. In addition, even in those programs with racial and ethnic data collections design and content vary widely as to quality, scope, frequency of issue, and above all, in usefulness as management tools.

Virtually none of the systems developed to date provides an objective basis for management to determine whether grant allocations are being made by program officers and the recipients of the funds in compliance with Title VI. In addition, the feasibility of evaluating specific grant programs to determine program effectiveness by racial and ethnic composition of the beneficiaries is even more unlikely.

The crucial questions which a program manager needs to answer are: What is the relationship between the population eligible for assistance from his program and the population actually receiving such aid? Where this total population is composed of different racial or ethnic groups, is the size of the benefits received by each group consistently and equitably related to the size of its eligible population? Unless some progress has been made that students of the subject are unaware of, it is likely that virtually no government department or agency has yet collected the information that would enable any of its program managers to answer these questions about their specific programs adequately. Prior to 1973 none of the agencies collected data systematically by racial and ethnic group on the number of persons eligible to receive assistance. Very few had systems for recording applicants or applications for such aid by racial and ethnic group although a larger but still limited number of agencies received periodic reports on the number of people receiving benefits according to racial and ethnic group.

In order to be able to appraise the extent of equality of opportunity in federal programs, to gauge the extent to which such assistance is actually reaching minority beneficiaries, and to determine whether the process is equitable, it is necessary to gather data both on beneficiaries of programs and on applicants for program benefits. Information on personal demographic characteristics as they relate both to need and to eligibility for the benefits of programs is also required, as is the collection of data on the size and the quality of benefits allocated.

Only two of the six agencies studied by the Commission on Civil Rights, the Department of Agriculture and the Department of Labor, have stated explicitly that racial and ethnic data should be collected for persons who are beneficiaries of federal programs. HUD requires that all recipients "furnish whatever minority group identification is needed by the Secretary in order to carry out his civil rights responsibilities."[4] On the other hand, Transportation, HEW, and the Veterans Administration do not have policies requiring the collection of beneficiary data by race or ethnic origin. Consequently, any data assembled by the latter three agencies are collected on an ad hoc basis, and are not likely to be used to measure the extent to which program benefits reach members of minority groups.

Program beneficiaries are distinguished from recipients by the fact that they are the persons who ultimately receive and use the assistance. The recipients, on the other hand, are the intermediaries through whom federal assistance (except that provided directly to the beneficiary) passes. The recipient is required to provide assurance of nondiscrimination in the administration of its program, and the beneficiary is supposed to be protected by this assurance.[*] Beneficiaries can be divided into two groups, participants and users. Participants are those beneficiaries who receive assistance as a result of an application made in person or in writing, membership in a group, or participation in an activity receiving federal assistance. Examples of participants are Social Security pensioners, families receiving Aid to Dependent Children, woodland owners receiving grants for forest improvement, and HUD mortgagers.

The participant type of beneficiary status generally entails record keeping by the recipients and/or the federal agency involved. When assistance is received as the result of an application, records are usually maintained concerning that application. When federal assistance is provided to persons as a result of their membership in a group or their participation in an activity, membership or participation records are generally maintained. Examples of such beneficiaries are children attending schools which participate in the DOA's

_____

[*] Beneficiaries are exempt from the requirements of Title VI of the Civil Rights Act of 1964 because they receive but do not distribute federal assistance.

Food and Nutrition Service's school breakfast programs and students living in dormitories constructed with HUD funds. Applicant or membership records for these beneficiaries do not necessarily include racial and ethnic data, but racial and ethnic information about them can often be collected by merely adding this information to existing records.

People who use federally funded facilities and programs open to the general public are also beneficiaries. Examples of such beneficiaries are those who drive cars on highways, airline passengers using airports, and vacationers visiting national parks. Records are not usually kept on individual users, and thus the collection of racial and ethnic data on users can be a more difficult problem than the collection of data on the beneficiaries classified as participants. In general the collection of racial and ethnic data on users requires the institution of special forms. [5]

Of the six agencies studied by the Commission on Civil Rights, only the Departments of Agriculture and Labor have been explicit in stating that racial and ethnic data should be collected on persons who are beneficiaries of federal programs. Former Secretary of Agriculture Clifford M. Hardin directed each constituent agency within DOA to "establish and maintain a system for collecting and reporting racial data on participation in USDA programs."[6] The Department of Labor directed that records of race and national origin of enrollees and participants in all Manpower Administration programs be kept. [7] In general, HUD now collects racial and ethnic data on all program beneficiaries, who are primarily purchasers and tenants. [8] In contrast, the Department of Transportation, HEW, and VA have no policies requiring the collection of beneficiary data by race and ethnic origin.

The kind of beneficiary data collected most often is participant data; user data are infrequently collected. Of the six agencies studied, the Transportation Department serves the greatest number of beneficiaries who could be classified as users. It does this through its programs administered by the Federal Aviation Administration, [9] the Federal Highway Administration, [10] and the Urban Mass Transportation Administration. [11] Only the Urban Mass Transportation Administration collects racial and ethnic information on the use of federally funded transportation; maps indicating any substantial concentration of minorities in an area affected by the programs financed by UMTA must be submitted by potential recipients of a Capital Grant project. [12] HUD grants funds to facilities which are open to neighborhood use such as parks, civic centers, and recreational centers, [13] and is requiring a one-time survey conducted by visual observation on the race and ethnic origin of the users of such facilities. The Forest Service of the DOA provides assistance for recreational facilities including playgrounds, boating and swimming facilities, camp-grounds, hotels, resorts, and visitor centers, and information on the use of these facilities by race and ethnic origin is sent to the DOA by the forest rangers in charge of these sites. Data are collected for only two groups, minority and white. The data are submitted annually, and the ranger is not instructed to make his count on any particular day, nor is he instructed to keep a cumulative record of visitors to the sites.

Inasmuch as the social benefits or products of grants-in-aid are really the total net benefits of federal assistance, there are frequently social costs as well as benefits involved in the operation of grants programs. If management's tools of measurement are to be complete and equitable, they must include the negative consequences resulting from federal activity as far as this is technologically feasible. The civil rights interest in such records is that they be maintained in such a way as to show whether the social costs, potential as well as actual, are borne equitably by race, color, national origin, and sex of the beneficiaries.

APPLICANT DATA

Racial and ethnic data on persons making application for participation in grants-in-aid programs are needed to disclose who is applying and whether the acceptance or rejection of applications is determined on a discriminatory basis. If applications from members of minority groups are not received with the frequency that would be expected from their proportion in the population eligible to participate in the program, this fact may indicate that information about the program has not reached the minorities, or that there is restriction of some kind on the application to benefits by such persons. While the Office of Management and Budget has recognized the need for such information, it has not made any government-wide recommendations or issued requirements for the collection of applicant data.

The Department of Labor is the only agency that requires the collection of applicant data, but it handles this in such a way that the data are virtually useless as a tool for planning and management. For example, it requires that all operating agencies of the Manpower Administration keep racial and ethnic records for applicants and beneficiaries of Manpower Administration programs, but although this information is recorded on application forms the applicant data are never tabulated until the applicant has been accepted for participation in the program. Without knowing the totals both of applicants and eventual participants, there can be no comparison made between the racial and ethnic origins of these groups.

ELIGIBILITY DATA

The periodic collection of eligibility data classified by racial and ethnic group is critically important to the effective management of federal programs operating under Title VI. Nevertheless, the collection of this type of data by departments and agencies having major responsibilities for grants-in-aid programs was almost completely absent some eight years after the passage of the Civil Rights Act of 1964. There is a strong suspicion that there may be a conspiracy to withhold information at a point critical to the effective implementation of Title VI, but nothing can be proved at this time.

The difficulties involved in assembling completely accurate eligibility data, do not explain the apparent absence of even crude measures of the size of the potential beneficiary groups, classified by racial and ethnic origin. The Census of Population and the Census of Housing, to name but two of several possible sources, provide important beginnings for the collection of data. With the large number of data banks available and the Automatic Data Processing (ADP) resources and techniques at hand, we have reached a state of the arts where such information of a quality and amount adequate for effective management is available at a reasonable cost.

To assess the extent to which program benefits are reaching intended beneficiaries on an equitable basis, program officials must also know the race and ethnic origin of person eligible for their programs.

Virtually no agency can compare its potential participant population with its acutal participant population. The Department of Agriculture is the only agency that has a requirement that the racial and ethnic composition of eligible beneficiaries be determined. It requires that every agency in the department set up ways of determining the number of minority group members in the population who are eligible for each program. However, according to the Commission on Civil Rights, this policy position does not require the actual collection of eligibility data by DOA programs, but permits "the use (of) data from the Census of Housing or the Census of Population. Despite this requirement, however, there is, even within the Department of Agriculture, very little data available or used on the population of persons eligible to benefit from specific Federal programs."[14]

Eligibility is defined by meeting criteria of income, education, military status, and so forth for program participation. A person eligible to participate in a program is one who meets these criteria regardless of whether he has applied for or received certification of his eligibility. To restrict data on eligible beneficiaries to those who have actually been certified by program staff as eligible for participation would defeat the purposes of the data collection suggested here. Not all persons who meet the criteria of eligibility may know about a program or realize that they are eligible for it, but they should be included in any analysis of the extent to which program benefits are reaching the people for whom they were intended. The data on persons certified as eligible for program participation can also be useful in assessing the extent to which there may be inequities in the process of certification of eligibility. In other words, the population of eligible beneficiaries includes both those who are served by a particular program and those who are not.

OTHER DATA: AMOUNT OF BENEFITS

In order to get an accurate measure of the extent to which benefits are equitably distributed to minority beneficiaries, it is also essential to examine the amount of benefits received by members of each minority group—for example, the size of the loan, the number of hours of training or counseling, the number of job referrals made, or the dollar value of services—in order to appraise the equity of the distribution of federal benefits. It is not sufficient merely to know the number of beneficiaries, eligible beneficiaries, or applicants by racial and ethnic origins. Variables affecting the value of the benefit to the beneficiary—such as interest rates, number of years allowed for repayment of a loan, frequency of training or counseling services—must be calculated as must the extent to which services are provided across racial lines. The impact of the benefit must be calculated separately for each racial and ethnic group.

OTHER DATA: NUMBER OF BENEFICIARIES

HEW and DOL prepare data on the amount of program benefit regularly. Programs at HEW are required to submit data on the distribution of program dollars by racial and ethnic group of the beneficiaries, but the value of these data is limited because program officials are not required to submit data on the number of beneficiaries in each racial and ethnic group. The Manpower Administration requires a similar collection of data on services provided by the State Employment Service such as the duration of training programs and the nature of the service provided. However, this information is not analyzed in connection with beneficiary data and, consequently, no analysis of service by racial or ethnic group can be carried out. The DOA, on the other hand, only requires data that measure the extent of service across racial lines, but even this information is

not generally collected at the DOA. No other agency provides for
the systematic collection of information on program benefits. The
collection and use of such data as are furnished are on an ad hoc and
infrequent basis for all other agencies.

DEMOGRAPHIC DATA

Statistics on the characteristics of the minority groups involved
constitute the final type of information necessary for the development
of a system of racial and ethnic data collection which would contribute
to effective decision making by management. Such data concerning
beneficiaries, applicants, and eligibles must be collected in order
that benefits can be allocated consistently with the needs of the members of the various minority groups, and in order to determine whether
the eligibility requirements for program participation of these groups
are equitable. The pertinent characteristics will vary from program
to program, depending on the benefit offered and the criteria for eligibility. Among the characteristics that should be considered are
income, past earnings, education, and family size. It is odd, to say
the least, that information of this type, which is among the most frequently assembled for use in the administration of federal programs
and is readily available is, according to the Commission on Civil
Rights, "rarely collected for use in measurement of equal opportunity
in Federal programs." Only the Labor Department collects such information on a regular basis and in conjunction with racial and ethnic
data.

It seems abundantly clear from the findings of the Commission
on Civil Rights study of racial and ethnic data collection systems that
there is not even a nucleus for a government-wide system, nor is
there a comprehensive system in any of the departments studied.
Furthermore, such data as have been assembled are not linked together in such a way that they can be used by management for program
evaluation or compliance appraisal. In fact, up to the time of the
establishment of the OMB, there seemed to be almost a conspiracy
of foot dragging among various departments and in the Bureau of the
Budget to guarantee that program managers would be unable to make
managerial decisions that were valid, rational, and timely on the
basis of data permitted and available.

DATA COLLECTION: HOW FREQUENTLY
AND IN WHAT DETAIL

The effectiveness of a racial and ethnic data collection system as a management tool depends in part on the frequency with which such information is gathered, the amount of detail collected, and the manner and speed with which it is analyzed. The needs vary from agency to agency, depending on the nature of the programs involved. An effective system must specify how often the data are to be collected or how current the data used must be. None of the agencies studied, however, had issued instructions as to the frequency of data collection, and as a result some programs appeared to be operating with data that were outdated for the purposes at hand. The appropriate frequency of collection for a particular program depends on such factors as the method of collection, the expected rates of change in program participation, and the desired rates of change in minority group practices deemed feasible and appropriate by the unit or program agency.

Extent of the Change Expected

The frequency of collection should be adjusted to the frequency of turnover in program participation. The larger the change in program participation, the more often the data should be collected or tabulated.

Extent of Change Necessary

The frequency of data collection will also depend upon the program goals and the timetables for reaching these goals. Even when the racial and ethnic composition of the groups participating in a particular program remain the same from year to year, if this composition has involved inequities in distribution of services by the program, data should be collected frequently until the inequities have been eliminated. Whenever numerical goals are set, data should be required to determine the extent to which these guidelines have been met.

Detail Required

The amount of detail collected in such a system should be the quanity and kind of information necessary to enable the manager to make an objective, rational decision as to whether the program under

his supervision is in compliance with Title VI. It is important to
determine whether data aggregated at the state level supply sufficient
information, if program managers need data which summarize the
information on particular recipients, or if program offices should
store information on each program beneficiary.

Programs of direct assistance, such as those administered by
the Social Security Administration and the Veterans Administration,
generally have access to data on individual beneficiaries. Programs
administered through recipients, however, tend to receive only ag-
gregate data; in some cases, totals may be provided for each recipient within a state and in others data may be aggregated at the state
level before being made available to the program office.

Whether such data contain sufficient detail for equitable func-
tioning in the program office depends upon the purposes of the data
collection. When data are collected to measure the extent to which
there is equitable distribution of program benefits to minorities, this
equity must extend to the local level, and to all recipients. Data
aggregated at the state level seldom provide information about the
local geographic location of inequities. These local inequities, including those which occur in isolated places, are rarely disclosed
through an examination of aggregated data. Data on individual beneficiaries may also be necessary for the program office when it wishes
to investigate a particular recipient, whether as a part of a complaint
investigation or a part of a compliance review.

FEDERAL AGENCIES:
TITLE VI RESPONSIBILITIES

While many reasons have been given for the failure to collect
the information needed by program managers to fulfill their Title VI
responsibilities, the single most important explanation for this failure
is the absence of an agency-wide or federal policy requiring that
it be collected and used.

The Role of the Funding Agencies

Well defined operating policies requiring the collection of
racial and ethnic data on program participation exist in the Departments of Agriculture, Labor, and Housing and Urban Development,
where considerably more data are collected for assessing the distribution of program benefits to members of minority groups than in the
Department of Health, Education, and Welfare, in the Department
of Transportation, and in the Veterans Administration. There was

only one assistance program (HEW's) in the three latter agencies
which systematically gathered and used racial and ethnic data to
appraise the extent to which program benefits were equitably distributed. But these data are collected for the programs administered
by the Manpower Administration in the Labor Department for selected
programs in several of the DOA constituent agencies, and such a
system is being established for all HUD programs.

In 1971 HEW required that dollar outlays be reported for each
program by racial and ethnic origin of its beneficiaries, but HEW
program managers have not interpreted this as a requirement that
they collect data on this matter. Instructions implementing this policy
of reporting have allowed the use of estimates on some "reasonable
basis." Also, to date there has been virtually no monitoring of this
reporting system, and some program officials have admitted that the
quality of these data is poor, resulting from the limited and obsolete
basis of the collection.

The Role of OMB

The predecessor of the Office of Management and Budget—the
Bureau of the Budget—was a neutral, if not negative, factor in pro-
moting the development of a racial and ethnic data system which
would foster compliance with civil rights laws and executive orders.
Its leadership did not facilitate management's ability to appraise the
level of compliance and to evaluate effectively the civil rights aspects
of its grants programs. The role of OMB in practice to date does not
appear significantly different from BOB in terms of results achieved,
though changes have been made in the part OMB can play in requiring
Federal agencies to secure compliance from recipients of federal
funds.

With regard to its form clearance procedure, OMB's role has
been to eliminate unnecessary data gathering and improve the collection of essential information. It has not, however, encouraged the
collection of additional statistics in order to increase the information
available for the effective operation of programs. Consequently, its
procedures have not promoted an increase in the amount of racial and
ethnic data available for program planning and evaluation. OMB has
judged forms primarily on the basis of their statistical merits rather
than upon the extent to which they would fill the administrative needs
of program officials. However, form clearance responsibility has
been shifted from the Statistical Policy Division to the Budget Examination Divisions within OMB, increasing the possibility that a new
clearance procedure may encourage agencies to collect and use data
relating to the distribution of program benefits to minorities.

According to the Commission on Civil Rights, "When an agency presents a data collection plan to OMB for approval, the Budget Examiner with responsibility for the particular program involved will participate in the clearance procedures to insure that approved forms are in 'full accord with agency program objectives.' "[15]

In its role as the regulator of federal statistical procedures, the OMB is showing some signs of positive attitudes if not action in this area, and some of the revisions which it appears to have in mind might bear positive fruit. The OMB has the authority to issue such regulations, and presumably can use Circular A-46, which was issued by the BOB in March 1952 and established requirements for federal statistics in more affirmative ways. However, this authority has not been used by OMB specifically to improve the quality of racial and ethnic statistics, except with respect to the specification of racial designations—that is, the terms to be used for the various racial and ethnic groups in federal statistics.

There remains a need for guidelines to govern the methods of collecting racial and ethnic data, but there is no indication that the OMB will use Circular A-46 to establish standards for all aspects of racial and ethnic data collection. Thus one may conclude from an analysis of the U.S. Commission on Civil Rights' study of the subject that no semblance of a nationwide system of collecting racial and ethnic data has been established, and the top management echelons of the federal government have given limited, uneven, and completely inadequate support to the development of a government-wide system or even to the promotion of agency-wide and program-wide systems.

NOTES

1. U.S. Commission on Civil Rights, To Know or Not to Know: Collection and Use of Racial and Ethnic Data in Federal Assistance Programs, February, 1973 (Washington, D.C.: Government Printing Office, 1973), p. 23.

2. Ibid.

3. Department of Health, Education, and Welfare, Long Range Planning System: Program Planning Structure, mimeographed, 1971. While HEW does not require the actual collection of racial and ethnic data on program participants, it does require submission of data on the dollar value of program outlays by the racial and ethnic origin of program participants.

4. U.S. Commission on Civil Rights, op. cit., p. 26, footnote 34.

5. U.S. Commission on Civil Rights, op. cit., p. 26, footnote 32. Since collection of racial and ethnic data on users can often be done by headcount, and thus will not link the racial or ethnic origin

of users with other identifying information, some of the issues discussed in the first section of this report do not apply to these data.

6.   Ibid., p. 26, footnote 33.

7.   Ibid.

8.   Ibid., p. 27, footnote 36.

9.   Ibid., p. 27, footnote 37. The Federal Aviation Administration provides assistance to state and local agencies for the development of airports, including assistance for planning, site acquisition, and construction.

10.   Ibid. The Federal Highway Administration provides assistance to state highway departments for the planning, construction, and improvement of highways.

11.   Ibid. The Urban Mass Transportation Administration provides assistance to state and local agencies for planning, development, and construction of urban transportation service. Data on actual use are not recorded. The Urban Mass Transportation Administration requires recipients to submit data in advance of the proposed project.

12.   Ibid., p. 27, footnotes 38 and 39. The Capital Grant Program provides assistance to state and local public agencies for the development and improvement of public transportation.

13.   Ibid., p. 27, footnote 40. Funding of such facilities is made by HUD's Model Cities Program, Neighborhood Facilities Program, and Metropolitan Development Program.

14.   Ibid., p. 28.

15.   Ibid., pp. 71-72.

10

USE OF RACIAL AND ETHNIC DATA AS A MANAGEMENT TOOL

The woefully limited systems for collecting racial and ethnic data developed by all levels of management in the federal government culminate inevitably in an even more dismal level of achievement in their actual use as tools for decision-making in civil rights compliance and program development. There is abundant evidence of the paucity of government agency efforts to employ racial and ethnic data in the analysis of the distribution of benefit programs. According to a CCR report, federal agencies have generally failed:

> . . . to establish mechanisms for the use of racial and
> ethnic data, and failed to direct that the analysis of
> racial and ethnic data should be conducted as part of
> on-going agency activities. Equally significant is the
> failure of federal agencies to hold program officials
> accountable for knowing the answers to questions re-
> garding the extent to which program benefits are pro-
> vided to minority beneficiaries and potential beneficiaries,
> the extent to which information about program benefits
> is reaching minority potential beneficiaries, and the qual-
> ity of the benefits received by minority beneficiaries.[1]

This situation exists in face of the fact that the long-range civil rights and equal opportunity goals of government agencies are clearly established by statutory law, executive orders of the president, and judicial interpretations of the laws. Since civil rights enforcement units have the broad responsibility under Title VI of assuring that equal opportunity is afforded all beneficiaries, clients, and certain employees in federal programs, it is essential that they relate their compliance and educational activities to budgets of program agencies

165

in such a way as to exert maximum surveillance. Compliance and program priorities should be compatible, and all resources of the departments should be directed to the achievement of the stated goals.

Effective management of civil rights and equal opportunity enforcement agencies requires that intermediate and short-range objectives be clearly developed and initiated by the top policy-making manager, who takes into consideration the basic laws and the resources, and techniques available to him. The goals established should be stated in objective terms, and should be measurable as far as possible. Of course, the intermediate (one to five years) and short-range (one year) objectives are influenced by many other factors than the law and the available resources. These include the interpretation of the law by a department or agency (or its subordinate offices established by these edicts), the scope of its implementation objectives, and the size of its resources and input know-how. But, whether departmental management (particularly the top level policy-making decision makers) is positively committed to the spirit and letter of civil rights and equal opportunity laws and the organizational structure is the decisive factor.

The role and significance of the civil rights enforcement unit of a federal agency can be well illustrated by observation of the development and changes in the Office for Civil Rights of HEW as a unit of management charged with the ultimate responsibility for Title VI and the Civil Rights Executive Order 11246 (as amended) throughout HEW. Despite the relatively high rank of HEW among the major federal departments in its civil rights and equal opportunity activities, its deficiencies in racial and ethnic data collection and use emerge as major factors limiting the participation and effectiveness of major program agencies in implementing the secretary's equal opportunity goals for 1971 and for 1972. No doubt there are deeper reasons for this lack of interest in civil rights goals but they will be discussed elsewhere in this study.

Whatever the reasons might have been, and whether they are justifiable under the existing circumstances, it is clear that the Office for Civil Rights was systematically and progressively eliminated from any meaningful participation in the Planning and Evaluation System (P&E) and subsequently in the Operational Planning System (OPS), which began on an experimental basis about July 1, 1969 (FY-1970), and became fully operative on July 1, 1970. This system has continued and expanded in its scope and significance since that time, but not until late 1972 was systematic attention given to OCR inclusion or participation in this system. Since then, OCR has begun to participate in the planning stage.

The virtual exclusion of the Office for Civil Rights from a planning and evaluation process was significant in that it conveyed to

program managers the view that the performance of their civil rights
responsibilities in program activities would not and could not be
appraised objectively by the secretary's staff. Despite the statement
of civil rights goals, the exclusion of OCR suggested that the department somehow did not consider compliance with Title VI by program
managers as a crucial factor in judging their program plans or results.
In addition, for HEW as a whole an excellent opportunity was lost
for developing an overall departmental policy on the collection and
use of racial and ethnic data. This meant that there was no mechanism
for collecting, analyzing, and using such information for civil rights
compliance, program evaluation, and budgeting purposes. A comprehensive and efficient department-wide racial and ethnic data system
would have been in operation had the department had the foresight
to allow OCR to participate appropriately in its operational planning
program as it evolved.

OPERATIONAL PLANNING SYSTEM

It is important to understand the phase of the Operational Planning System currently under consideration and the HEW Office for
Civil Rights involvement or lack of involvement which has emerged.
This OPS comes into operation shortly after the president's budget
is announced by the issuance of departmental program and management priorities designated as the secretary's priorities. It lists
approximately 12 to 15 major program objectives to which the president wishes the department to address itself during the coming fiscal
year plus others chosen by the department to meet its unique needs.
The second step is the issuance of major agency-wide objectives by
the head of each operating agency in the department. These include
the objectives from the secretary's list applicable to his agency, and
is considered an agency-wide high priority objective.
Agency heads at HEW are asked to develop approximately eight
to ten specific operational objectives for eventual transmittal to the
secretary. It is at this point that the planning, programming, and
budgeting process comes into play with reference to each of the operational objectives recommended. For each of these objectives,
the agency head—after careful consideration with his staff—is asked
to indicate the plans by which he will achieve each of his objectives,
the resources required for achievement, the sources from which resources can be obtained, and the steps that will be taken in carrying
out the plan, with a timetable of progressive dates culminating in
completion. This latter step is of utmost importance because it provides the basis upon which the secretary can systematically and regularly track progress toward the achievement of the objectives

established. Thus it has the promise of giving the secretary some
objective basis for relating the output of his department and his
agency heads to the input of resources, know-how applied to a given
objective.

The third step is the review, revision, and acceptance of agency
objectives by the secretary and the initiation of programs aimed at
achieving such objectives at the beginning of the fiscal year. Thereafter, regular reporting sessions of operating agency heads with the
secretary or his representatives are conducted in order to track the
progress toward the objectives which have been determined for each
agency of HEW.

Obviously, this process moves from the top of each HEW agency
down through the various bureaus involved and includes participation
by the regional offices of each agency as well as the HEW regional
director and his staff. This system has been developed and refined
over a period of years since 1969, but the basic characteristics described are applicable to all. During the fiscal year 1970 (beginning
July 1, 1969), the process was begun experimentally under the name
of the P&E System (Planning and Evaluation System) and was confined
to the major operating agencies and selected regions. The system
in revised form was put into HEW-wide operation on July 1, 1970
(for fiscal year 1971) under the name Operational Planning System
by then Secretary Robert H. Finch, and with some further refine-
ments and changes has been in operation since that time. In each of
these years, an equal opportunity priority statement was included in
the secretary's departmental priorities list. *

In preparation for the first government-wide application of the
system beginning July 1, 1970, the newly appointed director of the
Office for Civil Rights was rather belatedly requested by the assistant
secretary for management of HEW to submit a statement of civil
rights priorities covering all activities of the department and of
strategies for achievement of these aims for inclusion in the overall
statement of the secretary's priorities.

---

*The civil rights statements are listed in sequence. For FY
1971 HEW Goal No. 7 was as follows: "To enforce the applicable
laws and to otherwise assure that all persons regardless of their
social, educational or economic background, race, color, national
origin, religion, or sex, have an equal opportunity to participate in
financially assisted programs, activities and contracts, and HEW
employment." Statement by Secretary Robert H. Finch, HEW, March
26, 1970. For FY 1973 HEW, Goal No. 6 is the same except for the
number.

was prepared by John Hope II and, with some nonsubstantive revisions, accepted and sent to Secretary Finch. The statement reads:

The primary role of OCR in the Operational Planning System (OPS) and its predecessor, the Planning and Evaluation System, has been to provide technical assistance to program agencies and offices concerning the civil rights and equal opportunity aspects of their various programs. By this means we are trying to anticipate and prevent violations of Title VI and E.O. 11246 and, thus, reduce the incidence of overt noncompliance by recipients of Federal grants-in-aid and Federal contractors. Program agencies need to know and have adequate and demonstrable evidence that the Federal financial assistance administered by them is in compliance with applicable civil rights and equal opportunity laws and regulations.

On the other hand, since OCR is a compliance rather than a grant administering agency, it has been determined that is is not appropriate for OCR to participate in the reporting aspects of the OPS, although we fully support the basic objectives and techniques of this System and use them in our interval management processes.

Federal grant administering and contracting agencies have the direct responsibility for assuring that the recipients of funds dispensed by them are spent without discrimination because of race, color, national origin, or sex (contractors, E.O. 11246). However, the OCR has the ultimate responsibility and, consequently, the primary authority to impose and recommend sanctions for noncompliance with applicable laws and executive orders. Therefore, OCR's objectives tend to be (or should be) an integral part of the goals of all programs or activities receiving Federal financial assistance from HEW where minority groups are involved either as beneficiaries of services, as employees of Federal contractors, or as applicants for either.

The Secretary's Operational Planning Priorities for FY-1972 establishes twelve (12) national programmatic priorities one of which (No. 6) is Equal Opportunity. One of the important innovations of this Priorities program is that a coordinating office (s) has been designated for each priority. OCR, Office of the Assistant Secretary for Administration and Management (ASAM), and the Women's Action Program are the coordinating offices for the Equal

Opportunity Priority. Each coordinating office is to
"designate a person (1) to help in the development of
operational objectives and (2) to monitor progress in
achieving these objectives. The coordinators will
help operating agencies develop strategies for inte-
grating and coordinating their efforts. The coordinators will also be principal participants in my (The
Secretary's) review of progress toward meeting the
objectives and will report to me regularly on the status
of our efforts in each priority area. " (Secretary's
Operational Planning Priorities for FY-1972, Memo
April 27, 1971, pp. 2-3.)

I consider this an important breakthough for
OCR planning prospects since it should increase our
opportunities to give technical assistance regarding
high priority programs of operating agencies in HEW.

The Office of the Assistant Secretary for Administration and Management has corresponding compliance responsibility for in-house HEW employment.

The Secretary's Operational Planning Priorities
for FY-1972 adds "Age" to the attributes covered by
the FY-1971 Civil Rights Goals. However, specific
responsibility for implementation has not been assigned.
It has been recommended, however, that the Administration on the Aging handle complaints of discrimination
because of age.

I am attaching a copy of DHEW Goal No. 7 of the
Departmental Goals for FY-1971 and the five (5) basic
strategies for achieving it. These strategies remain,
in my opinion, sound means by which HEW can achieve
equality of opportunity and protection of the civil rights
of all its employees, clients, and beneficiaries. [2*]

This statement was quoted in its entirety because of its expected significance as a basis for more effective implementation of Title VI by
OCR and (as far as the writer knows) because it is probably the first
statement which delineates and separates the roles of the civil rights

---

*The writer was Assistant Director for Planning at OCR/HEW
and was the director's representative in all matters relating to OPS
and its predecessor from their inception until October 31, 1971 when
he became a Brookings Federal Executive Fellow and took a leave of
absence from HEW. Consequently, the chronology of the events
described ends at about this date.

personnel (particularly OCR) and that of program personnel in implementing the civil rights laws, particularly Title VI. [3]

The five ways which were proposed by HEW to meet its equal opportunity goals were: first, sanctions; second, negotiation; third, monitoring; fourth, assistance, persuasion, and education to assist in moving to a free and open society; and fifth, leading by examples.

Among the five ways HEW proposed to meet its equal opportunity goals, the fourth way emphasized the goal of equal opportunity as an integral part of every program and stated that it was to be stressed in all program activities: "Each HEW program office will stress the importance of providing equal opportunity in its program whether the recipient is a state, municipality, or private organization."[4]

The requirement concerning monitoring was explicit in placing responsibility on the program office to develop the tools, and presumably the racial and ethnic data, necessary to determine if the program was being conducted in conformity with Title VI and other civil rights laws. It was apparent that it was the secretary's intention to indicate that civil rights goals and program goals were not separate or separable, that program agencies had responsibilities for assuring compliance with civil rights laws, and that they, not the Office for Civil Rights, had the direct and primary responsibility for (in the Secretary's words) "developing an effective means of monitoring equality of opportunity in their programs, activities, and contracts." Clearly, then, the virtual exclusion of the Office for Civil Rights from participation in the Operational Planning System was not consistent with the secretary's goals, which have been in operation since July 1, 1970.

In like manner, the negotiation performance of program agencies required by the secretary in this document fell far short of the requirement in their day-to-day practices. It is apparent from his statement on negotiation that program agencies should not only take the initiative in determining whether their recipients were in compliance, but should take steps to assist and persuade them to eliminate such violations and, if unsuccessful, "must at once report the failure to the Office for Civil Rights and work out with that office an appropriate strategy for conducting negotiations with the recipient or contractor. Program officers must exercise initiative in meeting the department's goal." Finally, the statement indicated that if voluntary efforts to eliminate discrimination were unsuccessful, sanctions must be applied and that the Office for Civil Rights "has the primary authority to impose and recommend the sanctions provided under Title VI and Parts II and III of Executive Order 11246."

Despite the protestations of mutual interest and responsibility of HEW program and civil rights personnel for the effective implementation of Title VI and other civil rights edict, in practice the rigid division between civil rights and program functions, particularly in the minds of program personnel, continues to foster an atmosphere of separation, mutual suspicion, lack of cooperation, and sometimes hostility between these two groups. Indicative of this situation is the fact that during the whole period of development of the Operational Planning System from early 1969 to the fall of 1971 when the writer left this position, neither the assistant director for planning of the Office for Civil Rights, who was designated by its director as liaison with the office of the assistant secretary for management (OSM) of HEW, nor any of his staff was called into a meeting to participate in the discussion of these goals with the OSM staff, which had primary responsibility for developing the secretary's goals. The planning director of OCR was only asked to develop or agree to the statement having to do with civil rights and equal opportunity.

Moreover, after the OPS was completely formulated and the manual for its operation prepared, OCR staff was excluded from the rather sizeable staff dispatched to all regional offices to train regional personnel in the administration of the system. Likewise, the regional OCR directors were not invited—as were all of the regional program agency directors and their staffs—to participate in these training sessions until the apparent oversight was called to the attention of the Office of the Assistant Secretary for Management. Then the invitation was issued by word of mouth that OCR regional directors might attend the training sessions if they wished, but no specific assignments were given and there was no discussion of the civil rights and equal opportunity implications of the development of program objective plans and other aspects of the OPS at the training sessions.

On the other hand, when the agency objectives were completed and submitted by their agency heads to the Office of the Assistant Secretary for Management for review on behalf of the secretary, copies were sent to the director of OCR for review. When these statements were reviewed by the assistant director for planning at OCR for their civil rights implications and found inadequate, he wrote the following memorandum to the director of field operations on April 30, 1970, but no response or reaction was ever received from any source.

> In reviewing the statements from various regions, I
> must confess that we were somewhat surprised to find
> that some HEW regions did not include any aspects of
> the departmental civil rights Goal (No. 7) among their
> Regional Priorities for FY-1971. On the basis of our
> knowledge and experience, I doubt that we would have
> come to this conclusion for any region, though we might
> be considered a "Special Interest" agency in this regard.

Regions VII (Ark., La., NM, Okla., Texas),
VIII (Colo., Idaho, Mont., Utah, Wyo.), and IX
(Alaska, Ariz., Calif., Guam, Hawaii, Nev., Oregon,
Wash.) were in this category. All three of these re-
gions have multi-minority situations which complicate
their implementation processes. Two of them (Regions
VII and VIII) did, however, include some aspects of
Goal No. 3 concerned with improved services to Indians.

Of the remaining seven regions that had some
civil rights priorities, only two (Regions I and II) clearly and specifically included HEW-assisted programs in
general while one (Region III) included a regional civil
rights priority which was confined to its elementary and
secondary school program and gave primary emphasis
on Title IV assistance. The remaining regions' civil
rights priorities were restricted to employment, some
comprising in-house and contract employment, some
one or the other of these types, and some were not clear
as to how far their employment priorities would extend
in practice.

We would suggest that the civil rights priorities of
Regions IV and V be further clarified to make certain the
scope of their civil rights goals, i. e., whether they include both in-house employment and that by HEW contractors.

The civil rights priority of Region IV is stated in
such general and long-range terms that one might wonder what specific program objectives they plan to pursue.
However, the rather clear and specific statements of
'General Approach' reflect their broad and thoughtful
approaches to implementing their phase of the secretary's
Goal No. 7. Consequently, we do not suggest any change
in wording, provided it can be assumed that their specific
program objectives and plans will be based upon the 'General Approach' stated in their Priority No. 7.[5]

With regard to the use of equal opportunity by HEW program
agencies during the next year, the assistant director for planning,
Office for Civil Rights, reported the following:

My staff has reviewed statements of operational objectives received from nine agencies in the Department of
Health, Education, and Welfare.

Only one of these agencies, the Office of Education,
has indicated a priority related to the responsibilities of

the Office for Civil Rights. One other included in-
house employment which is under the jurisdiction of
the EEO staff director for the department who is in
the Office of the Assistant Director for Administration
and Management.

It is as disappointing this year as it was last
year that the Equal Opportunity Priority area with
which we have so much concern and which has received
so much emphasis from the secretary himself seems
to have little importance to the major grant administering agencies in the department.

You will note that the attached copy of the secretary's June 7, 1971, memorandum emphasizes his belief that the agencies must work together at the headquarters level but, so far, it does not appear that OCR
can make its contribution to the OPS program if priority No. 6 is so widely omitted from the operational objectives programmed by the agencies of this department.

I am enclosing a copy of my memorandum of April
30 to William Page based on my report to you of the paucity of agency-wide interest in equal opportunity during
FY-1971, but somewhat more interest than appears to
be forecast for FY-1972. [6]

This apparent insensitivity to the civil rights aspects of HEW
program activities and either ignorance or nonacceptance of the role
of the OCR as a participant in program matters of HEW were by no
means confined to regional offices and program agency officials.
Even after OPS had been fully operative for a year, the staff of the
assistant secretary for administration and management which is responsible for administering the OPS could not seem to comprehend
(or did not want to) the differences between the roles of program agencies and a compliance agency such as OCR in the OPS and related
matters. This lack of comprehension persisted despite the fact that
the writer had interpreted the difference by memorandum and in person over a two year period to various members of that staff. Yet in
a memorandum of April 28, 1971 from the assistant secretary for
administration and management, a request was made for OCR to submit its program objectives and priorities as a part of its submission
to the OPS as a participant. In his reply, J. Stanley Pottinger, the
director of the Office for Civil Rights, indicated the appropriate role
of OCR in this system and the willingness of OCR to cooperate in monitoring program plans, in providing technical assistance regarding
civil rights aspects of high priority programs of HEW agencies, and
in other matters:

The primary role of the Office for Civil Rights in the Operational Planning System and its predecessor, the Planning and Evaluation System, has been to provide technical assistance to program agencies and offices concerning the civil rights and equal opportunity aspects of their various programs. By this means, we are trying to anticipate and prevent violations of Title VI and EO-11246 and, thus, reduce the incidence of overt noncompliance by recipients of federal grants-in-aid and federal contractors. Program agencies need to know and have adequate and demonstrable evidence that the federal financial assistance administered by them is in compliance with applicable civil rights and equal opportunity laws and regulations.

On the other hand, since OCR is a compliance rather than a grant administering agency, it is not appropriate for OCR to participate in the reporting aspects of the OPS, although we fully support the basic objectives and techniques of this system and use them in our internal management processes.

Federal grant administering and contracting agencies have the direct responsibility for assuring that the recipients of funds dispensed by them are spent without discrimination because of race, color, national origin, or sex (EO-11246). However, the OCR has the ultimate responsibility and, consequently, the primary authority to impose and recommend sanctions for noncompliance with applicable laws and executive orders. Therefore, OCR's objectives are an integral part of the goals of all programs or activities receiving federal financial assistance from HEW where minority groups are involved either as beneficiaries of services, as employees of federal contractors, or as applicants for either.

I am designating John Hope II, Assistant Director (Planning) to help in the development of operational objectives and to monitor progress in achieving objectives.

I consider OPS an important breakthrough for OCR planning prospects since it should increase our opportunities to give technical assistance regarding high priority programs of operating agencies in HEW. [7]

Within six months the Office for Civil Rights was brought into OPS, and is now in the process of developing this kind of management capability.

In concluding this discussion of HEW's experience with management by objective, the role of OCR in this process, and implications for the development and effective use of racial and ethnic data, it is important to emphasize that this department probably remains one of the more effective of the federal departments in its use of racial and ethnic data, despite all of its imperfections.

Again, it is necessary to consult a document of the U.S. Commission on Civil Rights for the latest and most comprehensive treatment of this subject. As to the use of racial and ethnic data, the Commission summarizes as follows:

> Racial and ethnic data are essential tools in combatting discrimination and for planning and monitoring affirmative action to remedy past discrimination. The collection and analysis of these data are the most effective and accurate means of measuring federal program impact upon minority beneficiaries, and for assuring that equal opportunity policies are working effectively. [8]

However, these tools are frequently unavailable for use by those concerned with achieving equality of opportunity in a variety of federal programs, not because social statistics concerning the particular activity are not collected, but because they are not collected and classified in such a way that clear differentiation of practices can be made on the basis of minority status. For instance employers, both public and private, routinely gather statistics on such practices as recruitment, hiring, training, remuneration, promotion, demotion, transfer, assignment, or termination of employees, but seldom are these data classified by racial and ethnic groupings, even less frequently are analyses made of these specific practices in such a way as to determine whether discrimination is being practiced in specific types of activities.

So far the collection data for both federal employment and private employers with federal government contracts has been confined to a periodic census of the number of employees by racial and ethnic group classified by grade level for specific geographical areas. The same deficiency applies to the field of housing; information on the location, age, condition, financing, and cost programs, housing, and rentals or sales by builders and real estate brokers is no doubt assembled, but it can be of only limited value in assuring equal opportunity in existing housing or the planning and construction of additional facilities unless this and other related data are classified and analyzed by racial and ethnic origin.

It is also necessary that data concerning various educational programs include information on pupils, staff, participants in extracurricular activities and supplementary programs, and information

about capital facilities and equipment should be available by racial
and ethnic groups. Moreover, for programs of federal assistance,
estimates of the probable number of potential participants as well as
the number actually receiving benefits are likely to be assembled because they are needed in such matters as preparing budgets and planning. Similarly, in many cases the records of the number applying
for such benefits are maintained.

But all too often the collection and analysis of such data by racial
and ethnic grouping are confined to the number actually receiving benefits, so that managers of such programs have no way of determining
whether their activities are being conducted in compliance with Title
VI. People who might have questions about these activities can have
no concrete basis for determining whether their suspicions are valid
or not.

In addition to those program statistics which are assembled in
connection with and in order to improve the administration of particular programs, federal general purpose statistics are frequently
essential as background for equal opportunity programs, policy formulation, and program planning. There are various sources of general
purpose statistics; among the largest is the Bureau of the Census
statistics on population and housing.

RECOGNITION OF THE NEED
FOR RACIAL AND ETHNIC DATA

In previous years there was some difference in the views of
leaders of various minority groups as to whether racial and ethnic
data should be collected. Of principal concern was the potential
for both the invasion of privacy and the use of the information to harm
minorities. These objections have generally been dissipated now that
the leadership of most groups such as professional associations concerned with social conditions, civil rights groups, and civil liberties
organizations have generally agreed that it must be done to provide
information about the working of the political, economic, and social
systems and to deal effectively with social problems.

In addition, the OMB has recognized the significance of racial
and ethnic data collection in federal programs of assistance and has
stated to the Commission on Civil Rights, "in order to effectively
carry out the policy of nondiscrimination, it has become necessary
for federal agencies to obtain considerable information on race."[9]
However, OMB has not gone so far as to require that federal programs
collect such information. In the past year, there has been at least a
temporary breakthrough in regard to the use of racial designations in
compliance surveys of federal agencies.

Four of the secretaries of the six agencies included in the
Commission's study of racial and ethnic data collection have made
statements about the necessity to collect racial and ethnic data in
order to operate effective equal opportunity programs. These included the DOA, HEW, HUD, and DOL, while the Veterans Administration and the Department of Transportation have never expressed
such a policy. The following are descriptions of these four statements:

DOA. Clifford M. Hardin, Secretary of Agriculture, 1968-71,
    Secretary's Memorandum No. 1662, September 23, 1969. In this
    memorandum, Secretary Hardin enunciated departmental policy
    on civil rights with regard to racial and ethnic data. He stated
    that it was crucial for the department to develop a system of meas-
    uring the quantity and quality of services delivered to minority
    groups in all important and sensitive program areas.
HEW. Memorandum from Wilbur J. Cohen, Secretary of Health,
    Education, and Welfare, 1968-69, to HEW agency heads, Jan-
    uary 17, 1969, "The Collection and Use of Racial or Ethnic Data."
    Secretary Cohen endorsed the collection and use of racial and ethnic
    data as a "vital tool" for determining whether HEW programs are
    reaching the intended beneficiaries and for fulfilling the congress-
    ional mandate of nondiscrimination in federally assisted programs.
HUD. Memorandum from George Romney, Secretary of Housing and
    Urban Development, to all HUD assistant secretaries and the
    general counsel, "Collection of Racial and Ethnic Data," April 8,
    1970. Secretary Romney stated that it is impossible to carry out
    departmental civil rights responsibilities affirmatively without in-
    formation as to the racial and ethnic composition of applicants for,
    and recipients of, HUD assistance. He also indicated that such
    information could be of use in dealing more effectively with com-
    plaints received by HUD. He directed that a uniform data collec-
    tion system be implemented by all HUD programs.
DOL. W. Willard Wirtz, secretary of labor, 1962-68, address
    at the convocation of the NAACP Legal Defense and Education
    Fund, New York, NY, May 18, 1966. Secretary Wirtz described
    the civil rights responsibilities of his agency and the resulting
    need to know the racial distribution of participants in Manpower
    Administration programs. He announced that inclusion of racial
    identifications on employment records subject to the control of
    the Department of Labor would henceforth be required whenever
    this was necessary or helpful in combating racial discrimination
    and in promoting affirmative action programs to end discrimi-
    nation.[10]

These statements of policy express the need for such data to
meet the civil rights requirements of the department, to reveal

whether agency programs are actually reaching the intended
beneficiaries, and to learn about the quantity and quality of the benefits received by minorities.

WHO USES RACIAL AND ETHNIC DATA
COLLECTIONS, AND HOW ARE THEY USED?

The principal types of administrative units that use racial and
ethnic data for managerial purposes are the federal agencies responsible for administering grants-in-aid and other types of federal financial assistance programs and the recipients of federal assistance.
These recipients are "any state, political subdivision, or any public
or private agency, institution, or organization, or other entity, or
any individual in any state to whom federal financial assistance is
extended directly, or through another recipient, for any program
including any successor, programs, federal program officials, and
departmental civil rights specialists. . . . No agency officials in
charge of activities such as program planning, evaluation, research,
or civil rights compliance have been instructed to make the analysis
of racial and ethnic data an integral part of their responsibilities,
assignee or transferee thereof, but such term does not include any
ultimate beneficiary under any such programs."[11]
Up to this point agencies have given limited guidance to program
or civil rights managerial personnel as to which of them should be
responsible for tabulating, analyzing, and interpreting the racial and
ethnic data assembled. No agency-wide directives have indicated the
breakdown of this responsibility. In addition, the data which are
gathered are rarely made use of. Illustrative of the underutilization
of racial and ethnic data is the practice of the Department of Health,
Education, and Welfare. Information on the dollar outlay for federal
HEW programs according to the racial and ethnic origin of the beneficiaries is, according to the CCR report quoted below, "reported
annually to the HEW Office of the Assistant Secretary for Planning
and Evaluation, but program officials have not been instructed to
analyze and evaluate the data submitted, nor has this responsibility
been assumed by the Office for Civil Rights."[12]   The report continues:

> Even more significant, however, is the fact that there
> has been no instruction indicating what should be meas-
> ured with the racial and ethnic data collected.
>   Although there is no doubt that racial and ethnic
> data are to be collected to measure, in general, the
> extent of nondiscrimination in federal programs, and the
> extent to which program benefits are distributed equitably,

there have been few official suggestions to program
managers as to how racial and ethnic data might be
used systematically to locate possible sources of discrimination. [13]

The statements by DOA and HUD on this subject have consisted only of general directives that the collection of racial and ethnic
data is required to fulfill the civil rights responsibilities of the departments. The one exception to this lack of specific directives in
policy guidance was a statement of Secretary Wilbur J. Cohen of
HEW on the eve of his resignation at the beginning of the Nixon administration. At that time, Cohen directed the department to use
racial and ethnic data to show where program services and facilities
were underused by minority groups and where program goals were
not achieved in the case of minority group participants.
    If racial and ethnic data are to be used by managers more
effectively than in the past, it is necessary for all parties to receive
clear instructions as to what kinds of data are to be systematically
used at each stage in the channel of movement of federal financial
assistance funds, from source to the ultimate beneficiary. This requires that specific assignments be made to each management unit
along the way. If such an approach were adopted, it would become
readily apparent that the civil rights responsiblities of an agency
were not easily divisible between so-called program personnel and
civil rights and equal opportunity personnel. The crucial necessity
for close cooperation between these two groups would be recognized
and, in some cases, the need to integrate or merge the personnel
would be a managerial necessity. In the words of the CCR report:

Racial and ethnic data can and should be used at several
points in the process of distribution of federal assistance.
They may be used by recipients of federal assistance,
both in making application for federal assistance to show
the possible effect of the proposed project on minority
beneficiaries, and in examining the extent of nondiscrimination in the distribution process. They may be
used by federal program managers and by agency planning and evaluation offices for program development
and for assessment of the extent to which federal programs are meeting their stated objectives with regard
to minority beneficiaries. They are also essential to
other agency units such as the civil rights office for
the purposes of compliance review or complaint investigation, or administrative offices for appraising overall
allocation of resources, formulating requests for

additional appropriations, and drafting legislation.
Racial and ethnic data should also be used by the Office of Management and Budget (OMB) in its assessment of the effectiveness of distribution of federal
funds and in an overall evaluation of federal programs. [14]

This statement raises important questions about the appropriate
role of the civil rights and equal opportunity staffs of agencies in
cases where the need for using racial and ethnic data by administering
agencies and grant recipients has been fully recognized. Should civil
rights and equal opportunity unit personnel—for example OCR—be
involved at each of these stages in the progress of grant distribution?
If not, at what points should such involvement be focused, and what
should be its nature? What should be the status, location, and size
of civil rights and equal opportunity staffs in relation to program
personnel operating at the same point in the managerial chain of distribution of grants-in-aid funds?

USE OF RACIAL AND
ETHNIC DATA COLLECTIONS

The managerial channel through which federal financial assistance funds ultimately reach the beneficiary begins at the point when
grants-in-aid and similar grants are appropriated by Congress to a
particular executive department or agency. The department or agency
then allocates these funds among recipients (public or private), who
in turn distribute them among the ultimate beneficiaries or users of
such funds. The federal administering agency is responsible for
funneling funds from the federal treasury to the recipient according to
criteria and conditions established by law, one of which is that there
shall be no discrimination because of race, color, or national origin.
The recipient, or administering agency of direct grants, is the line
management unit which has the responsibility of distributing such
grants equitably to individuals or groups who will actually use the funds.
Systematic, mandatory, and universal collection of racial and ethnic
data constitutes one of the most efficient tools for initiating efforts
to eliminate inequities in access to federal funds arising from minority status. Such information is not merely a tool for determining the
presence of arbitrary differentials in the amounts or quality of benefits; but it also provides an objective basis for remedial action.
The role of the civil rights program manager in an agency is to
determine whether federal financial assistance funds are being distributed without discrimination because of race, color, national origin, or sex. This requires that he ferret out those programs where

discrimination is occurring or is likely to occur, take corrective
action where possible and, if necessary, initiate steps to cut off such
aid.

Observation of the method by which program management and
civil rights and equal opportunity units use racial and ethnic data at
each stage in the channel of grant distribution, can determine whether
the practices of managerial units result in differentiation based on
minority or ethnic status and, if so, at what stage in the process and
to what extent. The following is an analysis of the management practices of the federal funding agencies and the recipients of federal
funding in fulfilling their Title VI responsibilities.

Federal Funding Agencies

The administering federal agencies of grants-in-aid programs
are generally bureaus of offices of a federal department or independent agency which are covered by Title VI of the Civil Rights Act. They
are usually accountable directly to the heads of their departments or
agencies who, in turn, report to the president. As grantors of federal financial assistance provided by federal appropriations to them
for distribution to recipients, these federal agencies are responsible
for assuring that their recipients comply with Title VI. Consequently,
in order that administering agencies make objective, accurate appraisals as to whether their recipients are in compliance, it is ab-
solutely essential that they gather racial and ethnic data as a basis
for such appraisals.

Federal administering agencies have two major sources of information which can be used to determine the compliance status of
their recipients: first, the compliance review, which is a primary
tool and provides such information directly; and second, program
planning and evaluation, a process which more indirectly provides
civil rights compliance information and is an effective tool for both
civil rights and program purposes in situations where the functions
are effectively coordinated and properly integrated.

The compliance review is a periodic on-site review of activities
or facilities which are getting federal assistance. Its purpose is
to find out if the recipients are operating in compliance with Title VI
of the Civil Rights Act. Such reviews may be of the pre-grant
(or pre-award) type conducted prior to release of funds to the grantee,
or post-grant (or post-award) which are conducted after the fact.
Unfortunately, the vast majority of such reviews are at present of
the latter type. The use of racial and ethnic data is important in at
least three phases of the compliance review: first, to help determine
which recipients or potential recipients of federal aid should be chosen

for a full compliance review; second, to provide evidence pertinent and useful in the findings of the review; and third, to be used in setting up goals and timetables for affirmative action to correct violations where findings of noncompliance have been made.

One of the greatest obstacles to the optimum use of civil rights and equal opportunity staff resources is, in the opinion of the writer, the way agencies select recipients for a full compliance review. They should be chosen in such a way that each unit of investment of resources by the civil rights and equal opportunity staff maximizes the extent of elimination of discrimination in a given program. A full compliance review obviously requires the development of effective, sophisticated, reliable, stratified sampling procedures well adapted to the program to which it is applied. Sampling is necessary, given the vast number of grants-in-aid programs in operation. Even under the best of circumstances agencies will never provide civil rights and equal opportunity resources of the size and quality necessary to monitor all programs within a reasonable time. Consequently, within a given year, only a small proportion of the recipients of any given program are likely to be reviewed and, therefore, those chosen should be selected in such a way that they are most representative of the total group of recipients involved.

There is a question as to whether the sample chosen should be representative of the recipients that are the least effective and therefore need a review most urgently, or of all recipients, good and bad combined. The Commission on Civil Rights appears to favor the latter. It recommends a census-type review, including racial and ethnic data about the target population of applicants and of beneficiaries. Such a census using well established criteria would serve to locate systematically both potential recipients and recipients for whom further reviews are necessary, and to whom priorities for compliance reviews should be given.

In practice, only HEW has conducted large scale racial and ethnic surveys under the authority of Title VI of the Civil Rights Act of 1964. These have been surveys of hospitals, extended care facilities, and elementary and secondary schools, and have served as a basis for the identification of recipients whose status with regard to Title VI was most questionable—an identification which would have been more difficult, more costly and less accurate on any other basis.

In the opinion of the author, these noteworthy operations of HEW still fall short of the potential for full scale and effective sampling. One of the weaknesses of these efforts has been that the top management of the Office for Civil Rights has never permitted a level of control and consistency in handling data necessary for making accurate statistical inferences applicable to the total population from the sample chosen and manipulated. There might however be a question whether such action is politically feasible in the minds of the departmental executive and the president in light of the nature of the program and its controversial character.

The Commission summarizes its position on sampling in compliance reviews in the following terms:

> Federal agencies rarely have sufficient staff to conduct compliance reviews on every recipient or potential recipient of federal assistance. Consequently, such reviews are typically done for only a small proportion of recipients, and federal agencies achieve only limited familiarity with recipient's operations. Thus, racial and ethnic data may play an important role in three phases of the review process. They may be used in determining which recipients should be the subject of a compliance review; and used as a means of establishing goals and timetables for affirmative action.
>
> In the agencies studied, only HEW conducted large-scale racial and ethnic surveys in conjunction with assessment of civil rights compliance. These covered, for example, hospitals, extended care facilities, and elementary and secondary schools and have served as a basis for identification of recipients whose Title VI status was not questionable.
>
> Compliance reviews, whether conducted as pre-award or post-award reviews, involve the examination of pertinent records, the interview of witnesses, the review of relevant statistical data, and the personal observations of the compliance officer. Statistical data may provide information about the race and ethnic origin of the population to be served, applicants and beneficiaries. They may also assist in documentation of any differentials in benefits or service provided to minority group beneficiaries, and in documentation of the impact of the recipient's operation on minority beneficiaries. Such data may provide prima facie evidence of discrimination, or lack of it, or may be used as the basis for further investigation. [15]

The treatment of the subject of program planning and evaluation by the U.S. Commission on Civil Rights study of racial and ethnic data indicates how intensively and pervasively overall program and civil rights and equal opportunity functions of federal agencies are interrelated and intertwined in situations where the potential

beneficiaries of the respective grants-in-aid programs in force are
significantly mixed as to race, color, or national origin.

Moreover, it suggests some of the difficulties, if not the utter
futility, of departmental management achieving reasonably effective
civil rights and equal opportunity compliance where such functions
and the respective resources assembled to administer them are so
demonstrably separate and frequently noncooperative. And yet, under present circumstances, the merging of such functions presents
the prospect of less, rather than more, effective application of civil
rights and equal opportunity laws and policies than where they are
distinct, sometimes competitive, and on occasion, hostile.

It is obvious that, to date, departments and agencies with a
clear and distinctive top management mandate and specialized civil
rights and equal opportunity staffs reporting directly to such an
executive or to his designee, and not to specific program managers,
have been more effective. It is equally clear that program managers
have frequently tended to avoid, minimize, and sometimes even re-
nounce their civil rights and equal opportunity responsibilities and,
consequently, to provide no leadership or resources for the enforcing
of Title VI.

Even where executive management manifests no evidence of
prejudicial attitudes in its action, program planning and evaluation
are likely to result in minority group inequities unless certain distinct conditions prevail. These conditions are: first, the existence of
specific plans for administering the grant which serve to maximize
the benefits available to majority group participants and which, in
turn, will fully and equitably meet the needs of each of the corresponding minority groups involved; second, the existence of regulations, guidelines, and criteria that are developed by the administering agency to govern the distribution of grants to beneficiaries
and which, when applied to minorities, will assure their full participation without discrimination of any kind.

Insofar as program management effectively includes all potential beneficiaries in its planning and programming, it can facilitate the achievement of equal opportunity by preventing discriminatory
practices in contrast to the currently prevailing method of taking
a variety of remedial measures after the fact. In principle the former
procedure has advantages over the compliance review approach which,
with rare exceptions, has been concentrated on post-grant rather
than pre-grant compliance reviews. However, there is little in
practice to date to encourage civil rights and equal opportunity management to adopt such an approach without explicit assurances that
the immediate effectiveness of its ultimate authority to enforce the
civil rights laws and regulations will not be eroded.

Program evaluation is a standard means by which program management and sometimes overall departmental management judge effectiveness in the use of resources to achieve the predetermined objectives of the program being appraised. But insofar as the civil rights and equal opportunity objectives of that program, particularly Title VI, are either ignored or are inadequately or ineptly applied, the resulting performance cannot be efficiently or fairly appraised.

Since planning begins with goal setting and evaluation is aimed at the measurement of results, the formulation of goals and timetables is an obviously desirable means of judging the quantity and quality of results of the application of resources. It must be re-emphasized, however, that this concept of results is a rather complex one which, from the point of view of department-wide management, ultimately involves the combination of both program and civil rights objectives. At the program operational level of HEW, for example, the program and civil rights objectives are not fundamentally separate or even separable, and they become more complementary and less mutually competitive as the full and comprehensive impact and acceptance of the the civil rights laws and policies are more fully comprehended and more faithfully applied by top management of the department. *

Recipients of Federal Assistance

Frequently the ultimate responsibility for gathering racial and ethnic data belongs to the recipient of federal assistance. Consequently, before the recipient can legally make a grant to an individual or facility, it should have information for ascertaining whether that person or facility is providing equality of opportunity to all eligible beneficiaries from all eligible parties. This assurance obviously requires a determination as to the distribution of these funds between beneficiaries of different racial and ethnic groups in order for the recipient to judge whether the planned distribution is equitable.

Program data on people served are analyzed at the state level in some cases, and the data submitted by state agencies to federal

---

*In cases where racial and ethnic data collected by government agencies were made available to universities, research organizations, and private groups, these groups have often made significant contributions to securing compliance with the Civil Rights Act by grant recipients and federal government administrators of federal financial assistance programs by supplementing and, in some cases, challenging the practices of both recipients and granting agencies. They have sometimes also given special insights into particular problems which a government bureaucy cannot provide.

agencies are frequently computerized by the submitting state agency
for purposes of analysis. In the case of employment information
assembled by the State Employment Security Agency funded by the
Department of Labor, the data are analyzed by the various states in
order to show the extent to which minority applicants to state employment services are accepted for employment to which they are
referred.

Particularly in experimental projects, recipients of federal
aid are sometimes required to carry out evaluations of their project
effectiveness to ascertain to what extent the project attains program
objectives or the degree to which specific techniques for meeting
these objectives are successful.

Indicative of the unrealistic distinction frequently made between
program and civil rights functions of agencies is the fact that evaluations concerning Title I of the 1965 Elementary and Secondary
Education Act have been made for some time which simply ignore
the minority ethnic data. Even though the racial and ethnic inequities
were flagrant in this program, they were not corrected by program
personnel. An amendment was finally passed providing that funds
could not be shifted in such a way as to discriminate on the basis of
minority status or degree of poverty, but it was not put into operation
until July 1972.

Where racial and ethnic data concerning a program are computerized on a statewide basis, their value to civil rights compliance
officers may be severely limited. It would be important in a given
situation to determine how such information could be further broken
down in such a way as to reveal the pattern of practices, particularly
in program management units. If this step is not required on a mandatory basis, the shared cost in time and energy of the compliance
officers necessary to put the data in proper form may well make their
use prohibitive.

In cases where project reports include information about program participants—for example, school children or trainees—and provide such information as the number of participants or the results of
a particular program, these data should be broken down separately
by racial and ethnic groups included. This kind of information would
assist the federal agency program office in making plans for future
programs which would deal equitably with minority participants.

The analysis of racial and ethnic data gathered to measure the
distribution of program benefits could be organized in three different
ways. First, federal agencies could set up an agency-wide mechanism
for data analysis. Second, each program manager could be required
to conduct his own analysis of the pertinent data concerning his operations. For instance, in the words of a CCR report, each program

manager could be held "responsible for knowing answers to particular questions such as the extent to which program benefits and information about program benefits are provided to minority beneficiaries and potential beneficiaries, and the quality of the benefits received by minority beneficiaries."[16] Generally speaking, federal agencies have not made such requirements of their program staffs. Third, in order to be certain that racial and ethnic data collected are actually used, the same report suggests:

> . . . federal agencies could provide technical assistance to Program Directors. Again, this is infrequently done and even where assistance is offered . . . some program managers have been slow to enlist the suggestion of that office and then not used the data they have collected. In the agencies studied, where there has been analysis of racial and ethnic data to determine the extent of distribution of program benefits to minorities, this analysis has often been conducted at the direction of a few far-sighted managers rather than as a part of an agency-wide study of the extent of nondiscrimination in Federal programs.[17]

Ultimately, whether racial and ethnic data should be collected and whether they can be used will depend upon the manner in which they are analyzed for the purpose of implementing civil rights requirements, how incisive and imaginative such analyses are, and how efficient and uncluttered their results are. A rather resourceful discriminating beginning in this direction was made by the U.S. Civil Rights Commission which, in the course of refining and condensing the results of its broad study of many agencies and many practices provided illustrative material to sharpen the discussion of the various analytical methods applied to "program participation, receipt of applications, acceptance of application, quantity or quality of services for benefits, differing needs of particular minority groups, program results, integration of services, and time comparison."[18]

Failure to make the analysis of racial and ethnic data an integral part of a department's or an agency's responsibility reflects the attitudes prevailing in these government departments and agencies. Any tendency to isolate the managerial processes affecting civil rights from other managerial functions of the department or agency concerned defeats the purpose of Title VI of the Civil Rights Act of 1964, since the civil rights aspects of all government programs are an integral part of the total management process.

NOTES

1. U.S. Commission on Civil Rights, <u>To Know or Not to Know:</u> <u>Collection and Use of Racial and Ethnic Data in Federal Assistance</u> <u>Programs</u>, February, 1973, first draft manuscript, 1973, p. 244.

2. Memorandum of May 4, 1971 from John Hope II, Assistant Director for Planning at OCR/HEW, to J. Stanley Pottinger, Director, OCR/HEW.

3. Memorandum of May 10, 1971 from J. Stanley Pottinger, Director, OCR, to Rodney H. Brady, Assistant Secretary for Administration and Management, Subject: Operational Objectives Submission.

4. For HEW equal opportunity goal, see Appendix 5.

5. Memorandum of April 30, 1970 from John Hope II, Assistant Director of Planning, OCR, to the Director of Field Operations, HEW.

6. Memorandum of June 24, 1971 from John Hope II, Assistant Director of Planning, to J. Stanley Pottinger, Director, OCR.

7. Memorandum of May 10, 1971 from J. Stanley Pottinger, Director, OCR, to Rodney H. Brady, Assistant Secretary for Administration and Management, HEW.

8. United States Commission on Civil Rights, <u>To Know or Not</u> <u>to Know: Collection and Use of Racial and Ethnic Data in Federal</u> <u>Assistance Programs</u>, February, 1973 (Washington, D.C.: Government Printing Office, 1973), p. 3.

9. Ibid., pp. 5-6.

10. Ibid., pp. 6-7.

11. Department of Health, Education, and Welfare regulations to implement Title VI of the Civil Rights Act of 1964, 45 CFR 80.13 (i). These regulations are similar to the Title VI regulations of all other federal agencies.

12. United States Commission on Civil Rights, <u>To Know or Not</u> <u>to Know: Collection and Use of Racial and Ethnic Data in Federal</u> <u>Assistance Programs</u>, February, 1973 (Washington, D.C.: Government Printing Office, 1973), p. 8.

13. Ibid.

14. Ibid., p. 9.

15. Ibid., p. 10.

16. United States Commission on Civil Rights, <u>To Know or Not</u> <u>to Know: Collection and Use of Racial and Ethnic Data in Federal</u> <u>Assistance Programs</u>, February, 1973 (Washington, D.C.: Government Printing Office, 1973), p. 15.

17. Ibid.

18. Ibid., pp. 15-22.

THE CONTINUING GAP IN MINORITY ACCESS TO
GRANTS-IN-AID BENEFITS

The federal government has been so lax in enforcing Title VI of the Civil Rights Act of 1964, which requires the recipients of grants-in-aid to follow nondiscriminatory practices in the delivery of services, that it has not even developed a general government-wide system for checking on the delivery practices of the agencies and institutions receiving federal assistance. As a result it is impossible for anyone to make a valid assessment of the performance of most of the managers of these funding programs; the Office of Management and Budget and the operating administrators have failed to develop effective systems for gathering the information which they themselves need for making objective appraisals of Title VI compliance of programs under their supervision. The prevailing pattern of virtual absence of systematic collection and analysis of data on the delivery of services to racial and ethnic groups has led most agencies and organizations which are recipients of federal grants-in-aid to act as if the federal government does not seriously intend to enforce the law and regulations against discrimination in the delivery of services.

Despite the regulations requiring assurances of recipient compliance with Title VI (either in advance of granting financial assistance or through compliance reports and on-site investigations after the funds have been received and spent) federal departments and agencies have largely failed to devise an effective way of monitoring the nondiscriminatory use of federal financial assistance. This is the situation more than ten years after the responsible federal officials were required to implement the equal opportunity regulatives in the delivery of services financed through federal grants-in-aid. Although no one knows how many thousands of government agencies and private institutions have been permitted by funding agencies to flout the Title VI requirements for receiving federal financial assistance, very few recipients, with the notable exception of some elementary and secondary schools in the South, have been prevented from receiving grants-in-aid because of failure to comply with Title VI. In most cases where federal departments and agencies have taken any kind of action at all against offending recipients, they have negotiated with recipients of federal funding far past the deadlines set by the regulations for ending negotiations and cutting off funds. Still hoping for voluntary compliance, most federal agencies have continued for years to give funds to recipients who were not in compliance with the law.

Government program managers accept recipients' plans for delivery of services without requiring that they submit adequate proof that they have given goods and services to beneficiaries fairly in the past, or that they have objective ways of appraising and evaluating their actual practices. When complaints are filed by people who have alleged that they were discriminated against, the complaints are referred for investigation to the civil rights units in departments and agencies granting the funds. The civil rights units in turn are put in the position of having to take action against program managers in their own agencies, with whom they usually have little contact and who have failed to assume their own share of the legal responsibility to integrate civil rights and equal opportunity requirements into the ongoing administration of their programs. Federal agencies in effect treat the CR/EO laws and regulations which apply to their programs as if they were not their legal obligations—until they are taken to task by complaints from members of minority groups and by departmental civil rights specialists. The latter are almost powerless to change these illegal practices in any substantial way because they rarely possess the power and authority to make much of a dent on the systematic discrimination against minorities in the delivery of services by the widespread network of state and local agencies using federal monies.

The principal fund-granting federal departments and agencies, that gave recipients a total of about $50 billion in 1975 are the Departments of Health, Education, and Welfare, Labor, Agriculture, Housing and Urban Development, Interior, Commerce, Justice, Transportation, the Veterans Administration, and the Environmental Protection Agency. In some of these departments several programs have gained prominence for their Title VI enforcement efforts. However, these enforcement efforts have usually been in response to the pressure of outside groups and the persistent efforts of experienced insiders, usually the civil rights officials within departments.

In general, efforts to enforce Title VI have been either ineffectual, extremely slow in coming, or nonexistent. While the government was busily adopting new business management techniques (for example, management-by-objective, or MBO) for tracing the work of the federal bureaucracy through the use of written goals, timetables, milestones, and other means, the enforcement of the civil rights and equal opportunity goals of the country was somehow left out of the sophisticated management control devices. Elaborate data collection systems were organized for monitoring the management of most government programs, and could easily have included the racial and ethnic data needed to monitor the nondiscriminatory delivery of services by federally funded agencies. Indeed, in some departments, racial and ethnic data on users and participants of departmental programs and services are already collected. The Department of Agriculture, for example, requires the Food and Nutrition Service to collect racial and ethnic information about the children who each lunch at schools with federally assisted school lunch programs, but a breakdown in the effective use of the data occurred since the FNS has failed to use them to compel the local school lunch programs either to comply with Title VI or lose their funding. In the HEW programs giving financial assistance to elementary and secondary schools, statistics were eventually gathered on the race of the children attending schools as proof of the dsicriminatory use of educational resources in federally assisted school districts, but the data were not collected until outside pressure was put on HEW.

The apparent need for outside pressure on the federal bureaucracy to get enforcement of the civil rights and equal opportunity laws raises a number of questions. What are the sources of effective pressure for improving the delivery of services to minorities? Have the available internal management devices for assuring fair access of minorities to the benefits of federally funded programs been explored? Is it possible to move the federal bureaucracy in the direction of enforcing the civil rights and equal opportunity laws on the books even in an unfavorable political climate?

When the Civil Rights Act was passed it established a national policy banning discrimination because of minority status in several areas of activity, including public accommodations, public and private employment, and the distribution of federal financial assistance to eligible beneficiaries. The latter was provided for in Title VI of the act, which defined equal treatment in the delivery of services and instructed the federal executive to assure that no minority person "be excluded from participation in, be denied the benefits of, or be subjected to discrimination under any program or activity receiving Federal financial assistance." Since the bulk of the grants-in-aid monies was going to state and local governments and their subsidiaries, the statute appeared to signal an end to government complicity in racial discrimination in many public services, at least in those which had financial assistance from the federal treasury.

The new policy had a nationwide jurisdiction, covering all regions of the country whether or not local custom and practice had been traditionally discriminatory, and whether or not the opinion of the people controlling local government favored the new civil rights and equal opportunity laws. A national policy promising equal treatment by governments of all citizens regardless of race, color, and national origin was to make illegal the discriminatory practices deeply inbedded in local institutions and individual behavior. The weight of government was to be thrown on the side of equal treatment wherever it supported activities and programs with federal tax monies.

Control over the purse strings was to be a powerful tool in the hands of the national government, which would use it to get rid of deeply entrenched discriminatory practices. Title VI was this tool. It consisted of the time-tested technique of using grants-in-aids to set national standards of operation in local programs. It was a promising idea, and probably the sleeper in the Civil Rights Act. Whether the Congress seriously intended that it be faithfully administered is a debatable question, but in any case a majority voted for it and the president signed it into law.

It is important to remember that at the time of the passage of the Civil Rights Act of 1964, most public attention was probably focused on the largely symbolic provisions of the law to desegregate public accommodations. The protests of the civil rights movement had taken the form of sitting in at lunch counters and in the front of segregated buses and of swimming at beaches reserved for whites as means of asserting the right of equal access by blacks to public accommodations. This right was important to the dignity of blacks, but asserting it would probably not take much money out of white pockets. Still the civil rights battle was drawn up largely by confrontations between blacks asserting their rights to use public facilities and whites resisting changes in the patterns of social segregation of the races. The impact of the ban on segregation in public accommodations was therefore the most disturbing aspect of the Civil Rights Act to whites who were segregationists. Giving blacks a fair chance to compete with whites for employment also had potential for desegregating the places of work, and this was perceived with alarm and opposed by many whites. However, as long as minorities were discriminated against in education, on-the-job training, and all of the other services that develop job qualification, minorities would not make much progress in the job market, and the economic and social costs to whites would be limited.

The potential effects of Title VI were much less easy to grasp, and they did not appear likely to entail changes in social segregation. However, if minorities did indeed receive their fair share of the program benefits funded by the billions of dollars poured into local governments in every city and town in the 50 states, the impact on both the majority and minority populations would be immense. The cumulative effects of receiving their deserved portion of the education, health care, housing, recreational and vocational training, aid to farmers and businessmen, and the rest of the many local programs assisted by the federal government would be far-reaching, were it to come about. It had the potential for eventually bringing minorities into the mainstream of American society.

If in fact the minority population had participated in all the programs and activities receiving federal financial assistance to the extent that it was eligible, and relative to its numbers in the population, a profound change in its position in society would have occured. The amount of public investment in the development of the human resources of the minority populations in educational and health care alone would have done much to aid minority children during the past decade—if not the adult population—in competing in the market place for jobs and other benefits of the society. Equal access to the delivery of services could have done much to close the gap between the life chances of whites and those of minorities.

The new civil rights laws were passed in a climate and context that had at the same time both positive and negative prospects for implementation. The factors affecting the probability that they would be forcefully put into operation were basically political, but they were also to be influenced by the organizational characteristics and the management practices of the bureaucracy whose job it was to administer the law. As with all large bureaucracies, the federal executive often has a vested interest in not changing its old ways of doing things, particularly when this involves more work. It goes without saying that the policies and priorities of the incumbent president and his administration have considerable impact on the way the federal bureaucracy administers particular laws; at the same time civil servants have been known to defeat the intentions of presidents and their Cabinet officers, who head the federal departments.

In the Kennedy and Johnson administrations, the new civil rights and equal opportunity programs were faced not only with the usual reinterpretation and dilution of policy practiced by the members of the permanent bureaucracy, but with oppostion by influential members of the Congress and with resistance in many sectors of the society. Knowing that the civil rights and equal opportunity programs would likely be lost in the shuffle if they were handed over to the mercies of an old line department, President Kennedy created an independent agency known as the President's Committee on Equal Employment Opportunity, and appointed Vice President Johnson as its chairman. In this way he was able to emphasize his commitment to a strong civil rights policy, particularly as it applied to employment, and to give it the prestige and power it needed to accomplish its mission. Giving it a separate administrative structure, under the wing of the White House, invested it with a status that it would not have enjoyed if it had operated as a part of one of the regular federal departments.

But the new civil rights agency ran into immediate trouble with Congress, which passed an amendment denying it an adequate budget for its activities. In typical fashion, Johnson as chairman of the committee responded by finding a way around the Congress: he used the technique of putting people from other agencies on temporary assignment in order to staff the agency. The staff was able to take advantage of the deep commitment of the administration to civil rights and equal opportunity and of its direct access to Vice President Johnson to open the doors of recalcitrant departments. The executive departments learned rather quickly that the White House meant business on civil rights issues, and they responded to investigations of their discriminatory practices accordingly.

This was the heydey of effectiveness in civil rights enforcement, and many people still believe that a return to this kind of independent structure for civil rights and equal opportunity matters would be beneficial and preferable to the present decentralized form of organization. Johnson as president entertained the idea of a civil rights superagency, which was activated by Executive Order 11197 on February 5, 1965, and named the President's Council on Equal Opportunity. It never became fully operational. As events evolved during the first year of the Johnson administration, the time and attention of the president and his advisers shifted gradually from the Great Society to the war in Southeast Asia. Word spread rapidly through the bureaucratic grapevine that "We shall overcome" had taken a backseat to Vietnam. Doors began to close to the civil rights staff, who woke up one morning to the news that the president had disbanded the agency altogether and divided up its functions among various departments: equal employment was put into the Civil Service Commission, contract compliance into the Labor Department, and Title VI grants-in-aid into the Justice Department. In the future, whoever happened to be head of these three agencies would be the titular head of the CR/EO program assigned to his department, whether he had any expertise in or concern with civil rights issues or not. The problem with reconstituting and centralizing civil rights and equal opportunity activities in an independent agency in the image of the President's Council on Equal Opportunity is that it needs the backing and prestige of the president in order to succeed. If it turns out to be a sterile, undermanned, underfinanced agency, it would be worse than what exists in the decentralized form today, as inadequate as that has turned out to be.

Undoubtedly the Title VI program was assigned to the Justice Department because President Johnson thought he had an attorney

general sympathetic to its aims and ready to enforce it. But the
attorney general had many other matters to attend to, and had to
delegate the supervision of Title VI activities. It fell into the hands
of DOJ lawyers, who interpreted their relationship to the agencies
with Title VI programs as advisory and took the position that advice
was to be given only when Title VI program managers asked for it.
DOJ coordinated Title VI activities only in a permissive and advisory
way, so in effect no one managed Title VI. The Civil Service Commission and the Labor Department were a good deal more responsible
about assuming their coordinating managerial roles for equal employment opportunity for jobs in the federal government and in state and
local agencies and other organizations holding government contracts,
but results in those programs have been only moderately better than
the woefully inadequate DOJ performance in coordinating Title VI
grants-in-aid.

Absence of presidential leadership and ineffective management
by DOJ put the program in grave jeopardy during the Johnson administration. In the Nixon and Ford administration the civil rights and
equal opportunity programs not only lacked the necessary leadership
of the chief executives and their staffs at the top, but suffered the
negative consequences of presidential lack of commitment to the policies. Still, the enforcement of the civil rights laws was a part of
their constitutional obligation, and a whole new machinery of government has been created over the last decade to administer civil rights
and equal opportunity laws. Subsequent legislation and executive
orders and judicial decisions have specified and extended the jurisdiction of the agencies protecting minorities most notably to include
discrimination on account of sex and disability.

Although the federal government has been required for many
years to manage grants-in-aid programs so that the benefits of the
programs reach the final beneficiaries without prejudice on account
of race, ethnic origin, and sex, there remains a significant gap between the policy avowed by law and its application. The deviation of
the day-to-day practices from the policy norm varies widely from
program to program, from one federal administering department to
another, and from one geographical area to another within the same
department. These differences stem ultimately from actions taken
by decision-making managers of grant programs at all levels of the
governmental hierarchy, starting from the executive Office of the
President and descending through the various layers of management
to the line management unit, which makes the final delivery of grant
services to the ultimate beneficiary.

The central and pervasive basis for the deviation in practice
from the legal mandate is that decision makers dealing with mixed
populations give advantages to one group over another because of

such unchangeable and legally irrelevant traits as race, color, national origin, and sex. The elimination of this gap ultimately depends upon whether program managers let such assumptions of differences affect their decisions on delivery of services. The more their actions reflect a perception of difference, the greater the gap between policy and performance is likely to be, other things being equal. The converse is also true.

Title VI programs all over the country are supposed to give services to people without making race, color, national origin, or sex a factor in determining eligibility to enter programs or the extent and quality of services to be received from the programs. Unfortunately, this rarely happens. The following may serve to illustrate what goes on daily in many kinds of programs in all parts of the country. In the federally funded vocational rehabilitation programs, a paraplegic may qualify for education at federal expense to the fullest extent that he is capable of benefiting from, from high school to graduate education in a Ph.D. program, medical school, or whatever interests him. If two applicants come into a local rehabilitation office, one of whom is white and the other black, their color as far as the law is concerned is supposed to be extraneous to the decision about the amount of education a federal stipend will cover. But when a counselor habitually sends black applicants to trade school and white applicants to college and graduate school, indicating that the former should be prepared for skilled labor and clerical jobs and the latter for professional employment, it would be logical to wonder whether the judgment of the local official has been influenced by race and color. The consistency with which he makes one kind of decision for whites and another for blacks suggests that the decision is not based on the assumption that there is no difference between the two applicants, who happened by chance to be of different races, but has in fact been made on the basis that in reality there is a difference between them that he must as a professional counselor take into account. When questioned the interviewer argues that he must recognize the realities of the job market in his city and has used his knowledge of this for the benefit of the black applicant. With the best of intentions the interviewer has taken race and color into consideration and limited the access of the minority person to program services based on that distinction.

But there is a policy based on law that says that the interviewer at the desk in the vocational rehabilitation center is supposed to act as if there is no difference in race, color, national origin or sex that plays a part in his decision, even though he may consider this an unrealistic policy. That is the Title VI requirement for the administration of federally funded programs. The supervisor of the interviewer and those in the bureaucratic hierarchy at all levels above him may not

legally permit him to continue to administer the program any other
way, even though he may mean well.

The decent man who sits at his desk interviewing people and
determining their stipends from the government effectively keeps
the program from operating in compliance with Title VI by routinely
applying his personal and local standards and judging the eligibility
of white applicants one way and blacks another. Using race and color
as an element in the decision is illegal in federally assisted programs.
The managers of local programs and the federal managers of grants-
in-aid programs have the responsibility to insist that a person who
makes decisions about delivery of services does not thwart the Title
VI policy.

Obviously, occasional instances of discriminatory decisions
made by a vocational counselor or an agricultural extension agent,
do not constitute an adequate basis for assessing the access of minorities to grants-in-aid programs. Only regularly and systematically
collected information about all decisions on the delivery of services
can reveal a pattern in regard to the race and ethnic identity of the
beneficiaries and the types and amounts of services received. Where
records are already kept on applicants to programs it is a simple
matter to add a racial and ethnic identification which can eventually
be cross-tabulated with the outcome of the application to show the
pattern of benefits given to applicants and participants of various
backgrounds. Where records of participants are not ordinarily kept,
such as for children eating federally funded school lunches, people
swimming in public pools, and families who may be displaced from
their homes by highway construction, a racial/ethnic census of potential beneficiaries can be taken to determine whether minorities
share fairly in the benefits of such programs and facilities or suffer
unduly from the negative consequences of such programs.

Collecting, analyzing, and using racial and ethnic data are the
only ways of monitoring Title VI programs objectively. Only on the
basis of such figures can program managers know whether they are
complying with the law. The improvement in equal access can only
be measured by comparing rates of participation by all groups. These
figures can then be cross-tabulated with benefits received in order
to make a valid judgment about whether progress has been made in
closing the gap between majority and minority access to services.
This is not a mysterious or esoteric procedure. Management officials
from the Office of Management and Budget down to the line manager
in the regional office use equivalent methods for monitoring their
objectives in other programs.

No report on performance in other areas is acceptable without
factual evidence to support it. When reporting on Title VI compliance,
however, managers often make misleading claims about improvements

by supplying the wrong kind of data. They report increases in expenditures on minority populations in Title VI programs, citing the higher
figure from one year to the next or over five year spans. Suppose,
for example, that a manager reports that his program has doubled
the amount of money spent on blacks in the last year. That may be,
but it is not the issue that the equal opportunity program under Title
VI is supposed to deal with. The measure of progress for access of
minorities to services is not the absolute amount of improvement for
each group, because in this instance the amount spent on whites might
have also doubled or even increased fourfold or more. The issue is
whether the gap is being closed between what the minority group gets
out of the system compared with what the whites get. Absolute amounts
are thus irrelevant; only the comparative figures are pertinent to the
question whether there is equal opportunity to receive benefits. A
manager might find that the gap in his delivery of services has been
narrowed to some degree; he can then measure whether the goals and
timetables that have been set for his program in the future continue
to make progress in closing the gap. On the other hand, if the gap
which was supposed to be narrowing is staying the same, closing only
slightly, or widening, the equal opportunity effort is a failure and
needs remedying.

The Civil Rights Act was passed in the United States when the
gap between minority and majority participation in the benefits of the
economic and social system were perceived as intolerable. But the
policy adopted to remedy this injustice was not one of merely improving the conditions of life of minority Americans; and was explicitly a
policy of working toward equality of benefits received from the system
between minorities and the majority. It can be compared to the situation in South Africa today, where more people are awakening to the
idea that apartheid has created an intolerable gap between the life
situations of blacks and whites. This discrepancy is perceived as
intolerable even though the black gold miner, for example, may be
making more money than he was previously. In fact, it is likely that
he is making three times or more than he did several years ago. But
the question of working towards greater equality is not answered by
knowing whether the black worker is getting better wages. The equality question is whether the gap is narrowing between what the black
miner gets for the same job and what the white miner working along-
side him—or in a segregated section of the mine—gets for doing
the same job. If this gap is not narrowing, the wage level is increasing across the board. Although increasing wages of black miners in
South Africa by any amount may be a social change of some importance
and should be applauded, it is not an improvement in equal opportunity
if they do not come closer to making the same wages for the same
work as whites receive. If the relationship between the wages stays

the same and the supply and demand conditions remain identical, then the relative position between the two groups has remained the same, and all that can be said is that as far as the gap between them is concerned, it has not worsened.

To keep the focus on equal opportunity in access to Title VI benefits, differential participation has to be measured. If program managers and line officials are complying with this standard, there should be no detectable relative difference by group membership in the extent to which people of various groups are served by the programs, activities, and facilities.

Even civil rights officials have frequently lost the real focus and purpose of the equal opportunity programs. It is easy to understand why this has happened. They have often been too caught up in making investigations and taking people to court to realize that there is a mundane but significant alternate method they could use to enforce Title VI. They have failed in particular to recognize the potentiality of collecting, analyzing, and using racial and ethnic data to monitor the programs they are associated with. They are committed to a kind of activist implementation of the law, as they see it, while not understanding the role the gathering of data and the use of various other management devices could play in implementing the civil rights laws. They have failed to understand the value of becoming an integral part of the procedures that OMB has been fostering in order to secure more effective control of all government operations. Becoming a part of this management system offers the possibility of including civil rights and equal opportunity objectives in the goals and timetables of all programs instead of being kept outside and used merely to handle complaints and act as watchdogs.

Inclusion of civil rights in the Operational Planning Systems of the various departments and agencies with civil rights units has been slow to come and has barely begun, but the benefits to civil rights bear close watching. When civil rights are included in the regular planning processes, the secretary of a department puts civil rights and equal opportunity objectives on his list of departmental goals for the fiscal year. His top agency and program administrators are then required to write down how they plan to meet these goals in their particular agencies, how much they are going to spend from their budgets to accomplish this, and when they expect to achieve the goals. The staff of the various administrators must in turn write down goals and timetables for meeting the objectives of not only their substantive programs, but of the civil rights and equal opportunity aspects of them as well. They are then accountable to the heads of their agencies just as the chief administrators are accountable to the heads of their departments for carrying out their stated plans within a certain time for a stated purpose and using a particular amount of the resources from their budgets within certain time intervals.

When a secretary of one of the federal departments calls for a report on the progress made toward achieving his departmental objectives at monthly senior staff meetings, the administrators do not wish to be vulnerable to criticism for failing to carry out their stated goals according to the timetables planned. Once civil rights and equal opportunity have specific goals and timetables set for them in the Operational Planning System of each department, agency heads can no longer use the techniques of rhetoric and meaningless accounts of meetings attended and speeches given to gloss over not reaching their Title VI goals on time.

When civil rights and equal opportunity have been integrated into the major goals of an agency, several things happen. Program chiefs are required to take the goal and apply it to their particular programs, deciding what they are going to do to fulfill it and how they are going to do it and the speed with which they are going to finish various parts of it. Once this has happened, the civil rights staff can go to the program manager to ask him what he has accomplished in reaching his Title VI objectives. The answer has to be specific in terms of the written goals and timetables, not just rhetorical, as it has too often been in the past. The civil rights staff then has the basis for bringing the attention of the secretary to shortfalls in meeting departmental civil rights and equal opportunity objectives. In other words, the secretary's administrators and program managers can be called to account for letting the secretary down by not doing their jobs.

The significance of being integrated into the OPS, with the secretary's goal system and the tracking of the departmental work according to goals and timetables, is that it sets the stage for accountability in the civil rights and equal opportunity areas. If written goals and timetables of Title VI program managers indicate what they have specified they will achieve in the CR/EO aspects of their programs, they can then be called upon to explain their shortcomings and to take corrective action. Unfortunately in the past the civil rights units that wished to bring program managers to account have not usually been able to do so, unless they went to court. However, the combination of the integration of CR/EO goals into the OPS and the collection, analysis, and use of racial/ethnic data in Title VI programs could provide the means for an effective implementation—or at least an improvement in the implementation—of the nondiscriminatory grants-in-aid policy.

OPS and a racial/ethnic data system set the stage for external as well as internal accountability. It is true that the federal departments and agencies think of themselves as mainly accountable to the head of the executive branch who is the president. But the president is accountable to Congress for the administration of the laws, and Congress looks into the various parts of the executive operation.

Any congressman can request the General Accounting Office to conduct investigations of the work of federal departments and agencies and to report deficiencies and make recommendations for change to the departments themselves and to the Congress. The Congress also calls department heads and agency administrators to testify before their committees.

One of the ways of getting accountability internally and forcing accountability from the top of the executive branch is to get outsiders to bring pressure by raising questions about failures in performance. This makes the person with the responsibility protect himself from censure by demanding that his subordinates carry out the law regardless of whether he personally favors the policy or not. One reason for neglect or laxity in the administration of the CR/EO policies has been ineffective use of this kind of pressure on administrators in charge of federal grants-in-aid programs. In the climate of benign neglect during the Nixon and Ford administrations there was little reason for the Cabinet officers who headed the federal departments and their appointed assistants in the bureaucracies or the career civil servants to feel that there was a presidential priority on using grants-in-aid as an incentive to make the recipients of funds comply with Title VI. In fact, the judiciary branch brought Nixon up short on several occasions when he attempted to prevent the implementation of the law.

The oversight capabilities of the Congress and political capabilities of civil rights groups would be greatly enhanced by the integration of civil rights and equal opportunity objectives into the management system of the entire federal government. When these objectives become an integral part of the Operational Planning System, and at present they are not, then Congress and citizens groups can ask specific questions about performance and demand answers on such specific topics as the number of people working on Title VI, the number of field visits, the number of people changing their practices, the comparative figures on racial and ethnic eligibility, participation, and extent of benefits received. This cannot be done now, and without monitoring devices of this level of sophistication both oversight and citizen pressure will fail to stop the continuing failure to make any serious inroads on putting Title VI of the Civil Rights Act into effect.

Office Memorandum No. 71-53

March 25, 1971

OFFICE OF MANAGEMENT AND BUDGET

TO OFFICE OF MANAGEMENT AND BUDGET STAFF

Subject: OMB Civil Rights Activities

Last October, I stressed the importance of identifying civil rights issues in the budget process and evaluating agency performance in this critical area. In order to insure that this initial step is followed up throughout the year, a number of additional actions are needed. Otherwise there is considerable danger that the civil rights thrust will recede under the press of other considerations. It is necessary to build into OMB's institutional processes an ongoing concern with civil rights so that this concern becomes a part and parcel of the regular activity of the agency.

Certain civil rights leadership responsibilities currently center in the GGPD. The Division is already responsible for a number of identifiable civil rights programs, i.e., EEOC, Civil Rights Division Justice, Community Relations Service, etc. It has also been developing expertise and undertaking leadership in the evaluation of the Civil Rights Commission report. Many other programs, however, such as each agency's own internal equal employment program cannot easily be separated from the agency's other personnel programs. Still other substantial programs such as housing, food distribution, etc., have vital civil rights implications, but cannot be readily separated from other policy goals or consideration within the agency's overall functions.

Rather than attempt to establish a single civil rights unit, it is much more desirable to insure that all OMB examiners and management staff are conscious of their civil rights responsibilites and carry out such responsibilites in the course of their regular assignments. On the other hand, a central point for the review of the OMB effort to insure that the appropriate actions are being taken is essential. Mark Alger, Chief of the General Government Programs Division, will monitor the overall program outlined below and report to me on the progress of this effort.

Under the following approach all the major functional areas within OMB will have a coordinated role in the overall civil rights efforts. The following assignments are made:

    1. Revise Circular A-11 to include approriate requirements relating to civil rights activities—BRD and GGPD, consulting with appropriate OMB staff. OMB (GGPD) has been collecting data on agency expenditures for civil rights activities for the past several years. However, this has been done under the authority of a BPM rather than A-11. This more informal approach has led to a low visibility for this effort and does not invest it with an appropriate sense of priority.

Revision of A-11 might also focus on Federal agency equal employment opportunity employment practices, affirmative action plans and supporting budget data. While the question of collecting employment information must be carefully coordinated with similar responsibilities of the Civil Rights Commission, an appropriate revision to A-11 is highly desirable to insure that adequate data is gathered by the agencies and to highlight for OMB examiners these civil rights responsibilities. It may also be desirable to require data on agency procurement set-asides as well.

    2. Publish a Special Analysis on Civil Rights Activities—GGPD. Although OMB has been collecting data on civil rights activities for several years, the results have never been published for public review. While some of the data appears in the budget message in summary form, there is no exposure comparable to that in the Special Analysis on Law Enforcement, for example.

A special analysis for civil rights activities would give those interested this area a much fuller appreciation of the President's programs for civil rights, including equal employment opportunity in Federal employment, contract set-asides, school desegration, fair housing, Federal deposits in minority banks, etc.

3. <u>Revise the Examiners' Handbook—BRD, GGPD,</u> consult <u>with appropriate staff.</u> The Examiners' Handbook provides basic guidance for examiners in their examining functions. At the present time there is no guidance for reviewing agency equal opportunity programs or other civil rights agency activities. An appropriate revision of the Handbook will provide all examiners with standard policy guidance in examining agency programs.

4. <u>Institute information sessions on civil rights for OMB staff—</u> <u>GGPD.</u> Most Federal agencies have undertaken a variety of programs to acquaint employees with the concepts and practices in the civil rights area. No such activity has been undertaken in OMB. Examiners and other staff members have had to gain their knowledge—if any—of Title VI enforcement programs and equal employment opportunity programs as instances have arisen in the course of their review activities rather than through any systematic exposure to problems, concepts, practices and solutions. An appropriate program of information should be developed and an intensive scheduling of examiners, management, and other staff undertaken to achieve maximum coverage of staff before the next budget season.

5. <u>PCD, OMSD and ED should insure that civil rights elements</u> <u>are considered in their efforts.</u> In order to insure that civil rights issues are given appropriate recognition in the issue process, ED should include in the criteria for policy issues, elements which will insure that civil rights issues, particularly with respect to program impact, are at least as carefully considered as other types of issues. Inhouse equal employment opportunity and procurement set-aside efforts should receive attention equivalent to other crosscutting issues.

OMSD and PCD should also include these concerns in administering field coordination with the Regional Councils and FEB's.

6. <u>Revise Circular A-19—LRD and GGPD.</u> Circular A-19, which covers legislation clearance procedures, should be revised to require a review of civil rights issues in the legislative review process, such as that required in the case of environmental impact and cost analysis.

7. <u>Increase the flow of information between other central agen-</u> <u>cies with civil rights responsibilities and OMB staff—GGPD.</u> There are other agencies with across-the-board civil rights activities, notably the Civil Service Commission and the Civil Rights Division of Justice, which compile useful information that should be made available to OMB personnel on a systematic basis. The CSC collects

employment data for all agencies on minority employment. It also
reviews the agency affirmative action programs to insure their adequacy. The Justice Civil Rights Division evaluates the Title VI efforts of affected Federal agencies. Additional useful data is available from the Civil Rights Commission, the Equal Employment
Opportunity Commission and the Office of Federal Contract Compliance.

GGPD should insure that this type of data is passed on to OMB staff
in a systematic, timely fashion in order to assist examiners and others
in their evaluation efforts.

8. Evaluate and improve civil rights statistics—SPMISD and
Divisions. One important gap in evaluation of civil rights efforts is
the paucity of meaningful data on program performance in civil rights
terms. SPMISD should review agency programs for civil rights data
collection and develop a program, in collaboration with examining
division, to improve the usefulness of such performance data.

In constructing the new system for performance management, SPMISD
should insure that the achievement of civil rights goals is clearly
and specifically included among the performance responsibilities of
program managers.

9. Selective Review of Civil Rights Policies and Programs—PCD.
As part of its ongoing responsibilities for monitoring the implementation of major new initiatives and coordinating programs which cross
agency boundaries, PCD will be responsible for selective reviews of
agency activities which involve civil rights problems in areas of interest to the Executive Office of the President. In these reviews,
PCD will work with the GGPD to insure the civil rights issues are
given explicit attention at an early stage in program planning and that
agency civil rights policies and programs are consistent with overall
policy and with the policies of other agencies in terms of impact at
the field level.

George P. Shultz
Director

Office Memorandum No. 72-17

October 19, 1971
Document 15

OFFICE OF MANAGEMENT AND BUDGET

TO OFFICE OF MANAGEMENT AND BUDGET STAFF

SUBJECT: Civil Rights

Background and purpose. This memorandum is intended primarily for the guidance of Program Division examiners, although all divisions should be mindful of the need to pay special attention to the active implementation of the President's civil rights policies in all phases of internal and agency operations. It expands upon the recent changes made in the Examiner's Handbook (Sec. 401B, 428, 431, 433, and 443) and Office of Management and Budget Circular No. A-11 (Sec. 13.2).

Responsibilities for making Federal programs and internal management more responsive to and more effective in meeting the needs and desires of all Americans were set out in Office of Management and and Budget Office Memorandum No. 71-53. Ultimately, though, it is the job and responsibility of each representative of the Office of Management and Budget to insure that the full attention of agency management is being devoted to this important area of concern and that this concern extends equally to all minorities.

Responsibilities. Office staff should familiarize themselves with the civil rights considerations outlined in the attachment. Within the executive branch, the administration of civil rights responsibilities is essentially reserved to the departments and agencies. Oversight and coordination of these activities rests with the Office of Management and Budget and the Civil Rights Committee of the Domestic Council.

Office policy, as stated in the Memorandum referred to above, assigns all Office of Management and Budget examiners and management staff this civil rights responsibility. Although this responsibility covers program execution and departmental management year round, agency hearings relating to program review and budget formulation provide a unique opportunity to focus the attention of agencies' executive staff on civil rights performance and problems. The attached statement of civil rights considerations should be of use in that task.

Implementation and Review. Examiners and management staff should keep these considerations in mind so that they can from time to time advise agencies of those civil rights responsibilities which should be reflected in agency operations--both internal and external. Staff should review and evaluate agencies, civil rights performance at appropriate intervals consonant with their efforts to evaluate agency budgetary requirements and performance. This can be done in conjunction with such activities as reviews of proposed legislation, obtaining information and evaluating agency requirements during the spring and fall reviews, and while visiting all installations and observing programs.

                                        George P. Shultz
                                        Director

Attachment

CIVIL RIGHTS CONSIDERATIONS

1.   Federal Financial Assistance

Title VI of the Civil Rights Act of 1964 (P. L. 88-352), Section 601, provides for equal access to and benefits from all programs receiving Federal financial assistance:

No person in the United States shall, on the ground
of race, color or national origin, be excluded from
participation in, be denied the benefits of, or be subjected to discrimination under any program or activity receiving Federal financial assistance.

OMB examiners should be familiar with the Title VI regulations in their agencies in order to determine whether Title VI protections are being enforced. Some of the areas which they may wish to direct their attention to are listed below:

What is the approximate number of potential beneficiaries (total and by race) of a program?

What is the approximate number of actual beneficiaries (total and by race) in this program?

Is there racial or ethnic discrepancy between the number of potential and the number of actual beneficiaries? Why?

Are all beneficiaries receiving equal benefits?

What are the main problems of discrimination?

How can they be remedied?

How many Title VI complaints were received in Fiscal Year 1971, and thus far in Fiscal Year 1972?

What is the status of these complaints?

How many full-time professionals work solely in Title VI in your agency? How does this compare with Fiscal Year 1971 and estimates for Fiscal Year 1973?

Are they stationed in Washington, D. C., or in the field?

What is their racial breakdown?

How many Title VI compliance reviews were conducted in FY 1971? What about FY 1972, and plans for FY 1973?

What methods of investigations are used?

Were any instances of noncompliance disclosed?

What actions were taken against those found in noncompliance?

Does your agency current conduct pre-approval Title VI reviews? If not, are such reviews contemplated?

What sort of racial and ethnic program data are currently collected or being planned for?

2.   Contract Compliance

Executive Order 11246 provides for equal opportunity in private employment under contracts and subcontracts with the Federal Government. Contractors are also required to take affirmative action in regard to employment and on the job treatment and to establish targets and goals for equal employment opportunity. Although contracting agencies are primarily responsible for obtaining compliance, they are required to follow rules established by the Office of Federal Contract Compliance (Department of Labor).

Examiners should determine the nature and frequency of contract compliance reviews; the detail and effectiveness of such reviews; and their timing (pre-award or post-award). Has there been any change either in employment patterns on contracts or among contractors in recent years? Is the contract compliance staff adequate to handle the job? What sanctions have been imposed for noncompliance? In how many cases have sanctions been levied?

3.   Equal Opportunity in the Federal Service

Executive Order 11478 provides for equal employment and advancement opportunities for Federal employees without discrimination because of race, color, religion, sex, or national origin.

Agencies must have affirmative action programs for minorities and women.

What is the racial/ethnic and sexual breakdown of agency employees?

How many in each category are above the GS-11 grade or wage-board equivalent by grade? What is the category relationship to ageency totals?

How many above and below GS-11 or wage-board equivalent in each category are located in Washington, D. C., and in the field by grade? What is the category relationship to Washington, D. C., and field totals?

What are the main elements of your agency's affirmative action plan?

How effectively are they being implemented?

Does the agency plan include goals and timetables in order to help implement equal opportunity and does it provide special employment programs for both hiring and upward mobility?

To what extent are opportunities for advancement and career training available to secretaries and clerks?

4.   Fair Housing and Site Selection

Titles VIII and IX of the Civil Rights Act of 1968 (P. L. 90-284) and Executive Order 11063 provide for equal opportunity in housing and affirmative action in housing and urban development. In addition, Executive Order 11512 provides for the planning, acquisition and management of Federal space. Site selection for either the acquisition or leasing of land and/or structures should conform to the criteria set out in this order. Special attention should be paid to the availability of low and moderate income housing on a non-discriminatory basis and to relocation considerations when Federal installations or projects are involved. The process of acquisition and leasing must give due consideration to the civil rights considerations involved in such projects early enough so alternative arrangements can be made to shift projects from areas not meeting Federal criteria. Examples should be identified of site locations changed because of this policy.

Is the agency civil rights office consulted when relocation of Federal installations or projects are planned?

5.   Minority Procurement

Section 8 (a) of the Small Business Administration Act (P. L. 85-536) provides for channeling Federal agency procurement to minority businesses. Examiners should determine if agencies are using this mechanism to procure construction, services and supplies to the fullest extent possible to advance minority business enterprise.

6.   Minority Bank Deposits

An OMB Memorandum (Ocotber 2, 1970) to heads of departments and agencies called attention to the vital role played by minority banks in expanding the opportunities for minority business enterprises. "Departments and agencies of government can and should help strengthen these minority banks by utilizing their services to a greater extent than has been the case up to now." Examiners should determine to what extent agencies have increased their deposit of official funds in minority banks and whether increased participation in this important effort is feasible.

7.   DHEW Goal: To enforce the applicable laws and to otherwise assure that all persons regardless of their social educational or economic background, race, color, national origin, religion or sex, have an equal opportunity to participate in financially assisted programs, activities and contracts, and HEW employment.

This nation was founded on the principle of equal opportunity for all Americans. It is now seeking to assure that this principle applies to all Americans --to build a free and open society.

Title VI of the Civil Rights Act of 1964 imposes a specific responsibility on HEW to assure that no person is subject to discrimination on the ground of race, color or national origin in program or activities receiving Federal financial assistance from HEW. Also, under Executive Orders 11478 and 11246, HEW is responsible for assuring that there are equal employment opportunities, respectively, for in-house HEW employment and under the contracts for which HEW is responsible.

This Department also has a general duty to assure that all Americans participate equally in its programs and activities, including those for which it has been delegated authority and jurisdiction. In meeting this general goal, the Department recognizes that many Americans do not achieve their full potential because of prejudice based on race, color, national origin, religion, sex or a particular social, economic or educational background. These factors and mistaken assumptions often cause minority groups and underprivileged people to live in frustration, to the damage of both themselves and their society, and deprives society of the benefits of talents it otherwise would have. If the American society could enable all Americans to live their lives at their full

---

From, secretary's operational planning priorities, D/HEW, civil rights goal no. 7 for fiscal year 1971.

potential, our nation would be far richer, both in a material and a spiritual sense.

HEW will meet its equal opportunity goal in five ways:

1. Sanctions

    When HEW has evidence that there is discrimination con-
    trary to law and negotiations to correct that discrimination
    have failed, HEW will impose one of the sanctions authorized
    by Title VI, Executive Order 11246 or other provisions of
    law. (The Office for Civil Rights has the primary authority
    to impose and recommend the sanctions provided under Title
    VI and Parts II and III of Executive Order 11246.) Such sanc-
    tions will be imposed only when all reasonable attempts to
    achieve changes through negotiation have failed. In seeking
    solutions, the Department will be guided by the President's
    Principles of Enforcement (Statement by the President on
    Elementary and Secondary School Desegregation, March 24,
    1970).

2. Negotiation

    When a recipient of an HEW financed program, activity, or
    contract fails to provide equal opportunities, HEW will
    attempt to achieve a change in the recipient's or contractor's
    practices through negotiation. When an HEW program office
    discovers the failure of a recipient or contractor to provide
    equal opportunity, it must at once report the failure to the
    Office for Civil Rights and work out with that Office an appro-
    priate strategy for conducting negotiations with the recipient
    or contractor. Program offices must exercise initiative in
    meeting the Department's goal. However, ultimate respons-
    ibility for such negotiations lies with the Office for Civil
    Rights, and that Office will move with dispatch and firmness
    to achieve equal opportunity in all HEW programs, activities
    and contracts.

3. Monitoring

    Each HEW program office will develop an effective means
    of monitoring equality of opportunity in its programs, activi-
    ties and contracts. These monitoring programs will be used,
    among other things, to determine the effectiveness of the

program office's equal opportunity activities and to identify areas which require more equal opportunity work.

4. Assistance, Persuasion, and Education to assist in moving to a free and open society.

Each HEW program office will stress the importance of providing equal opportunity in its programs whether the recipient is a State, municipality or private organization. The equal opportunity goal will be an integral part of every program, and will be stressed in all program activities. Maximum use will be made of Title IV funds and DHEW technical assistance to develop an equal opportunity environment. The Department's efforts will be guided by the President's Policies for Progress (Statement by the President on Elementary and Secondary School Desegregation, March 24, 1970).

5. Leading by Example

HEW will provide equal opportunity in all its own in-house practices, particularly employment. Specifically, the Department will strive to increase substantially the number of minority group members and women employed in middle and upper level positions by the following actions:

a. Improve current staffings and placement procedures so that more qualified minority and women employees will be identified for middle and upper level positions. To achieve this goal may involve modification or development of new efforts in the areas of data information systems, Career Service Boards, New Careers, and Career Development programs.

b. Identify dead-end jobs and jobs of limited promotion potential so as to assure that employees possessing greater promise are not unnecessarily placed in them; and, to identify shortage occupations in order to determine whether they are dying or growing occupations, and to encourage career placement and training of minorities and women accordingly.

c. Establish and provide career ladder positions in suitable occupations so that the underutilized can be placed in them and/or specific recruitment efforts may be developed.

d. Encourage and give assistance to state agencies, universities, and other non-Federal sources of direct executive recruitment to hire and develop qualified minorities and women who may be considered for executive placement in HEW.

e. Assure that all HEW recruitment efforts and hiring practices are designed to promote contacts with minority and female sources on a realistic basis in filling real vacancies.

GUIDE FOR INTERVIEWS
WITH
EQUAL OPPORTUNITY PROGRAM HEADS
Prepared by John Hope II

1. (a) What Equal Opportunity (EO) laws, Executive Orders, etc.,
   are applicable to respective programs of your Department,
   e.g., (grants-in-aid, housing and development subsidies,
   training, employment, etc.)?

   (b) List the major programs and indicate which of these edicts
   governs each of them.

   (c) State what Rules and Regulations, Guidelines, and/or statements of standards or criteria for appraising the compliance
   level attained which have been developed in your Department
   (or Agency), by whom (e.g., EO unit or program offices),
   and to which program(s) each applies.

2. What is the scope of the program mission of the EO unit which
   you head?

   (a) Substantive activities under your management? (e.g., EEO,
   EO in participation in benefits of grants, business activities).

   (b) Organizational--(e.g., bureau, agency, Department).

   (c) Geographic--(e.g., local, regional, national).

3. (a) What are the major implementation methods, techniques, and
   devices used by your Department (or Agency) (e.g., complaint processing, recipient or applicant reviews, recipient
   reporting of racial and ethnic data).

   (b) What is their relative importance in your overall program
   (rank the most important, "1", next "2", etc.,)?

4. Describe the organizational structure of the EO unit which you
   head and the position your unit (office or agency) in the overall

organizational structure of the Department (or Agency) of which your unit is a part.

(a) In terms of line authority, to whom do you report <u>directly</u> regarding the administration of your EO program?

(b) What is the process and procedure by which you have access to the head, e.g., Department Secretary or Agency Director?

(c) If it is not direct, who are the parties (and their titles) with whom you deal or through whom you pass in order to see the Secretary (or Director)? What generally is the basis for this chain of relationships?

   (1) On day-to-day Administration problems, crisis, etc.?

   (2) On matters concerned with policy, rules and regulations, etc.?

5. How would you describe the accessibility of the head of your Department (or Agency)?

(a) Under normal conditions?

(b) When a matter of policy concerning EO problems is at issue?

(c) On day-to-day matters where EO implementation is involved?

6. Has the overall <u>management</u> of the activities and functions of your Department been decentralized? If so, how and to what extent?

(a) Headquarters?

(b) Program policy decisions made at Agency or Bureau level?

(c) Program policy decisions made at regional (district or state) level?

7. (a) Are the activities of the EO unit decentralized or not? If so, to what extent and how?

(b) Is there full-time EO personnel in field offices of your Department (e.g., Regional area, or state)? If so, to whom do they report (e.g., to you or program executive)?

8. Indicate the relationship between the EO manager (or executive) and the program managers (executives) at all levels of Departmental management, e. g. , Headquarters, Regional offices, Area or District offices.

   (a) What is the nature and scope of decision-making authority of EO and program managers in EO matters?

   (b) What is the EO executive's status in the departmental (or agency) heirarchy relative to his program executive counterpart?

   (c) His grade level?

   (d) The degree of directness and speed of access of the EO executive to the Secretary?

9. (a) Are there specialized full-time professional EO personnel employed in your Department? If so, by whom are they supervised in carrying out their regular responsibilities and to whom do they report normally? (e. g. , to program management? EO management? Other?).

   (b) Indicate the number by grade level, location (headquarters, regional or district office), classify by racial/ethnic group and occupational levels of jobs.

10. The classic role of the manager (or executive) in our society is to maximize the attainment of his (pre-determined) objectives from the combination and use of the resources (labor and capital) and technology available to him. In this rather simplistic situation, it is assumed that he determines what his objectives are for the management for a given period and then arranges his personnel resources, chooses his equipment, techniques, etc. , and organizes his facilities with the aim of obtaining the largest return (output or result) possible per unit of input.

   (a) Does the manager of the EO unit of a Department have a more complex and less managerially precise responsibility than is assumed above? If so, what essentially is his role and what is its impact upon his ability to effectively manage?

   (b) Can he realistically set objectives and track the efficiency and effectiveness of his staff in reaching his goals; or are his activities so unpredictable and his organization so "crisis-oriented" that such planning is likely not to be productive? Not feasible?

(c) Should he set goals and objectives?

(d) Can he measure the results achieved by the use of his mixture? (resources, technology, etc.) How?

(e) Should he try to do this or is it more effective for him to rely primarily upon the collective subjective appraisals of his line program managers (e.g., division, branch, etc., chiefs) and their staffs in making decisions as to the effectiveness of his organization?

11. If measurements are to be used, what kinds do you suggest?

What kind(s) does your agency use? (e.g., measures of efficiency? effectiveness? goals and time tables?, etc.)

12. (a) Can the EO Agency executive rely on the collective judgment of his own EO program managers and the program and field offi managers of his department to provide him with sound basis for making the major policy, strategy, and operational decisions necessary for the effective administration of his agency?

Or, does he need some form of management reporting system that will provide measurable indexes of performance at regular intervals in such a form that it will give him an objective foundation for his executive decision making?

(b) Is there a middle ground? If so, describe it.

13. (a) Is an EO management reporting system feasible and realistic for your Department? For your EO unit?

(b) If not, why? Is such a system being planned? Where?

(c) If so, is such a system now in operation? Where? Prospective date will become operative?

(d) What is the general character of your system? (describe)

14. (a) How, if at all, does your Department use racial and ethnic data for management decision making? How does your EO unit use it

(b) At what level of management and in what unit or office is such information collected and processed?

(c) At what levels is it used for management purposes?

15. Invariably, Departments' and Agencies' EO executives claim that their unit is under-staffed in terms of its responsibilities and this receives some support from a study of the U.S. Commission on Civil Rights. But, I find little convincing factual justification for such views.

(a) In your experience, how is staff (and budget) size for EO units in Government agencies usually determined?

(b) What is the nature and scope of your relationship with the top budget officer of your Department (or Agency)?

(c) Do you (or to your knowledge, EO managers usually) have direct contact with the Departmental budget officer? If so, what kind?

(d) Do you have an opportunity to fully present your budget or is your participation in budget making of your unit limited, in-direct and/or peripheral? (e.g., submission to departmental budget office, directly or indirectly; appear before appropriate Congressional Committee, etc.)

(e) Specifically, how do you estimate the number of professional employees required for your EO agency or unit?

16. (a) In your judgment, what are the major program activities of the EO unit or agency which you head?

(b) How would you rank each of these in importance, and approx-imately what proportion of your total resources (or budget) now goes into the administration of each of these programs?

(c) Looking to the future, how, if at all, would you suggest that this division of resources-use be changed?

(d) Are there new priorities to be considered? If so, what are they?

17. Are there any other Equal Opportunity, Civil Rights, or Anti-discrimination programs, Offices, Agencies, not under your

direction, operating in your Department? If so, name them and give the name and title of their heads.

18. (a) What are the relative merits (and disadvantages) of the Compliance Review and the Complaint Processing techniques for achieving EO compliance in each of your programs (e.g., Title VI, E.O. 11246, E.O. 11478, etc.)

    (b) In your judgment, are they competing or complementing methods?

    (c) In your opinion, which of these techniques should generally be primary and roughly what proportion of your compliance action resources would you like to allocate to each? What is your present allocation? If different from your above stated preference, why?

    (d) In cases where neither of these methods can achieve voluntary compliance, which ultimate enforcement action, in your experience, is the stronger tool: fund cut-off, debarment, etc., based on noncompliance with the terms of a grant or contract; or court action based on alleged violation of a civil right?

19. EO agencies and units seek to bring about equal opportunity by various means. Some of these approaches are aimed at preventing or avoiding discrimination before it starts while others are mainly remedial, aimed at mitigating or eliminating already existing discrimination.

    (a) In which of these, in your opinion, is your program now concentrated?

    (b) What would be your rough estimate of the resource distribution in your EO agency between preventive and remedial techniques (i.e., estimated percent of total resources used for each of these)?

    (c) Looking to the future, do you think this distribution should be changed? If so, how?

LIST OF GOVERNMENT OFFICIALS IN FEDERAL
CIVIL RIGHTS/EQUAL OPPORTUNITY PROGRAMS
Interviewed by John Hope II

John Attaway, Executive Officer, Officer for Civil Rights, General
Services Administration

Joseph Bennett, Director of Equal Employment Opportunity (Civilian)
Department of the Army

Marion A. Bowden, Assistant to the General Manager for Equal Opportunity Atomic Energy Commission

Hal W. Boyles, Special Assistant to the Director for Equal Opportunity,
Department of the Navy

Stewart Broad, Director of Equal Opportunity (Civilian), Office of the
Secretary of Defense

Arthur A. Chapin, Director, Office of Equal Employment, Department
of Labor

Robert Coates, Chief, Public Programs, Departmental Office of Civil
Rights, Department of Transportation

Arnold Feldman, Chief, Compliance Division, Small Business Administration

James Frazier, Director of Civil Rights, Department of Transportation

Ruth Bates Harris, Director of Equal Employment Opportunity,
National Aeronautics and Space Administration

Samuel M. Hoston, Director, Equal Opportunity Staff, Department of
Health, Education, and Welfare

A. G. Huber, Staff Member, Office of Personnel, Department of
Commerce

Frank Kent, Director, Office of Human Rights, Office of Economic
    Opportunity

Wilma S. Klick, Chief, Equal Employment Opportunity Division,
    Small Business Administration

William Leonard, Budget Examiner, Executive Office of the President,
    Office of Management and Budget

Thomas McFee, Deputy Assistant Secretary for Management Planning
    and Technology, D/HEW

Jeffrey M. Miller, Director, Office of Federal Civil Rights Evaluation,
    Commission on Civil Rights

Edward Mitchell, Director of Civil Rights, General Services Admini-
    stration

David Norman, Assistant Attorney General for Civil Rights, Departmen
    of Justice

Judge William Parker, Director, Contract Compliance Division,
    Veterans Administration

Malcolm Peabody, Acting Assistant Secretary of Equal Opportunity,
    Department of Housing and Urban Development

Judge Samuel R. Pierce, Jr., General Counsel, Treasury Department

Frederick D. Pollard, Jr., Director, Equal Employment Opportunity
    Program, Department of State

Bernard D. Rifkind, Chief, Equal Employment Opportunity Office,
    Directorate of Civilian Personnel, Department of Air Force

James Robinson, Senior Budget Examiner, Executive Office of the
    President, Office of Management and Budget

Wade Ropp, Deputy Director, Personnel, Department of Commerce

David Sawyer, Director of Equal Opportunity Program, Treasury
    Department

William Seabron, Deputy Director of Equal Opportunity, Department
    of Agriculture

Edward E. Shelton, Director, Office for Equal Opportunity, Department of the Interior

Jerome Shuman, Director of Equal Opportunity, Department of Agriculture

Samuel Simmons, Assistant Secretary for Equal Opportunity, Department of Housing and Urban Development

Luther Steward, Special Assistant for Civil Rights, Department of Commerce

Velma Strode, Director, Office of Equal Employment Opportunity, Department of Labor

Carol M. Thomas, Director, Office of Civil Rights and Urban Affairs, Environmental Protection Agency

Joseph Walker, Chief, Public Programs, Departmental, Office of Civil Rights, Department of Transportation

Elliott Worley, Staff Assistant, Office of Equal Opportunity, Department of Navy

James R. Yancey, Chief, Policies and Program, Equal Employment Opportunity Staff, Veterans Administration

TABLE F.1

Number and Percentage of Blacks and Non-Blacks Government-Wide
and in Selected Regions by Grade Levels, 1970

	Government-Wide						Central Office (headquarters)					
	Total Employees	Percentage	Total Black Employees	Percentage	Total Non-Black Employees	Percentage	Total Employees	Percentage	Total Black Employees	Percentage	Total Non-Black Employees	Percentage
Total	1,283,991	100.0	142,466	100.0	1,141,525	100.0	228,180	100.0	47,971	100.0	180,209	100.0
GS 1-4	294,991	23.0	65,716	46.1	229,275	20.1	35,269	15.4	18,087	37.7	17,182	9.5
GS 5-8	373,932	29.1	52,257	36.7	321,675	28.2	70,462	30.9	21,976	45.8	48,486	26.9
GS 9-11	316,540	24.6	16,849	11.8	299,691	26.2	37,674	16.5	4,710	9.8	32,964	19.4
GS 5-11	690,472	53.7	69,106	48.5	621,366	54.4	108,136	47.4	26,686	55.6	81,450	45.2
GS 12-13	219,634	17.1	6,174	4.3	213,460	18.7	46,845	20.5	2,329	4.8	44,516	24.7
GS 14-15	73,308	5.7	1,378	1.0	71,930	6.3	33,862	14.8	796	1.6	33,066	18.3
GS 12-15	292,942	22.8	7,552	5.3	285,390	25.0	80,707	35.4	3,125	6.5	77,682	43.1
GS 16-18	5,586	0.4	92	0.06	5,494	0.5	4,068	1.8	73	0.1	3,995	2.2
GS 12-18	298,528	23.2	7,644	5.4	290,844	25.5	84,775	37.1	3,198	6.6	81,577	45.3

	Atlanta Region						Dallas Region					
	Total Employees	Per-centage	Total Black Employees	Per-centage	Total Non-Black Employees	Per-centage	Total Employees	Per-centage	Total Black Employees	Per-centage	Total Non-Black Employees	Per-centage
Total	149,684	100.0	9,210	100.0	140,474	100.0	115,584	100.0	6,032	100.0	109,552	100.0
GS 1-4	36,360	24.3	5,625	61.1	30,735	21.9	29,275	25.3	3,349	55.5	25,926	23.7
GS 5-8	44,648	29.8	2,164	23.5	42,484	30.2	34,103	29.5	1,576	26.1	32,527	29.7
GS 9-11	37,371	25.0	1,121	12.2	36,250	25.8	31,896	27.6	807	13.4	31,089	28.4
GS 5-11	82,019	54.8	3,285	35.7	78,734	56.0	65,999	57.1	2,383	39.5	63,616	58.1
GS 12-13	24,757	16.5	246	2.7	24,511	17.4	16,400	14.2	179	3.0	16,221	14.8
GS 14-15	6,297	4.2	51	0.5	6,246	4.4	3,794	3.3	21	0.3	3,773	3.4
GS 12-15	31,054	20.7	297	3.2	30,757	21.9	20,194	17.5	200	3.3	19,994	18.2
GS 16-18	251	0.2	3	0.03	248	0.17	116	0.1	0	0	116	0.1
GS 12-18	31,305	20.9	300	3.25	31,005	22.07	20,310	17.6	200	3.3	20,110	18.3

(continued)

(Table F.1 continued)

	Philadelphia Region						Boston Region					
	Total Employees	Per-centage	Total Black Employees	Per-centage	Total Non-Black Employees	Per-centage	Total Employees	Per-centage	Total Black Employees	Per-centage	Total Non-Black Employees	Per-centage
Total	145,949	100.0	21,922	100.0	124,027	100.0	46,427	100.0	1,562	100.0	44,865	100.0
GS 1-4	39,909	27.3	11,496	52.4	28,413	22.9	11,112	23.9	727	46.5	10,385	23.1
GS 5-8	41,711	28.6	6,913	31.5	34,798	28.1	13,281	28.6	479	30.6	12,802	28.5
GS 9-11	36,605	25.1	2,679	12.2	33,926	27.3	12,105	26.1	211	13.5	11,894	26.5
GS 5-11	78,316	53.6	9,592	43.7	68,724	55.4	25,386	54.7	690	44.2	24,696	55.0
GS 12-13	22,579	15.5	729	3.3	21,850	17.6	7,836	16.9	108	6.9	7,728	17.2
GS 14-15	2,951	3.4	103	0.5	4,848	3.9	1,996	4.3	36	2.3	1,960	4.4
GS 12-15	27,530	18.9	832	3.8	26,698	21.5	9,832	21.2	144	9.2	9,688	21.6
GS 16-18	194	0.1	2	0	192	0.2	97	0.2	1	.1	96	0.2
GS 12-18	27,724	18.9	834	3.8	26,890	21.7	9,929	21.4	145	9.3	9,784	21.8

	New York Region						Chicago Region					
Total	82,738	100.0	10,754	100.0	71,984	100.0	151,984	100.0	23,643	100.0	128,341	100.0
GS 1–4	18,640	22.5	4,975	46.3	13,665	19.0	40,523	26.6	11,532	48.8	28,911	22.5
GS 5–8	22,894	27.7	3,802	35.4	19,092	26.6	42,455	27.9	7,960	33.7	34,495	26.9
GS 9–11	21,282	25.7	1,307	12.1	19,975	27.7	36,472	24.0	2,885	12.2	33,587	26.2
GS 5–11	44,176	53.4	5,109	47.5	39,067	54.3	78,927	52.0	10,845	45.9	68,082	53.1
GS 12–13	15,953	19.3	560	5.2	15,393	21.4	26,163	17.2	1,123	4.7	25,040	19.5
GS 14–15	3,831	4.6	105	1.0	3,726	5.2	6,141	4.0	139	0.6	6,002	4.7
GS 12–15	19,784	23.9	665	6.2	19,119	26.6	32,304	21.2	1,262	5.3	31,042	24.2
GS 16–18	138	0.2	5	0.03	133	0.18	230	0.2	4	0.01	226	0.2
GS 12–18	19,922	24.1	670	6.2	19,252	26.7	32,534	21.4	1,266	5.3	31,268	24.4

Source: U. S. Civil Service Commission, Minority Group Employment in the Federal Service (Washington, D. C.: Government Printing Office, 1970).

229

TABLE F.2

Number of Employees (Total and Black) and Black Penetration Rates Government-Wide
in Selected Major Departments by GS Grade Levels, 1970

	Total	GS 1-4	GS 5-8	GS 9-11	GS 5-11	GS 12-13	GS 14-15	GS 12-15	GS 16-18	GS 12-18
Government-wide										
Total employees	1,283,991	294,991	373,932	316,540	690,472	219,634	73,308	292,942	5,586	298,528
Black employees	142,466	65,716	52,257	16,849	69,106	6,174	1,378	7,552	92	7,644
Penetration rate (% black of total)	11.1	22.3	14.0	5.3	10.0	2.8	1.9	2.6	1.6	2.6
Consumer and/or Work-Oriented										
DOL										
Total	10,535	1,346	2,997	1,464	4,461	3,098	1,528	4,626	102	4,728
Black	2,712	776	1,182	305	1,487	316	126	442	7	449
Penetration rate	25.7	57.7	39.4	20.8	33.3	10.2	8.2	9.5	6.9	9.5
D/HEW										
Total	94,502	24,893	32,960	19,805	52,765	10,725	5,796	16,521	323	16,844
Black	20,086	9,188	8,061	1,921	9,982	669	236	905	11	916
Penetration rate	21.3	36.9	24.5	9.7	18.9	6.2	4.1	5.5	3.4	5.4
D/HUD										
Total	14,721	2,292	3,567	3,837	7,404	3,506	1,416	4,922	103	5,025
Black	2,732	889	1,161	330	1,491	222	112	334	8	342
Penetration rate	18.6	39.2	32.5	8.6	20.1	6.3	7.9	6.8	7.8	6.8
Business-Oriented (with consumer elements)										
DOA										
Total	81,437	12,399	28,455	24,436	52,891	12,638	3,277	15,915	232	16,147
Black	4,507	1,522	1,994	767	2,761	192	28	220	4	224
Penetration rate	5.5	12.3	7.0	3.1	5.2	1.5	0.9	1.4	1.7	1.4
DOC										
Total	29,155	6,676	6,870	6,520	13,390	5,482	3,200	3,682	367	9,049
Black	4,212	1,890	1,498	486	1,984	253	83	336	2	338
Penetration rate	14.5	28.3	21.8	7.5	14.8	4.6	2.6	3.9	0.5	3.7

230

Resource- and Facility-Oriented

DOI										
Total	50,725	9,270	13,258	15,134	28,392	9,677	3,190	12,867	196	13,063
Black	2,020	562	844	506	1,350	83	24	107	1	108
Penetration rate	4.0	6.1	6.4	3.3	4.7	0.9	0.8	0.8	0.5	0.8
DOT										
Total	58,690	4,034	10,216	18,245	28,461	19,776	6,114	25,890	305	26,195
Black	3,185	856	1,282	548	1,830	400	84	484	15	499
Penetration rate	5.4	21.2	12.5	3.0	6.4	2.0	1.4	1.9	4.9	1.9
Other										
DOJ										
Total	36,945	8,497	11,916	7,878	19,794	6,432	1,911	8,343	313	8,656
Black	3,550	1,901	1,287	227	1,514	98	33	131	4	135
Penetration rate	9.6	22.4	10.8	2.9	7.6	1.5	1.7	1.6	1.3	1.5
DOD*										
Total	600,044	144,480	178,249	155,711	333,960	98,917	21,639	120,556	1,048	121,604
Black	46,800	20,265	17,177	6,835	24,102	2,307	213	2,520	3	255
Penetration rate	7.8	14.0	9.6	4.4	7.2	2.3	1.0	2.1	0.3	0.2
DOS										
Total	5,810	775	2,303	1,116	3,419	795	780	1,575	41	1,616
Black	1,829	448	1,063	248	1,311	60	10	70	0	70
Penetration rate	31.5	57.8	46.2	22.2	38.3	7.5	1.3	4.4	0	4.3
D/Treas.										
Total	82,318	18,867	23,826	19,950	43,776	15,612	3,720	19,332	343	19,675
Black	10,124	5,156	3,467	1,007	4,474	434	58	492	2	494
Penetration rate	12.3	27.3	14.6	5.0	10.2	2.8	1.6	2.5	0.6	2.5

* Excludes Army, Navy and Air Force Personnel
Source: U.S. Civil Service Commission, Minority Group Employment in the Federal Government (Washington, D.C.: Government Printing Office, 1970).

TABLE F. 3

Number of Employees (Total and Black) and Black Penetration Rates Government-Wide in Selected Major Departments by GS Grade Levels, 1965

	Total	GS 1-4	GS 5-8	GS 9-11	GS 12-18
Government-wide					
Total employees	1,126,101	335,832	311,363	265,077	213,829
Total black	106,706	64,727	30,039	9,125	2,815
Penetration rate (% black of total)	9.5	19.3	9.6	3.4	1.3
Selected Departments					
Consumer- and/or work-oriented					
DOL					
Total	8,962	1,890	2,395	1,885	2,792
Black	1,772	788	688	170	126
Penetration rate	19.8	41.7	28.7	9.0	4.5
D/HEW					
Total	70,979	25,992	19,661	16,330	8,996
Black	12,659	7,872	3,672	915	200
Penetration rate	17.8	30.3	18.7	5.6	2.2
D/HUD					
Total	13,092	2,915	3,047	4,114	3,026
Black	1,580	836	500	158	86
Penetration rate	12.1	28.8	16.4	3.8	2.8
Business-oriented (with consumer elements)					
DOA					
Total	83,152	23,379	26,575	20,974	12,224
Black	3,090	1,625	1,151	245	69
Penetration rate	3.7	7.0	4.3	1.2	0.6
DOC					
Total	27,011	5,676	7,239	6,253	7,843
Black	3,245	1,758	1,077	297	113
Penetration rate	12.0	31.0	14.9	4.7	1.4
Resource- and facility-oriented					
DOI					
Total	47,956	11,699	14,086	12,750	9,421
Black	1,395	587	539	226	43
Penetration rate	3.9	5.0	3.8	1.8	0.5

	Total	GS 1–4	GS 5–8	GS 9–11	GS 12–18
DOT[a]					
Total					
Black					
Penetration rate					
Other					
DOJ					
Total	30,196	7,415	10,534	5,345	6,902
Black	1,489	916	455	80	38
Penetration rate	4.9	12.4	4.3	1.5	0.6
DOD[b]					
Total	513,169	156,209	144,607	125,271	87,082
Black	38,260	20,579	12,243	4,185	1,253
Penetration rate	7.5	13.2	8.5	3.3	1.4
DOS					
Total	7,759	1,274	3,097	1,342	2,046
Black	1,797	601	1,029	126	41
Penetration rate	23.2	47.2	33.2	9.4	2.0
D/Treas.					
Total	80,552	23,521	19,412	22,460	15,159
Black	8,760	5,833	1,920	803	204
Penetration rate	10.9	24.8	9.9	3.6	1.3

[a]Department of Transportation not established until October 15, 1966.

[b]Excluding Army, Navy and Air Force GS Personnel.

Source: U.S. Civil Service Commission, Study of Minority Group Employment in the Federal Government (Washington, D.C.: Government Printing Office, 1966).

TABLE F.4

Number of Employees (Total and Black) and Black Penetration Rates* in Department of Health, Education, and Welfare and Its Agencies and Bureaus by GS Grade Levels, 1970

	Total	GS 1-4	GS 5-8	GS 9-11	GS 5-11	GS 12-13	GS 14-15	GS 12-15	GS 16-18	GS 12-18
Department of Health, Education, and Welfare										
Total employees	94,502	24,893	32,960	19,805	52,765	10,725	5,796	16,521	323	16,854
Total black	20,086	9,188	8,061	1,921	9,982	669	236	905	11	916
Penetration rate	21.3	36.9	24.5	9.7	18.9	6.2	4.1	5.5	3.4	5.4
Agency/Bureau										
Office of the Secretary										
Total	3,417	423	1,112	563	1,675	704	557	1,261	58	1,319
Black	906	216	461	77	538	97	51	148	4	152
Penetration rate	26.5	51.5	41.4	13.7	32.1	13.8	9.1	11.7	6.9	11.5
Office of Education										
Total	2,729	262	819	339	1,158	607	657	1,274	35	1,309
Black	663	127	373	59	432	60	42	102	2	104
Penetration rate	24.3	48.5	45.5	17.4	37.3	9.7	6.7	8.0	5.7	7.9
Food and Drug Administration										
Total	4,326	591	1,081	1,077	2,095	1,130	477	1,617	33	1,640
Black	754	239	287	136	423	74	18	92	0	92
Penetration rate	17.4	40.4	28.2	12.6	20.2	6.5	3.8	4.4	0	5.6
Social and Rehabilitation Service										
Total	1,676	212	589	139	728	348	367	715	21	736
Black	377	74	242	20	262	24	16	40	1	41
Penetration rate	22.5	34.9	41.1	14.4	36.0	6.9	4.3	5.6	4.8	5.6
Social Security Administration										
Total	50,917	16,690	16,741	12,080	28,821	4,088	1,281	5,639	37	5,406
Black	11,889	6,687	3,948	994	4,942	211	49	260	0	260
Penetration rate	23.3	40.1	23.6	8.2	17.1	5.2	3.9	4.8	0	4.8
National Institutes of Health										
Total	8,776	1,511	3,313	1,943	5,256	1,117	824	1,941	68	2,009
Black	1,926	858	758	237	995	52	14	66	7	73
Penetration rate	22.0	56.8	22.9	12.2	18.9	4.6	1.7	3.4	10.3	3.6
Health Services and Mental Health Administration										
Total	19,757	5,923	7,660	3,453	11,113	1,711	980	2,691	30	2,721
Black	4,604	2,074	2,103	341	2,444	59	25	84	2	86
Penetration rate	23.3	35.0	27.4	9.9	22.0	3.4	2.5	3.1	6.6	3.1

* Penetration rate = Total number of black employees divided by the total number of employees.

Source: Data provided by Equal Employment Opportunity Staff, HEW.

TABLE F.5

Number of Employees (Total and Black) and Black Penetration
Rates in Central Office and Selected Regions
by GS Grade Levels, 1965

	Total	GS 1-4	GS 5-8	GS 9-11	GS 12-18
Headquarters (central office)					
Total employees	201,290	45,444	62,280	32,081	61,486
Total black	35,800	19,243	13,022	2,441	1,094
Penetration rate	17.8	42.3	20.9	7.6	1.8
Selected regions					
Atlanta					
Total	126,157	39,497	34,824	30,296	21,540
Total black	5,133	3,865	1,019	354	75
Penetration rate	4.1	9.3	2.9	1.2	0.3
Dallas					
Total	98,852	30,302	28,339	26,302	13,909
Total black	3,754	2,645	788	294	27
Penetration rate	3.8	8.7	2.8	1.1	0.2
Philadelphia					
Total	123,713	42,978	32,336	30,383	38,126
Total black	14,856	9,439	3,511	1,509	297
Penetration rate	12.0	22.2	10.9	5.0	1.6
Boston					
Total	40,095	12,842	10,245	10,141	6,867
Total black	1,181	737	257	130	57
Penetration rate	2.9	5.7	2.5	1.3	0.8
New York					
Total	86,448	26,095	21,284	22,329	16,740
Total black	10,231	6,286	2,515	1,071	341
Penetration rate	11.8	24.1	11.8	4.8	2.0
Chicago					
Total	136,439	44,533	34,081	32,942	24,883
Total black	20,141	12,866	4,820	1,865	590
Penetration rate	14.8	28.9	14.1	14.1	2.4

Source: U.S. Civil Service Commission, Study of Minority
Group Employment in the Federal Government (Washington, D.C.:
Government Printing Office, 1966).

TABLE F.6

Number of Employees (Total and Black) and Black Penetration Rates in Central Office and in Selected Regions by GS Grade Levels, 1970

Area	Total	GS 1-4	GS 5-8	GS 9-11	GS 5-11	GS 12-13	GS 14-15	GS 12-15	GS 16-18	GS 12-18
Headquarters (central office)										
Total employees	228,180	35,269	70,462	37,674	108,136	46,845	33,862	80,707	4,068	84,775
Total black	47,971	18,087	21,976	6,710	26,686	7,329	796	3,125	73	3,198
Penetration rate	21.0	51.3	31.2	12.5	24.6	5.0	2.4	3.9	1.8	3.8
Selected regions										
Atlanta										
Total	149,684	36,360	44,648	37,371	82,019	24,757	6,297	31,054	251	31,305
Black	9,210	5,635	2,164	1,121	3,285	246	51	297	3	300
Penetration rate	6.2	15.5	4.8	3.0	4.0	1.0	0.8	0.9	1.3	0.9
Dallas										
Total	115,584	29,275	34,103	31,896	65,999	16,400	3,794	20,194	116	20,310
Black	6,032	3,449	1,576	807	2,383	179	21	200	0	200
Penetration rate	5.2	11.8	4.6	2.5	3.6	1.1	0.6	0.9	0	0.9
Philadelphia										
Total	145,949	39,909	41,711	36,605	78,316	22,579	4,951	27,530	194	27,724
Black	21,922	11,496	6,913	2,679	9,592	729	103	832	2	834
Penetration rate	15.0	28.8	16.6	7.3	12.2	3.2	2.1	3.0	1.0	3.0
Boston										
Total	46,427	11,112	13,281	12,105	25,386	7,836	1,996	9,832	97	9,929
Black	1,562	727	479	211	690	108	36	144	1	145
Penetration rate	3.4	6.5	3.6	1.7	2.7	1.4	1.8	1.5	1.0	1.5
New York										
Total	82,738	18,640	22,894	21,282	44,176	15,953	3,831	19,784	138	19,922
Black	10,754	4,975	3,802	1,307	5,109	560	105	665	5	670
Penetration rate	13.0	26.7	16.6	6.1	11.6	3.5	2.7	3.4	3.6	3.4
Chicago										
Total	151,984	40,523	42,455	36,472	78,927	26,163	6,141	32,304	230	32,534
Black	23,643	11,532	7,960	2,885	10,845	1,123	139	1,262	4	1,266
Penetration rate	15.6	28.5	18.7	7.9	13.7	4.3	2.3	3.9	1.7	3.9

Source: U.S. Civil Service Commission, Minority Group Employment in the Federal Government (Washington, D.C.: Government Printing Office, 1970).

TABLE F.7

Number of Employees (Total and Black) and Black Penetration
Rates in Selected Standard Metropolitan Statistical Areas
(SMSAs) by Grade Levels, 1965

SMSA	Total	GS 1-4	GS 5-8	GS 9-11	GS 12-18
Washington					
Total	201,290	45,444	62,280	32,081	61,486
Total black	35,800	19,243	13,022	2,441	1,094
Penetration rate	17.8	42.3	20.9	7.6	1.8
Atlanta					
Total	12,838	3,935	4,012	2,416	2,475
Total black	567	416	103	34	14
Penetration rate	4.4	10.6	2.6	1.4	0.6
Dallas					
Total	5,757	1,545	1,663	1,258	1,288
Total black	246	190	39	14	3
Penetration rate	4.3	12.3	2.3	1.1	0.2
Philadelphia-New Jersey					
Total	35,593	12,148	8,547	9,494	5,404
Total black	7,016	4,307	1,803	783	123
Penetration rate	19.7	35.5	21.1	8.2	2.3
Boston					
Total	16,177	4,752	3,884	3,819	3,722
Total black	621	379	128	79	35
Penetration rate	3.8	8.0	3.3	2.1	0.9
New York					
Total	43,058	13,055	10,799	11,065	8,139
Total black	6,876	4,267	1,838	654	177
Penetration rate	16.0	32.2	17.0	5.9	2.2
Chicago					
Total	29,621	10,353	7,437	6,959	4,872
Total black	6,431	4,310	1,443	553	125
Penetration rate	21.7	41.6	19.4	7.9	2.6

Source: U. S. Civil Service Commission, Minority Group Employment in the Federal Government (Washington, D. C.: Government Printing Office, 1966).

TABLE F.8

Number of Employees (Total and Black) and Black Penetration
Rates in Selected Standard Metropolitan Statistical Areas
(SMSAs) by Grade Levels, 1970

SMSA	Total	GS 1-4	GS 5-8	GS 9-11	GS 12-18
Washington					
Total	228,180	35,269	70,462	37,674	84,775
Total black	47,971	18,087	21,976	4,710	3,198
Penetration rate	21.0	51.3	31.2	12.5	3.8
Atlanta					
Total	16,102	3,700	5,484	2,986	3,932
Total black	1,687	984	411	162	130
Penetration rate	10.5	26.6	7.5	5.4	3.3
Dallas					
Total	6,350	1,287	1,708	1,514	1,841
Total black	441	226	123	56	41
Penetration rate	6.9	17.6	7.2	3.7	2.2
Philadelphia-					
New Jersey					
Total	42,270	11,260	11,347	11,715	7,948
Total black	8,973	4,225	3,005	1,381	362
Penetration rate	21.2	37.5	26.5	11.8	4.5
Boston					
Total	17,624	3,836	4,497	4,122	5,769
Total black	873	382	273	113	105
Penetration rate	5.0	10.0	6.1	2.7	2.0
New York					
Total	34,374	8,308	10,254	8,051	7,767
Total black	6,687	3,040	2,560	743	344
Penetration rate	19.4	36.6	25.0	9.2	4.4
Chicago					
Total	29,862	7,902	8,798	6,884	6,278
Total black	7,286	3,654	25.6	748	386
Penetration rate	24.4	46.2	28.6	10.9	6.1

Source: U. S. Civil Service Commission, Minority Group Employment in the Federal Government (Washington, D. C. : Government
Printing Office, 1970).

BOOKS AND MONOGRAPHS

Becker, Gary S. , The Economics of Discrimination Chicago: University of Chicago Press, 1957.

Blaustein, Albert P. and Robert L. Zawgrarendo, eds. , Civil Rights and the American Negro: a Documentary History. New York: Washington Square Press, 1968.

Blaylock, Jr. , Hubert M. Toward a Theory of Minority Group Relations. New York: Wiley, 1967.

Burkey, Richard M. Racial Discrimination and Public Policy in the United States. Lexington, Massachusetts: Heath Lexington Books, 1971.

Center for National Policy Review. Establishing A Federal Racial/ Ethnic Data System: A Report of the Interagency Racial Data Committee. Washington, D. C. : Center for National Policy Review, School of Law, The Catholic University of America , 1972.

Downs, Anthony. Inside Bureaucracy. Boston: Little Brown, 1967.

Flax, Michael J. Blacks and Whites: An Experiment in Racial Indicators. Washington, D. C. : The Urban Institute, 1971.

Fleming, Harold C. , Virginia Willis, and Ameliz Perazich. Affirmative Action: The Unrealized Goal. Washington, D. C. : The Potomac Institute, 1973.

Henderson, William L. and Larry C. Ledebur, Economic Disparity: Problems and Strategies for Black America. New York: The Free Press, 1970.

Huber , John. The Lost Priority: What Happened to the Civil Rights Movement in America? New York: Funk and Wagnalls, 1970.

Kain, John F. , ed. Race and Poverty: The Economics of Discrimi-
    nation. Englewood Cliffs, New Jersey: Prentice-Hall, 1969.

Krislov, Samuel. The Negro in Federal Employment. Minneapolis:
    University of Minnesota Press, 1967.

Marshall, Burke. Federalism and Civil Rights. New York: Columbia
    University Press, 1964.

Marshall, Ray and Virgil Christian. "Economics of Employment
    Discrimination. " In Negro Employment in the South, edited by
    Ray Marshall. Final report to the Manpower Administration,
    U.S. Department of Labor, Contract 81-46-70-24. Austin:
    Center for the Study of Human Resources, University of Texas,
    1973. Mimeographed.

Miller, Arthur S. Presidential Power to Impound Appropriated Funds:
    an Exercise in Constitutional Decision-Making. Chapel Hill:
    University of North Carolina School of Law, 1946. (Reprint
    from North Carolina Law Review 43, no. 3 (1965): 507-47.

Morgan, Ruth P. The President and Civil Rights: Policy-making by
    Executive Order. New York: St. Martin's Press, 1970.

National Urban Coalition. Counterbudget: A Blueprint for Changing
    National Priorities 1971-1976. Edited by Robert S. Benson &
    Harold Wolman. New York, Washington, London: Praeger
    Publishers, 1971.

Okum, Arthur M. Equality and Efficiency: The Big Tradeoff. Wash-
    ington, D.C.: The Brookings Institution, 1975.

Ott, David J. and Attiat F. Ott. Federal Budget Policy. Rev. ed.
    Washington, D.C.: The Brookings Institution, 1969.

Panetta, Leon E. and Peter Gall. Bring Us Together. Philadelphia:
    Lippincott, 1971.

Parsons, Talcott and Kenneth B. Clark, ed. The Negro American.
    Boston: Riverside Press, 1966.

Rankin, Robert S. The Impact of Civil Rights upon 20th Century
    Federalism. Urbana, Illinois: University of Illinois Depart-
    ment of Political Science, 1963.

Rivlin, Alice M. Systematic Thinking for Social Action. Washington,
    D. C. : The Brookings Institution, 1971.

Robinson, Joan. The Economics of Imperfect Competition. London:
    MacMillan and Co. , 1936.

Schultze, Charles L. The Politics and Economics of Public Spending.
    Washington, D.C. : The Brookings Institution, 1968.

Schultze, Charles L. , Edward R. Fried, Alice M. Rivlin, and
    Nancy H. Teeters. Setting National Priorities, The 1973 Budget.
    Washington, D.C. : The Brookings Institution, 1972.

Sklar, Morton H. and William W. Taylor. Civil Rights Under General
    Revenue Sharing. Washington, D.C. : Center for National
    Policy Review, Catholic University Law School, July 1975.

Thurow, Lester C. Poverty and Discrimination: Studies in Social
    Economics. Washington, D.C. : The Brookings Institution,
    1969.

Vaughn, Robert G. The Spoiled System: A Call for Civil Service
    Reform. Washington, D.C. : Public Interest Research Groups,
    1972.

Willie, Charles V. OREO: on Race and Marginal Men and Women.
    Wakefield, Massachusetts, Parameter Press, 1975.

Witherspoon, Joseph P. Administrative Implementation of Civil
    Rights. Austin: University of Texas, 1968.

Wolk, Allan. The Presidency and Black Civil Rights: Eisenhower
    to Nixon. Rutherford, N.J. : Fairleigh-Dickinson University
    Press, 1971.

Yette, Samuel F. The Choice: The Issue of Black Survival in
    America. New York: Putnam, 1971.

                         ARTICLES AND PERIODICALS

Alexander, Jr., Clifford L. "White Collar Help Wanted. . .Or Is
    It?" Personnel Administration 32, no. 4 (July-August 1969):
    4-9.

Brimmer, Andrew F. "The Black Revolution and the Economic Future of Negroes in the United States." American Scholar 38 no. 4 (Autumn 1969): 629-43.

Feischaker, Marc L. and others. "Racial Discrimination in the Federal Civil Service." George Washington Law Review 38, no. 2 (December 1969): 265-304.

Fleming, Harold C. "Riding Herd on Government Programs." Foundation News (May-June 1972): 5-9.

Kator, Irving. "The Federal Merit System and Equal Employment Opportunity." Good Government (Spring 1972): 1-6.

Krueger, Anne O. "The Economics of Discrimination." Journal of Political Economy 71, no. 5 (October 1963): 481-86.

Marshall, Ray. "The Economics of Discrimination: A Survey." Journal of Economic Literature 12, no. 3, (September 1974): 849-71.

Reeves, Earl J. "Making Equality of Employment Opportunity a Reality in Federal Service." Public Administration Review 30, no. 1 (January-February 1970): 43-49.

Rosenberg, Bernard and F. William Howton. "Ethnic Liberalism and Employment Discrimination in the North." The American Journal of Economics and Sociology 26, no. 4 (October 1967): 387-98.

Schick, Allen. "From Analysis to Evaluation." Annals of the American Academy of Political & Social Science 394 (March 1971): 57-71.

Schultze, Charles L. "The Reviewers Reviewed." The American Economic Review 61, no. 2, (May 1971): 46-49.

GOVERNMENT DOCUMENTS

Code of Federal Regulations: Title III - The President, 1964-65 Compilation. Washington, D.C., Federal Register, National Archives and Record Service, General Services Administration, 1967.

Executive Order 11478. Washington, D.C. Office of the White House
    Press Secretary, August 1969.

General Services Administration. U.S. Government Organization
    Manual 1967-68. Washington, D.C.: Government Printing
    Office, 1967.

General Services Administration. U.S. Government Organization
    Manual 1971-72. Washington, D.C.: Government Printing
    Office, 1971.

United States Civil Service Commission. Minority Group Employment
    in the Federal Government. Washington, D.C.: Government
    Printing Office, 1970.

- - - - -. Study of Minority Group Employment in the Federal Govern-
    ment. Washington, D.C.: Government Printing Office, 1966.

- - - - -. General Accounting Office, Office of Management and
    Budget and 17 Participating Agencies. Measuring and
    Enhancing Productivity in the Federal Sector. Mimeographed
    June 1972.

United States Commission on Civil Rights. The Federal Civil Rights
    Enforcement Effort. Washington, D.C.: Government Printing
    Office, 1971.

- - - - -. The Federal Civil Rights Enforcement Effort: One Year
    Later. Washington, D.C.: Clearinghouse Publication no. 34,
    1971.

- - - - -. The Federal Civil Rights Enforcement Effort--A Reassess-
    ment. Washington, D.C.: Government Printing Office, 1973.

- - - - -. To Know or Not to Know: Collection and Use of Racial and
    Ethnic Data in Federal Assistance Programs, February, 1973.
    Washington, D.C.: Government Printing Office, 1973.

- - - - -. The Federal Civil Rights Enforcement Effort--1974. Vol.
    II, To Provide For Fair Housing. Washington, D.C.:
    Government Printing Office, 1974. Vol. III, To Ensure Equal
    Educational Opportunity. Washington, D.C.: Government
    Printing Office, 1975. Vol. VI, To Extend Federal Financial
    Assistance. Washington, D.C.: Government Printing Office,
    1975.

- - - - -. Making Civil Rights Sense out of Revenue Sharing Dollars,
     Clearinghouse Report 50. Washington, D.C.: Government
     Printing Office, 1975.

United States Congress. Senate Subcommittee on Labor. Committee
     on Labor and Public Welfare. The Equal Opportunity Act of
     1972, 92nd Congress, 2nd Session, 1972.

United States Department of Health, Education, and Welfare. Long
     Range Planning System: Program Planning Structure, 1971.
     Mimeographed.

United States Department of Justice, Civil Rights Division. 1972
     Annual Report. Xeroxed. Washington, D.C.

United States National Advisory Commission on Civil Disorders.
     Report of the National Advisory Commission on Civil Disorders.
     New York: Bantam Books, 1968.

United States President. "Richard M. Nixon, 1970." Public Papers
     of the Presidents of the United States. Washington, D.C.:
     Office of the Federal Register, National Archives and Records
     Service, 1971.

                          OTHER SOURCES

Brimmer, Andrew F. "Economic Progress of Negroes in the United
     States: The Deepening Schism." Remarks at the Founders'
     Day Convocation, Tuskegee Institute, Tuskegee, Alabama,
     March 22, 1970.

- - - - -. "Education, Income, and Wealth Accumulation in the Negro
     Community." Commencement Address at the Booker T. Wash-
     ington Business College, Birmingham, Alabama, May 28, 1970.

- - - - -. "An Economic Agenda for Black Americans." Remarks at
     the Charter Day Convocation Celebrating the 105th Anniversary
     of Atlanta University, Atlanta, Georgia, October 16, 1970.

- "Race and Welfare: An Economic Assessment." Remarks at the
     70th Annual Commencement of San Francisco State College,
     San Francisco, California, June 3, 1971.

- "Jobs and Inequality: Progress and Stagnation in the Quest for an
     Open Society. " Remarks on presentation of the 56th Spingarn
     Medal at the 62nd Annual Convention of the National Association
     for the Advancement of Colored People, Minneapolis, Minnesota,
     July 6, 1971.

- "Regional Growth, Migration, and Economic Progress in the Black
     Community. " Convocation address at Bishop College, Dallas,
     Texas, September 15, 1971.

- "Education and Income in the Black Community. " Remarks at the
     58th Annual Convention of the Association for the Study of Afro-
     American Life and History, New York, New York, October 19,
     1973.

Brimmer, Andrew F. and Henry S. Terrell. "The Economic Potential
     of Black Capitalism. " Paper presented at the 82nd Annual
     Meeting of the American Economics Association, New York,
     New York, December 29, 1969.

Buggs, John A. "The Philosophy and Principles of Revenue Sharing:
     Progress for Whom?" Address before the Assembly for Action
     on Revenue Sharing, Lansing, Michigan, June 16, 1973. Wash-
     ington, D.C.: U.S. Commission on Civil Rights, 1973.

Marshall, Ray and James Hefner. "Black Employment in Atlanta. "
     Proceedings of the Industrial Relation Research Association,
     23rd Annual Meeting, Winter 1970.

National Clearinghouse on Revenue Sharing. Revenue Sharing Clear-
     inghouse, published bimonthly at the Center for National Policy
     Review, Catholic University of America, Washington, D.C.

Rittenoure, R. Lynn. "Negro Employment in the Federal Government. "
     Proceedings of the Industrial Research Association, 23rd
     Annual Meeting, Winter 1970.

and Welfare)

OSM (see, Office of the Assistant
Secretary for Management,
Department of Health, Educa-
tion, and Welfare)

other minorities: as census
category, 110

others: as census category, 110

Overall Economic Development
Programs, 31, 32

Page, William, 174

P&E (see, Planning and Evaluation System)

parity representation index:
definition of, 121, 134; in
federal departments, 121; in
regional offices, 134-37; in
subunits of Department of
Health, Education, and
Welfare, 121-23

parks, federally assisted, 155

participation records (see,
programs, federally assisted:
participants in)

penalties, 36-41 (see also,
Sanctions, Title VI; termination of funding)

penetration rate, black (see,
black penetration rate)

people orientation: of federal
departments, 114-17

Performance Management
System: application of, to
agencies, 12; purposes of,
11; and Title VI enforcement,
11-12

personnel, federal (see, employees, black federal; employment, federal)

Philadelphia (Civil Service
Commission) region: black
penetration rate in, 133;
blacks in supergrades in,

134; increase in black penetration rate in, 139-42; parity
representation index in, 136;
white-black ratio of federal
executives in, 131-32 (see also,
Civil Service Commission,
regions of; Philadelphia-New
Jersey SMSA)

Philadelphia-New Jersey SMSA:
black penetration rate in, 137-
38; growth in penetration rate
in 141-42 (see also, Civil
Service Commission, regions
of; Philadelphia [Civil Service
Commission] region)

Planning and Evaluation System,
166-68; and Office for Civil
Rights, 166-75

planning boards, 30-35

planning, programming, and
budgeting process, 167-68

PMS (see, Performance Management System)

police departments, 79

policy, civil rights, xvi-xvii, 88,
149

policy making, 91; at Office of
Management and Budget, on
civil rights, 6-7 (see also,
decision makers; decision
making)

political climate, 184, 192, 194

poor, the, 151

population categories, United
States Census, 110

post-approval compliance reviews
(see, reviews, compliance:
post-approval types of)

Pottinger, J. Stanley, 26-27, 174

poverty, 151

Poverty and Discrimination (Lester
C. Thurow), 103n

pre-approval compliance reviews
(see, reviews, compliance:
pre-approval types of)

JOHN HOPE II, Deputy Special Assistant to the Secretary for Civil Rights, Department of Health, Education, and Welfare, has conducted action-oriented research on minority-majority relations and held positions in this field in the federal government and universities.

Until 1965 Mr. Hope's activities were primarily focused on minority employment problems. He taught economics at Morehouse College, Spelman College, and Atlanta University before World War II and was a Fair Practice Examiner in a southern regional office of the President's Committee on Fair Employment Practices during the war. Later he was Director of Industrial Relations in the Race Relations Department of the Congregational Christian Churches, Fisk University, and Research Associate at the National Manpower Council, Columbia University. During the Kennedy-Johnson administrations, he was Assistant Executive Director of the President's Committee on Equal Employment Opportunity and Director of its federal employment program.

While at Fisk University Mr. Hope directed self-surveys of human relations in employment for several municipalities and an international labor union and served as consultant to various city and state government, federal agencies, unions, and intergroup relations organizations. Out of this experience came a number of articles in professional journals and two books on minority employment, Three Southern Plants of the International Harvester Company and Equality of Opportunity: A Union Approach to Fair Employment. Since 1965 when Mr. Hope joined the staff of the Department of Health, Education, and Welfare, he has concentrated on the problems of the arbritrary inequities in the distribution of the benefits of federal financial assistance.

This book on the gap between equal opportunity laws and policies and their enforcement is an impressive outgrowth of the author's long and varied experience in the broad field of civil rights and equal opportunity.

ETHNICITY AND SUBURBAN LOCAL POLITICS

David J. Schnall

A SURVEY OF PUERTO RICANS ON THE U. S. MAINLAND
IN THE 1970s

Kal Wagenheim

THE WELFARE FAMILY AND MASS ADMINISTRATIVE
JUSTICE

Daniel J. Baum

STATE GOVERNMENT PRODUCTIVITY: The Environment
for Improvement

Edgar G. Crane,
Barnard F. Lentz
Jay M. Shaflitz